HAMILTON AND THE LAW

HAMILTON AND THE LAW

*Reading Today's Most Contentious
Legal Issues through the Hit Musical*

EDITED BY LISA A. TUCKER

CORNELL UNIVERSITY PRESS
ITHACA AND LONDON

Dedication sources: Lin-Manuel Miranda, "Dear Theodosia," *Hamilton: An American Musical* (Atlantic Records 2015); Stephen Sondheim, "Finishing the Hat," *Sunday in the Park with George* (RCA 1984); Miranda, "Best of Wives and Best of Women," *Hamilton*; Miranda, "Satisfied," *Hamilton*.

First published 2020 by Cornell University Press

Library of Congress Cataloging-in-Publication Data

Names: Tucker, Lisa A., editor.
Title: Hamilton and the law : reading today's most contentious legal issues through the hit musical / edited by Lisa A. Tucker.
Description: Ithaca [New York] : Cornell University Press, 2020. | Includes bibliographical references and index.
Identifiers: LCCN 2020007218 (print) | LCCN 2020007219 (ebook) | ISBN 9781501752216 (hardcover) | ISBN 9781501753381 (paperback) | ISBN 9781501752223 (ebook) | ISBN 9781501752230 (pdf)
Subjects: LCSH: Law—Political aspects—United States. | Hamilton, Alexander, 1757–1804—Influence. | Miranda, Lin-Manuel, 1980– Hamilton—Influence. | Musical theater—Political aspects— United States—History—21st century. | History in popular culture— United States—History—21st century.
Classification: LCC KF211. H357 2020 (print) | LCC KF211 (ebook) | DDC 349.73—dc23
LC record available at https://lccn.loc.gov/2020007218
LC ebook record available at https://lccn.loc.gov/2020007219

CONTENTS

Part 2. "America, You Great Unfinished Symphony"

Part 3. "We'll Never Be Truly Free": *Hamilton* and Race

Part 4. "I'm 'a Compel Him to Include Women in the Sequel"

Part 5. "Immigrants, We Get the Job Done"

Part 6. "The Ten Duel Commandments"

Part 7. "Who Tells Your Story?"

Part 8. "What Is a Legacy?": Lessons from *Hamilton* beyond the Libretto

Preface: "Is This a Legal Matter?"

In April 2018, my daughter and I were on that road trip. You know the one: one high school junior; one proud but harried mom; ten days, five or six states, twelve colleges, and 1,100 miles on the SUV.

In this version of the road trip, both the junior and the mom were musical theater nuts. The junior played the French horn; the mom taught law; this road trip was their chance to immerse themselves in the revolutionary world of *Hamilton: An American Musical*. They sang their way through the original cast album at least once a day. One was Eliza, one was Angelica. One was Hamilton, one was Burr. One was excited to lead her own troops.[1] The other wanted to protect her from the truth that it's much harder when it's all your call.[2]

Around the second or third state, I was actively listening, passively driving, when it hit me. I turned to my daughter. "Take out your journal!" I said (she's *that* kid, the one who keeps a paper journal and sends snail mail letters and writes *Hamilton* quotes in beautiful calligraphy to hang on her walls). "I need you to take notes."

And so the anthology experiment began.[3] Over the next several days, my daughter and I tested a theory that *Hamilton: An American Musical* is a narrative not just about the Founding but about the law. And not just because Lin-Manuel Miranda has one of the most quintessentially legal names in the great name book of composers. And not just because the musical explains the writing of the *Federalist Papers* (although every lawyer I know is still gobsmacked about how *that* happened).

If you listen to the musical carefully, and if you're looking for it, the Easter egg is right there, plain enough for anyone (not just a law professor and her law-curious daughter) to hear. The story takes on any number of legal controversies. We know in the first ten minutes of the show that Aaron Burr shot Alexander Hamilton. The rest, as Rabbi Hillel famously said, is commentary. To lawyers? A legal commentary.

The road trip ended, as all good road trips do, but the theory begged to be tested. Over the next few months, I started talking to law professor friends. I posted on Facebook, "Law prof friends: Who's a huge *Hamilton* fan?" Among the thirty-nine almost immediate replies: "I am embarrassed to say how many times I saw it"; "Listen to the soundtrack more often than is polite to others"; and the simple, straightforward, "Who is not?" And it wasn't just law professors. At a gathering of Supreme Court lawyers, several said to me, "We quote it around the office all the time! And even in our briefs!" One federal judge told me proudly that she'd been the first to quote the musical in an opinion.

It's hardly a surprise that lawyers have responded enthusiastically to *Hamilton*. After all, Alexander Hamilton was a lawyer, and his passions matched those of today's lawyers in many ways. Hamilton, like lawyers across the ages, wrote like he was "running out of time" ("all day and night"), battled for clients (the U.S. Constitution, among others), tried cases (including the first murder trial in "our new nation"), fought for justice (in cabinet battles as well as his personal life), and sought to influence the formation of a new system of government in a way that would benefit the most people. He worked non-stop to write a Constitution that could survive the ages. He spoke out on the key issues of the day. And, in Lin-Manuel Miranda's version of the story, Hamilton—like so many of the characters Shakespeare created 400 years ago—rapped soundbites that have woven themselves inextricably into lawyers' vocabulary.

Initially, I thought of doing a symposium, or a conference, or even—why not?—a book. But symposia and conferences and books take participants. Many people, who I was told were fans, were well-known Act I Aaron Burrs to my Act I unknown Alexander Hamilton. People I didn't know, even as Facebook friends. People who, when I emailed them to introduce myself and say that I was working on a project in which I'd like to involve them, politely told me they were much too busy.

Until I said that it was about *Hamilton*.

Initially, just as John Jay, James Madison, and Alexander Hamilton thought there might be twenty-five *Federalist Papers*, evenly divided,[4] I thought this book might be a slim volume of ten or twelve chapters. But when all these big-time lawyers and professors and writers enthused about explaining their own *Hamilton*-based legal theories, I realized that I was coordinating a much bigger project. In the end, thirty-two people I respect and admire joined me in this project.

There is simply no question that *Hamilton* has captured the American imagination in a way that no lesson on civics, government, the Founding of the nation, and the development of the U.S. Constitution has ever achieved. Tickets are almost impossible to acquire, more than 1.4 million cast albums had been sold by 2018,[5] it was the most streamed and top Billboard cast album in 2019,[6] *Hamilton: The Revolution* has sold hundreds of thousands of copies,[7] and certain phrases from the musical have become part of the American lexicon. *Hamilton* has infused itself into the very essence of the American experience; the musical tells the story of the beginning of that experience, and that experience is forever altered because the musical came to be. This book tells the story of how the legal landscape has been affected and changed by *Hamilton: An American Musical*.

I'm proud beyond measure of this volume, of this collaboration among great minds, all of whom share three important qualities: they love the law, they love *Hamilton*, and they see a natural connection between their legal scholarship or advocacy and the musical. Otherwise, they could not be more diverse. Some are former solicitors general of the United States; some are law school deans; some are novelists; one is a student. Some are men, some are women; some are black, some are white, some are brown;

some consider themselves liberals, some conservatives. Some are experts in constitutional law. Some know pretty much everything there is to know about the law of copyright. Some are really into the Second Amendment, or legal history, or election law, or tort law, or immigration law. Some have spent their careers coming up with innovative ideas to help women, or people of color, or the poor.

And then there's me. I fit into some of the categories above. But can I be real a second? For just a millisecond? Let down my guard and tell the people how I feel a second?[8] As I write this introduction to this book about two great passions, I look around, and I realize how lucky I am to be alive right now.[9] How lucky I am to have worked on this volume with these thirty-three other lawyers—who have practiced the law, and pretty much perfected it,[10] and taught it to others—alright, alright! That's what I'm talking about![11]

Lisa A. Tucker

ACKNOWLEDGMENTS

Many thanks to the following people:

My husband, Adam Bonin, for taking me to see *Hamilton: An American Musical* for the first time, on a cold New York December evening, which ended with my deciding (but not telling you quite yet) that I was going to marry you;

My children, Zoe and Abby, and my stepchildren, Lucy and Phoebe, for loving *Hamilton* right along with me (OK, Zoe, you would if you'd give musical theater a chance);

My Drexel colleagues, Arianna Moriniere-Wilson, Dan Filler, Bret Asbury, Alex Geisinger, and Deborah Gordon, for their feedback, insights, support, and enthusiasm;

John Cannan, research librarian extraordinaire, for patiently tracking down about a million cites at the last minute and making it look easy;

Ian Zimmermann, my research assistant, who started out as a formatting-and-citation guru but then turned out to be an everything-else guru;

Sasha Rolon Pereira and Susan Zuckerman of EduHam, for encouraging
  me with this project;
and
Emily Andrew and Mahinder Kingra, for taking a risk on this project and
  talking me through the process of bringing it to life.

Hamilton and the Law

Part 1

"And so the American Experiment Begins"

The Constitution and the Three Branches of Government

1

Lin-Manuel Miranda and the Future of Originalism

Richard Primus

The summer of 2015, when *Hamilton: An American Musical* opened on Broadway, was also the summer when Donald Trump announced his candidacy for the Republican presidential nomination. The shared timing was more than coincidental; there was a reason why each of these projects came on the scene during the last phase of America's first nonwhite presidency. The birther-in-chief's campaign for high office and Lin-Manuel Miranda's rap opera about the man behind the *Federalist Papers* spoke to the same deep issues about American identity at a time when the nation's demography was increasingly coming to resemble that of the larger world. They just approached the subject from different perspectives. One sought to protect an America that was still mostly white and Christian against Mexicans, Muslims, and other outsiders deemed dangerous. The other was so confident in the multiracial future that it rewrote the American past in its image. Trumpism and *Hamilton* are, in short, the same national transition but from opposite sides of the looking glass. And the passions that each has inspired are rooted partly in the desire to reject a vision of America that the other represents.

The astounding success of each project has implications for the future of constitutional law. The effects of Trump's election are obvious: The Supreme Court is likely to have a Republican-appointed majority into the indefinite future, continuing an unbroken run that began in 1970. While Republican appointees control the Court, Miranda's project is unlikely to have significant effects on legal doctrine. But among the Court's liberal opposition—on and off the bench—*Hamilton* will contribute to a significant change. After several decades during which constitutional originalism has been mostly a right-wing art form, liberals will increasingly turn to a jurisprudence of original meanings—and not merely as a way of trying to appeal to the originalists on the bench. Instead, liberals will turn to originalism because they will increasingly believe, authentically, that originalist methods support liberal positions in constitutional law. Eventually, we'll see this development's ascendancy: when the day finally comes that the Supreme Court has a liberal-leaning majority, that majority will deploy originalism for liberal ends. *Hamilton* is part of the reason why.

Judges commonly understand the Constitution in light of their assumptions about the Founding generation. The writing of the Constitution is part of America's origin story. And if the history of constitutional law shows anything, it shows that the "original meaning" of the Constitution changes over time. Not the *actual* original meaning, of course. To the extent that the Constitution has an actual original meaning, that meaning is fixed by historical facts. But what shapes constitutional law is not the actual original meaning of the Constitution. It is the *operative* original meaning of the Constitution, meaning the original meaning as understood by judges and other officials at any given time. The operative original meaning of the Constitution is not entirely divorced from actual constitutional history, but it is also not a strict function of careful historical inquiry. Instead, how judges imagine the original meaning of the Constitution depends on their intuitions—half-historical, half-mythical—about the Founding narrative. If you can change the myth, you can change the Constitution.

Hamilton is changing the myth. Originalism in constitutional law has recently had a generally conservative valence not because the Founders were an eighteenth-century version of the Federalist Society, or the Cato Institute, or the Family Research Council, but because readings of Founding-era sources that favored right-leaning causes were generally predominant in the community of constitutional lawyers. Since 2015, however, the millions of Americans who have listened obsessively to *Hamilton*'s cast album or packed theaters to see the show in person have been absorbing a new vision of the Founding. The blockbuster musical narrative of our times has retold America's origin story as the tale of a heroic immigrant with passionately progressive politics on issues of race and issues of federal power. And so the balance shifts:[1] inspired in part by this retelling, a new orientation toward the Founding will come into view.

Hamilton offers this alternative vision at the dawn of a period when liberals will find themselves attracted to rediscovering the Founders as political and jurisprudential allies. The Court is likely to be distinctly conservative, or libertarian, or some mixture of the two. One of originalism's leading uses is as a tool of resistance to judicial authority. Within our legal culture, an appeal to the Founders is an appeal over the judges' heads. The Founders lack the power to reverse the Supreme Court, so in the here and now that appeal to higher authority is a bid for hearts and minds rather than damages and injunctions. But in a democratic society, hearts and minds are worth winning. Moreover, many liberals will be opposed to things the Court does, and they will want ways to articulate their opposition. Many liberals will accordingly do what many conservatives were motivated to do by the Court of the 1960s: tell stories about the Founding that vindicate their values against current judicial depredations. *Hamilton* will help that process along. So for everyone who has learned to expect originalist arguments to lead mostly to conservative results, here is your Miranda warning: within a generation, American liberals may have developed a jurisprudence of original meanings that, if deployed one day by a liberal Court, could underwrite progressive constitutional decision-making like nothing seen since the days of Chief Justice Earl Warren.

Twenty years ago, in an opinion curtailing the federal government's power to regulate gun sales, Justice Antonin Scalia described Hamilton as the most nationalistic of the Founders. It was not a compliment. It was a reason to discount an argument based on one of Alexander Hamilton's arguments in the *Federalist Papers*, an argument that would have upheld broad federal power to regulate in the case at hand. The true Founding view, Scalia wrote, was better captured in a different essay by James

Madison, who was (in Scalia's presentation) more skeptical of central authority.[2] Hamilton was out of step.

Scalia was not wrong to think of Hamilton as a fervent supporter of national government. But Hamilton's views were not as marginal as Scalia's treatment suggested. Any number of leading Founders were aggressive centralizers in 1787—Madison included. Writing for a majority of the Supreme Court, however, Scalia's confidence in the Founders as local-power, small-government types enabled him to imagine Hamilton as an outlier who could be dismissed. The same set of assumptions also framed Scalia's reading of Madison's essay—an essay that would easily bear a more nationalistic interpretation than Scalia gave it. I assume that Scalia and the rest of the Court's majority made these interpretive moves in good faith. Quite authentically, they thought of Hamilton as nonrepresentative and Madison as skeptical of central authority. Those attitudes supported an interpretation of the sources that blocked an exercise of federal lawmaking.

Hamilton, which opened in the last year of Scalia's life, will make it harder for the next generation of American lawyers to think of Hamilton as marginal. A large and ecstatic audience now knows a narrative of the Founding in which Hamilton is protagonist and hero. If that perspective prevails, then future readers of originalist source material will hear Hamilton's voice more loudly. Moreover, if Hamilton's ardent support for centralized power is taken as the view of a leading figure, it will be easier to read the writings of other Founders as leaning further toward national authority. The sources will bear more nationalist readings than the Court has given them in recent decades. The question is whether the judges and commentators who do the reading will continue to expect Founding texts to lean against federal power, as they have in the past generation, or whether a substantial portion of the next generation of readers will develop the intuition that the nationalism Hamilton represents was an authentic Founding view.

The question is not whether *Hamilton* will change the way dedicated conservatives view federal power. It is whether *Hamilton* will help people who might be open to robust conceptions of federal power to see the Founders as on their side and to deploy the cultural power of originalism accordingly. The answer to that question is probably yes. One cannot know in advance how any given influence will change people's intuitions about history, but in this case it is hard to overstate the preliminary indications. *Hamilton* is a Pulitzer Prize–winning production whose cast album went platinum faster than any album in the history of Broadway. The audience has not just been listening; it has been rapt. In cooperation with the Rockefeller Foundation, *Hamilton*'s production company has staged special performances for tens if not hundreds of thousands of students in New York City's public schools. My personal experience suggests that a significant proportion of teenage Michiganders can recite the lyrics. If art can change ideas—and it can—then it looks like a new vision of the Founding is ready to rise up.[3]

As a weapon of social change, *Hamilton* is trained directly on the intuitions that previously made the Founding the differential property of conservatives. In part, this is a matter of the substantive political values that Miranda's protagonist represents, both on the issue of federal power and on currently salient social issues like immigration. But *Hamilton*'s larger enterprise is exploding the politics of racial memory that have, in recent decades, made liberals queasy about embracing the Founding too closely. On that score, *Hamilton* attempts nothing less than regime change. Not in the sense of replacing the president with a different president, but by altering the way that Americans—of all races—think about the identity of the republic.

The show takes barely thirty seconds to establish its perspective on this issue. In the opening sequence, half a dozen rappers—all of them nonwhite in the original production—take turns contributing verses to an introduction of the title character. The third rapper in the series, describing Hamilton's adolescence in the West Indies, speaks these words:

> And every day while slaves were being slaughtered and carted
> away across the waves, he struggled and kept his guard up
> Inside, he was longing for something to be a part of
> the brother was ready to beg, steal, borrow, or barter.[4]

Americans have told countless stories about the framers that marginalize or omit slavery. Americans have also told many stories about the Founding that seek to take slavery seriously. *Hamilton* did something new. The same African American actor (in the original production at least) who announces, in the play's first minute, that this story will neither hide slavery nor deny its brutality also refers immediately to the white title character as a "brother."[5] Hamilton, announces the nonwhite cast communicating in a paradigmatically nonwhite genre, was *one of us*. Not because of some bizarre claim that the first Treasury secretary was actually not a white man. But because we—the cast members—see him as ours. (The next rapper calls Hamilton "our man."[6]) In full knowledge that Hamilton's race differentiated him from the slaves being slaughtered and carted away,[7] the cast uses racially laden terms of identification to describe its connection to the story's protagonist. *Our* race matters, the company implicitly declares. It shapes how we tell this story. But there is no hint that the historical Hamilton's race matters, one way or the other.

Scrambling prevailing intuitions about race and the Founding in the way that *Hamilton* does is not a method of helping audiences think accurately about the lives of nonwhite Americans in the eighteenth century. If you think that theater has a responsibility to help the public get those kind of historical understandings right, you might conclude that *Hamilton*'s casting and its use of paradigmatically black musical genres are gimmicks that whitewash historical injustice. But if you think that theater can legitimately play a myth-making role, the required analysis is different. The question is then not whether *Hamilton* does justice to the past by depicting it accurately but whether *Hamilton* builds justice in the present by reallocating the ownership of the republic. Broad public absorption of *Hamilton*'s vision would not replace a false picture of the past with a true picture. It would replace one false picture with a different false picture. In scholarship, that substitution would not be an appropriate aspiration. But in the politics of national identity, the practical alternative to the reigning myth is never a careful historical understanding. It is always some other myth.

The leading Founders are figures of myth. That's precisely what makes them potent in the rhetoric of law and politics. How people imagine mythical historical figures is at least as much a function of their own mental maps as it is a function of dispassionate history. As long as the mental maps of Americans feature deep social cleavages based on race, the historical fact that the Founders were white will figure in citizens' images of George Washington and Thomas Jefferson. But in a future America, one that was thoroughly multiracial and egalitarian, a nonwhite image of Washington might be no more jarring than dark-skinned images of Jesus have been among nonwhite Christian populations around the world. At that future juncture, the argument that *Hamilton* misrepresents the eighteenth century would be a bit like the argument that originalism is a bad way to make most constitutional decisions. As a matter of intellectual analysis, it's a good point. But it's a complex and inconvenient point, and it is unlikely to withstand the power of a good story. *Hamilton* tells a good story, with thumping good music to help it along. By the time you leave the theater, maybe even Washington is a little bit brown.

The success of *Hamilton*'s project would mark an inflection point in the politics of American memory. If nonwhite Americans can own the story of the Founding without selling out their racial identities, then the door is open for large numbers of Americans with liberal politics to claim the Founders as their own. In part, that is simply because the median nonwhite voter is to the left of the political center. But just as important is the effect on white liberals, whose ability to embrace the Founders enthusiastically has been tempered in recent decades by the fear that one cannot celebrate those dead white men without risking complicity in the continued marginalization of nonwhites. For the generations that revered Thurgood Marshall, a responsible perspective on the Founding had to show critical distance. But if Miranda's frame replaces Marshall's, or even just competes with it, then white liberals can be less ambivalent. Surely white liberals can lay as much claim to the Founders as their nonwhite allies do.

What's more, *Hamilton*'s demonstration that the story of the Founding can be told from a liberal perspective is not limited to the subject of race. The particular Founding Father whom Miranda's musical elevates was not just an opponent of slavery but a city dweller and a passionate supporter of strong central authority in the national government. The musical emphasizes all of these aspects of Hamilton's character. To be sure, *Hamilton* takes some politically motivated liberties with the historical record. The historical Hamilton's antislavery attitudes were real, but they are accentuated in the musical. Similarly, the musical's relentless characterization of Hamilton as an immigrant in an important sense anachronistic: it seems natural only because the audience thinks of the thirteen British colonies that became the United States as a distinct entity in the international order. (Hamilton's journey from Nevis to New York occurred entirely within colonies of the British Empire.) The musical also repeatedly uses the label "immigrant" to describe the Marquis de Lafayette, who was in no sense an immigrant. He was just a foreigner, a well-born Frenchman who fought the British without ever intending to settle in America. In short, *Hamilton* is a piece of musical theater, not an article in the *Journal of American History*. But as musical theater goes, *Hamilton* is well steeped in its historical sources. And a good musical can shape views of its subject matter, even when audiences ought to know that they are watching an exercise in myth-making. *Hamilton*'s version of the Founding story will accordingly creep into the consciousness of a large group of Americans.

That should have two mutually reinforcing effects. First, *Hamilton* will prime people in the audience who interpret the Constitution for a living—law professors, judges, and others—to think, consciously or otherwise, that the historical sources will bear politically progressive readings. Second, it will change who is inclined to tell the story,[8] rather than leaving that story for someone else. If liberals of all races become confident storytellers about the Founding, they will put their own spin on the sacred sources, consciously or subconsciously, and across a broad range of issues. That sense of connection and ownership will be more significant than *Hamilton*'s raising the profile of any Founder or reorienting public intuitions about how the Founders saw any particular issue. It is not that liberal views of constitutional law will on all issues come to track the views that the historical Hamilton held in the eighteenth century—many of which play no role in the musical, and some of which modern liberals might dislike. It is that by offering a version of the Founding that resonates with liberals today, *Hamilton* will encourage them to embrace the Founding rather than run away from it. And when liberals appropriate the Founding, they will (consciously or unconsciously) emphasize those sources that can be made to do work for liberal causes in modern constitutional law. Some of those causes will coincide with the politics of Hamilton, or those of *Hamilton*, or both. Others may not. But we can be confident that the meanings that liberals give to the Founding, once they are inclined to play the game of originalism, will be liberal-leaning meanings, just as the meanings that conservatives have given the Founding have mostly leaned conservative. What matters is who tells the story.[9]

Hamilton's reframing may not be powerful enough to convince people with conservative political principles that the framers of the Constitution were liberals. But it can persuade people with liberal politics that the framers have their backs, thus prompting them to tell the tale accordingly.

Hamilton is beyond compelling as art: people who hear the music once want to hear it again and to hum it walking down the street. And American liberals are not going to expend too much effort fighting the revised myth they are being offered. They are going to need resources of resistance to a conservative judiciary, and no resource has more capital in our legal culture than the Founders. In addition, in a noninstrumental way, deep down most liberals want to claim the mantle of the Founders just as much as most conservatives do. It is nice to have Washington on your side.[10]

The liberal originalism of the future will not rest on one rap opera alone. Cultural change has many inputs. *Hamilton* plays a role, and so do the other things in the environment that made the musical possible. The sheer fact of the Obama presidency helped nurture the intuition that nonwhite Americans are full owners of the republic, thus opening a door for Miranda to walk through—and provoking a white countermovement desperate to slam it shut. If the American republic eventually repudiates President Trump, the racial bigotry that brought him to power might be further discredited. Farther downstream, *Hamilton* will mix with other influences, some of which it will have directly nurtured and some of which might have arisen independently. The combined effect will be transformative. Nothing the Trump administration can do will prevent an American future that is demographically different from the one in which today's justices formed their worldviews. *Hamilton* is helping that future bring its origin story along with it. And in the field of constitutional law, originalism will keep the present connected to the Republic's Founding by making sure that the Founding adapts. Just you wait.[11]

Some Alexander Hamilton, but Not So Much *Hamilton*, in the New Supreme Court

John Q. Barrett

Supreme Court justices have long been reading, contemplating, debating, and quoting individual framers, perhaps opportunistically. As any fan of *Hamilton: An American Musical* knows, in 1787, the framers—including Alexander Hamilton—drafted in Philadelphia the document that state conventions then ratified over the next year, bringing into effect the U.S. Constitution. It decreed that the United States would have a "supreme Court" comprised of "Judges."[1] The members of the Supreme Court interpret their power and duty under the Constitution to include interpreting the Constitution.[2] In that task, they have often considered and invoked the words and views of the framers, who are in many ways omnipresent.

U.S. Supreme Court justices are particularly enamored with *The Federalist*, the seventy-seven newspaper essays Alexander Hamilton and James Madison penned together with their ally John Jay (Hamilton "wrote . . . 51!")[3], with Aaron Burr declining to participate in the project ("What if you're backing the wrong horse?")[4], in less than six months in late 1787 and early 1788. They sought to persuade their generation, and especially their readers in New York State, to ratify the Constitution.

In Supreme Court decisions since then, and especially in modern times, justices regularly cite to this or that numbered paper from *The Federalist*. According to one study, Supreme Court justices cited *The Federalist* in 324 Court decisions between 1789 and 2006.[5] Wise Supreme Court advocates, knowing of the justices' high regard for any view expressed in a *Federalist* essay, cite to them and quote from them in their written briefs,[6] and sometimes they invoke them in their oral arguments.[7]

One prominent example of framer-invoking, first to the Supreme Court by advocates and then by a justice explaining his vote, occurred in the 1952 Steel Seizure Case, one of the most high-profile, high-stakes cases in U.S. history.[8] Limiting executive power, the justices held, by a vote of 6–3, that the president's seizure of the steel companies, not authorized by legislation, was outside his constitutional powers.[9]

Justice Robert H. Jackson was one of the justices in that U.S. Supreme Court majority. Jackson both joined Justice Hugo L. Black's opinion for the Court and wrote his own concurring opinion, a majestic essay that has become, in Court decisions and constitutional law thinking and commentary since 1952, the core meaning and enduring analysis of the Steel Seizure Case.[10] Justice Jackson's decision contains important insights. Considering that the steel companies had cited James Madison's constitutional convention notes as proof that the framers feared executive power of all types, Jackson expressed his skepticism that any framer's view could be helpful to a Court seeking to answer presidential power questions as they arise in actual cases. Jackson lamented "the poverty of really useful and unambiguous authority applicable to concrete problems of executive power as they actually present themselves. Just what our forefathers did envision, or would have envisioned had they foreseen modern conditions, must be divined from materials almost as enigmatic as the dreams Joseph was called upon to interpret for Pharaoh."[11]

Jackson wrote that the history of partisan debates and scholarship since around 1800 supplied "only . . . more or less apt quotations from respected sources on each side of any question. They largely cancel each other."[12] And then, responding directly to the steel company lawyers' invocations of James Madison,[13] Jackson countered by turning face up a high card from the card deck of the framers. "A Hamilton may be matched against a Madison," Jackson wrote in his opening footnote, and he included a citation to Hamilton's collected works.[14]

Will it affect the justices, and also the advocates before them, that they now have, in addition to long-dead Alexander Hamilton's writings, a living, singing, captivating, much-memorized "Hamilton" of play and song? Will Lin-Manuel Miranda's creation increase the impact of Hamiltonian (be it written or sung) thinking on, and the deployment of Hamiltonian words by, our Supreme Court justices?

There was, just a few years ago, reason to think that would be the case. Richard Primus of the University of Michigan Law School, writing in *The Atlantic* in mid-2016, asked "Will Lin-Manuel Miranda Transform the Supreme Court?"[15] Primus answered his own question by speculating that it could happen—he noted that although in recent decades it had been conservative Supreme Court justices who tended to invoke the framers as support for narrow views of national government power, the success of the musical could give more liberal justices a newly powerful framer to follow. Alexander Hamilton had been, as Justice Antonin Scalia (no fan) noted in a 1997 Court opinion, "the most expansive expositor of federal [i.e., national government] power."[16] By 2016, for liberals, Miranda had made *Hamilton*, and thus Hamilton, newly prominent and compelling in culture, thought, and, it seemed, constitutional interpretations.

In mid-2016, President Barack Obama was successfully completing his second term—the Gallup poll at the end of that June showed that 52 percent of the public approved of his performance.[17] Justice Scalia had died suddenly that winter, and Obama's nominee to succeed him, Chief Judge Merrick B. Garland of the U.S. Court of Appeals for the District of Columbia Circuit, was awaiting Senate action. Senate Majority Leader Mitch McConnell had vowed that the Senate would not act on the Garland nomination—McConnell was determined that the next president, not Obama, should appoint Scalia's successor. But it was not clear that such unprecedented obstruction could succeed. In any case, former secretary of state Hillary Clinton was poised by early that summer to capture the Democratic Party's presidential nomination, and then to go on to defeat Republican candidate Donald Trump. If the Senate obstruction of Obama's Garland nomination did persist even after the election and to the 2017 inauguration, President "Clinton 45" was sure to nominate Judge Garland again, or someone else of his high caliber and constitutional orientation.

By the way, Clinton had seen and loved *Hamilton*—she called it a "beautiful piece of art" about the "fight for the heart and soul of our very nation."[18] In July 2016, Clinton even quoted from the play when she gave her speech accepting the Democratic Presidential nomination. She looked toward the future, remarking that "though 'we may not live to see the glory,' as the song from the musical *Hamilton* goes, 'let us gladly join the fight.' Let our legacy be about 'planting seeds in a garden you never get to see.' That's why we're here . . . not just in this hall, but on this Earth. The Founders showed us that."[19]

But, as Richard Primus notes in an updated version of his essay in chapter 1 of this volume, we are in a different future. Donald Trump is president. He has appointed two conservatives to the Supreme Court, Justice Neil M. Gorsuch in 2017 to succeed Justice Scalia and Justice Brett M. Kavanaugh in 2018 to succeed retired justice Anthony M. Kennedy. On the Supreme Court it is the more liberal justices, those who in different circumstances might have been part of a like-minded majority now and for the years ahead, who are fans of *Hamilton*, including as a guide to constitutional interpretation.

Not every justice's theater-goings and reviews get reported, but I have tried to find all such reports. We thus know that Justice Stephen Breyer, for example, saw the "American musical" in 2015. He called it "terrific," and noted that it "communicated the values that I believe from all I've read the Framers really did have. And it did so in a way that the next generation and the generation after that will understand and absorb and like it. And I thought that's such a good thing. And I learned a lot about [Alexander] Hamilton."[20] By contrast, Chief Justice John G. Roberts, Jr., who saw the show around the same time, offered no public comment on either its artistic merit or its constitutional law significance.[21] Justice Kennedy saw the musical in the summer of 2016 and called it splendid.[22]

Justice Gorsuch, back in 2017 when he was a circuit court judge and rising to be a short-list prospective Trump nominee to the Supreme Court, had not seen the play. He also, while attending (in Justice Kennedy's place) the Ninth Circuit Judicial Conference and participating in almost all of its sessions, "bowed out" of one, an education program segment on *Hamilton*'s usefulness in teaching civics, when panelists began to speak about the Trump administration and its views and treatment of immigrants.[23]

Justice John Paul Stevens, in retirement, did not see *Hamilton*, but he was briefed on at least some it.[24]

In the Supreme Court as an institution, *Hamilton* is not playing. The 2018–19 Court term featured little Hamilton and little *Hamilton*. Yes, Justice Clarence Thomas, writing for the Court in a decision on states' sovereign immunity, quoted the man—he quoted from Hamilton's *Federalist* No. 81.[25] Justice Thomas also stated that interpreting the Eleventh Amendment as preserving states' traditional immunity from private suits accords with the statements of the " 'Madison-[John] Marshall-Hamilton triumvirate' " when the original Constitution was ratified.[26]

Only Justice Breyer has mentioned the musical *Hamilton*. He did so in a dissenting opinion, in support of his argument that the word "describe," as used in federal immigration law, should be interpreted to mean more than, in the grammatical sense, "modify." Breyer explained that a noun can be "described" by more than just the adjectives that modify it. To illustrate the point, he crafted this sentence: "The well-behaved child was taken by a generous couple to see *Hamilton*." That sentence "describes," he explained, a child who was both "well-behaved" and who was "taken by a generous couple to see *Hamilton*."[27]

I am happy for that child, hypothetical though she is, as I am for any lucky theatergoer who sees a production of *Hamilton*. But there is a seeming disconnect between the nationalism of Alexander Hamilton and how a majority of today's Supreme Court justices regard the Constitution that he helped to draft and to explain to the public. That child, and we all, will be seeing *Hamilton* much more on stages and hearing it played and sung by thespians than we will be reading Hamilton, as revivified by *Hamilton*, in Supreme Court decisions.

3

Tragedy in the Supreme Court

"I'd Rather Be Divisive Than Indecisive"

Lisa A. Tucker

> They think me Macbeth, and ambition is my folly,
> I'm a polymath, a pain in the ass, a massive pain,
> Madison is Banquo, Jefferson's Macduff
> And Birnam Wood is Congress on its way to Dunsinane.
>
> — "Take a Break," Hamilton

In the fall of 2018, Americans watched, riveted, as a Supreme Court nominee, the Senate, three female accusers, and one "independent investigator" went toe-to-toe over allegations of sexual assault, blackout drinking, and political conspiracy. Many compared the controversy to the 1991 face-off between then-nominee Clarence Thomas and his former employee, Anita Hill. Indeed, there were parallels: a well-regarded nominee, charges of sexual harassment and violence, conservative versus liberal views of just what conduct constituted wrongdoing.

The parallels went back 250 years, to the infancy of our country, a time when wives and children left the city for the summer and the Founding Fathers (at least, those with a real job)[1] stayed home; when, in the words of Lin-Manuel Miranda, they said, "We gotta go, gotta get the job done, / gotta start a new nation."[2] Just as Alexander Hamilton and his foes, Jefferson and Madison, sought to start a whole new nation that would cement their ideologies in the documents of the nation's Founding, the Kavanaugh hearing was a battle not only about this nomination but about using the Court to establish ideological control over the American people.

Although *Hamilton: An American Musical* does not mention the Supreme Court—its focus is purely on the executive and legislative branches, cabinet battles, and getting plans through Congress[3]—the ideological "war" in America today largely focuses on the federal judiciary. And it is far from clear that we will ever see one another on the other side of it.[4]

The weapons are largely the same, no matter which side employs them. Typically, they involve exposure—of powerful men who have taken advantage of (less powerful) women. Indeed, the witches foretold Macbeth's rise to power, then downfall through a dangerous woman. It is when Hamilton is in his ascendancy (in part, perhaps, from listening to Angelica) that Madison, Jefferson, and Burr feel most threatened. And it is when he takes advantage of a woman that Hamilton's fall begins.[5]

In today's conservative America, there is one key difference: where a woman screws her courage to the sticking-place[6] and alleges misconduct by a powerful man, the right's immediate reaction is to discredit her, to stoke disbelief.[7] Just as Macbeth does not believe the witches at the beginning of the Scottish play (and just as the audience does, if it is familiar either with dramatic devices or with the play itself), many do not initially believe modern female accusers (those who do watch with alarm as the action plays out). And when a woman asserts that a man should fall because of his misdeeds,[8] men team up, in an illogical and often ferocious attack on the woman, in a Birnam Wood on its way to Dunsinane,[9] determined not to take down the king, but to keep a favored son in power.

Today, the female accuser is a more feminist version of Lady Macduff: "Why then, alas, do I put up that womanly defence?" Rather than being allowed to live her own truth, she is murdered for telling the truth and standing her ground. The accused men lie, and they are believed, or at least not disbelieved. And so, today, the woman is not the source of a Supreme Court nominee's downfall. After a woman challenges him, he becomes not a fool, but a tragic hero, persecuted by female and political weakness, but in the end prevailing.

At the Supreme Court, this has not always been so. Until the end of the twentieth century, a small "misdeed" in a nominee's past was enough to cause an uproar, sufficient to force the nominee out of the confirmation process ("never gon' be [a justice] now").[10] Yet in 1987, when Supreme Court nominee Douglas Ginsburg withdrew his name from consideration after it became known that he had smoked marijuana, Democrats controlled the Senate. To get a nominee through confirmation by the other party, it was then believed, the Republican president had to nominate someone squeaky clean, with no hint of scandal in his past. Still, an unblemished nominee was confirmable; at the time, the political parties understood the president's appointment power to encompass his choosing an acceptable nominee, even if that president (and therefore, almost certainly, his nominee) were on the "other side." The concept that "history has its eyes on you"[11] applied, not just to the nominee, but to the dignity with which the Senate treated an acceptable nominee.

Four years later, history had its eyes[12] on Clarence Thomas. Even though the nominee garnered less support from the American Bar Association than any other nominee in recent history, his confirmation—still by a Democratic-controlled Senate—seemed inevitable in this era of polite political resistance against, but in the end deference to, the president. Until the finger-pointer, Anita Hill, who sought to ruin her former boss's chances. At least, that was the narrative that Senate Republicans put forth.

The woman had a story to tell, a story about greed, and abuse, and harassment. It was powerful—powerful enough that the Republicans and the nominee needed a counter story. The Republican's best ammunition? Attack the woman. She was, at best, vengeful; at worst, a sociopathic liar. The nominee's best counternarrative? That the Democratic Senate's willingness to listen to his accuser's account was motivated by bad faith, even evil: "From my standpoint as a black American, as far as I'm concerned, it is a high-tech lynching for uppity blacks who in any way deign to think for themselves, to do for themselves, to have different ideas, and it is a message that unless you kowtow to an old order, this is what will happen to you. You will be lynched, destroyed, caricatured by a committee of the U.S.—U.S. Senate, rather than hung from a tree."[13]

What was the U.S. Senate to do? Proceed with what had now been called a lynching, perhaps confirming that they were, as Thomas alleged, racists? Or confirm the man? After all, there was no proof that what this woman said was true. Unlike Hamilton, Thomas had admitted nothing. There was no trail of checks to confirm Anita Hill's story. And Thomas had successfully reframed the story to make the Democratic senators into racists and Anita Hill into a crazed Lady Macbeth, determined to take him down, to sully his reputation with spots that could never be removed. In reframing the story, Thomas ensured his survival, even at the expense of the integrity of the highest court in the land.

With the Thomas confirmation, a new standard for the Supreme Court confirmation process—what some now call a "farce"[14] or "kabuki dance"[15] was established. The Republicans on the Judiciary Committee learned two important lessons. First, deny, deny, deny. Call anyone who criticizes your nominee crazy, vengeful, and out for political power. Second, nominate whomever you want. Democrats are polite. They will confirm because they believe that you'll do the same when it's their turn.

And then, when it is their turn? You can kick them in the ass. And you'll have all the power. And there will be nothing—nothing—that anyone can do about it, what with life tenure and the virtual impossibility of impeachment.

Enter Brett Kavanaugh stage right. He was a nice guy. He drove his kids' carpool and coached their basketball team. He had good hair. Totally acceptable.

He also had a Republican Senate considering his nomination.

When his accuser entered stage left, all Kavanaugh had to do was follow the playbook. Deny, call the woman deluded, and get angry. Really angry. "How dare you" angry. And remind the Senate Republicans that, if they silence the woman, they'll get the ideological power. They'll control the Supreme Court, and through that—maybe?—the presidency.[16] They'll set policy for the next fifty or sixty years.

The Republicans, through their leader, Mitch McConnell, became Lady Macbeth, determined to put their nominee in his rightful seat—his throne—no matter what the cost. Kavanaugh became a Hamilton figure in his brilliance, a Burr in his surface likeability, a Macbeth in his determination to seize power even at the expense of his party's integrity and the dignity of the position he sought.

After Hamilton published the *Reynolds Pamphlet*, admitting his misdeeds but insisting that he still deserved political power ("Yes, I have reasons for shame / but I have not committed treason and sullied my good name. / As you can see I have done nothing to provoke legal action. / Are my answers to your satisfaction?"),[17] his fall was nevertheless fated (or so it seemed), just as Ginsburg's marijuana consumption eventually prevented him from taking a seat on the Supreme Court. But the 2018 Republicans had learned from Alexander Hamilton and from Douglas Ginsburg—indeed, from Macbeth. Never admit your wrongdoing. Continue to insist that you deserve your rightful place in charge.

The confirmations of Clarence Thomas and Brett Kavanaugh demonstrate that natural law does not always exact justice. As Kenji Yoshino observes, Macbeth is the paradigmatic example of natural law at work, of the idea that "vaulting ambition"[18] will take you down.[19] Lin-Manuel Miranda retells Macbeth's story through Alexander Hamilton, and he does so explicitly, although Hamilton, in describing it, does not believe Jefferson and Madison to be correct in their assumed assessment of the power differential.

But what McConnell and his predecessors have achieved with the Supreme Court has changed the paradigm—in their version of the story, vaulting ambition installs you and your supporters in power. It's a very Burr way of doing things. "Don't let them know what you're against or what you're for."[20] Just win at all costs. As Miranda's George Washington says to Hamilton, "I know that we can win. / I know that greatness lies in you. / But remember from here on in, / History has its eyes on you."[21] Although the language may be the same, when McConnell gives his "son" Brett Kavanaugh the identical message, the intent behind it is different. Stay the course, win, because that's the way we will show history that you can't get rid of us. "We will fight up close, seize the moment and stay in it."[22]

In seizing power through refusing to confirm (or even consider) the other party's nominee and then pushing their nominees through, the Republicans on the Judiciary Committee have set a dangerous precedent both for the process and for the substance of Supreme Court confirmations. It is as if they have eaten on the insane root that takes the reason prisoner.[23] The danger to the process is that obstructionism will become the new normal, and a nominee's legal and ethical qualifications will matter little. The danger to the substance? That a right-wing Court will strip Americans of their basic freedoms—fair voting laws, privacy, criminal justice—through overruling existing legal precedent and establishing new, more restrictive law to take its place. Both of these dangers may endure for decades, as nominees become younger (Clarence Thomas was forty-three, and Brett Kavanaugh was fifty-three) and remain on the Court longer, and as the

Supreme Court vacancies become political prizes to be won, no matter what the "duel commandments" of fair play might dictate.

In *Macbeth*, the Scottish king is "cursed" by the witches' prophecies. In *Hamilton*, it is again the title character who is cursed, whether by naming the Scottish play or by flying "too close to the sun."[24] But today, if this pattern of "all or nothing" Supreme Court appointments—what a group of scholars recently called "cast in apocalyptic terms"[25]—continues, it is America that will be cursed.

"Angels and ministers of grace defend us!"[26]

ALEXANDER HAMILTON'S "ONE SHOT" BEFORE THE U.S. SUPREME COURT

Gregory G. Garre

There might have been a million things he hadn't done[1] when Alexander Hamilton stepped off a boat in New York Harbor in 1773 as an orphaned sixteen-year-old boy. But he did more to help found America over the next thirty-three years than almost anyone else. His contributions to our government are legendary. Less known is his career as a private lawyer. Here, too, he was a phenom. Hamilton established a reputation as one of the most gifted lawyers of his time. He began practicing in New York in 1782, quickly winning acclaim with a "melodious voice," "hypnotic gaze," and "towering passion that held listeners enthralled"[2]—all qualities that would make him an ideal subject for a musical some 230 years later.

Yet Hamilton was to make just one appearance before the nation's highest court, the Supreme Court of the United States. Although important, his case, *Hylton v. United States*, was hardly epic. In retrospect, however, this largely forgotten appearance was one of the most historic arguments presented before the Court. And Hamilton did not disappoint.

This chapter recounts the story of that day, when one of America's greatest champions made his case before its greatest court.

The story begins with Congress's enactment of the Carriage Act in 1794. The act imposed what amounted to a "luxury tax" on the personal use of carriages—the ultimate ride in the late 1700s—as a means of funding the fledgling federal government.

Controversy hounded the act from its inception. Many Americans were distrustful of the exercise of federal authority in general, and few (if any) liked to be taxed. Some—like Hamilton's political foe, James Madison—maintained that the carriage tax qualified as a "direct" tax,[3] which the new Constitution required to be apportioned among states.[4]

Daniel Lawrence Hylton, a wealthy Virginia businessman and carriage owner, shared this view and refused to pay the tax on the ground that it was an unconstitutional, direct tax. The local U.S. attorney promptly brought a debt action against Hylton to recover unpaid taxes—and the legal "duel" that would eventually be decided by the Supreme Court began.

By January 1795, Hamilton was in regular contact with the government's lawyers about the case. Not only had he almost single-handedly built the U.S. fiscal system, but Hamilton—who was "writing day and night"[5]—had also authored all nine of the Federalist Papers that discussed federal taxation.[6] In *Federalist* Nos. 12, 21, and 36, he had even already begun to sketch out the differences between direct and indirect taxes.

That spring, Virginia's circuit court heard arguments and issued an evenly divided opinion. Ordinarily, this would have triggered a rehearing. But to avoid further delay, Hylton admitted his liability so that he could then petition the Supreme Court to hear the case.[7] By the summer of 1795, *Hylton v. United States* had arrived at the Supreme Court.

The Attorney General William Bradford formally turned to Hamilton to defend the constitutionality of the carriage tax before the Court. Perhaps appealing to Hamilton's (not insignificant) vanity, Bradford said he considered the question presented by *Hylton* "as the greatest one that ever came before th[e] Court." He continued that it was of "last importance" that the Justices uphold the Act." As a result, Bradford said, the government lawyers would "all be rejoiced to see" Hamilton join "in defence of the act." Bradford added that "this too will be a proper occasion for you to make your debut in the Supreme Court."[8]

It was an offer Hamilton could not refuse. And roughly six months later, in February 1796, Alexander Hamilton—Revolutionary War hero, framer extraordinaire, and architect of the nation's fiscal system—made his debut before the Court.

At the time, the Supreme Court sat in Philadelphia's old city hall, a two-story brick building located next door to Independence Hall. Far from the august marble palace that the Court occupies today, the old Supreme Court chamber was a small, sparsely decorated courtroom with a table for counsel and a straight wooden bench. The architecture and trappings were in the Federal style—regal, but geometrical and with few frills.

The Court had just six seats at the time. And only five justices participated in *Hylton*. The chief justice, John Rutledge, had recently resigned, and Oliver Ellsworth did not take his seat as the new chief justice until just after *Hylton* was argued.

Hamilton traveled to Philadelphia, likely by carriage, in early February. It was a hectic time in the city—then the nation's capital—especially for the former Treasury secretary. The Treasury struggled to implement Hamilton's expansive fiscal vision, and his successor as head of the department, Oliver Wolcott, Jr., frequently sought his advice and approval. Congress was embroiled in a battle over funding for the Jay Treaty, one of Hamilton's great foreign policy achievements while in office.[9] And while Hamilton was in town for the *Hyland* argument, President George Washington called on his former "right hand man" to make an unexpected request—to draft a farewell address for the nation's first president.[10]

Meantime, Hamilton, who must have been working non-stop,[11] somehow made his final preparations for oral argument. On February 22, Hamilton "was admitted and sworn a Counselor of . . . [the Supreme] Court."[12] The *Hylton* argument, which lasted three days, began the following day. And, on February 24, Hamilton rose on behalf of the United States to present his first argument before the Court. Once again, history would have its eyes on Alexander.[13]

On the day of Hamilton's argument, John Adams wrote to Abigail to say that the city was experiencing "a spell of very cold weather."[14] But that did not deter what Justice James Iredell reported was the "most crouded Audience I ever saw [at the Court], both Houses of Congress being almost deserted by the occasion."[15] Hamilton spoke for three hours making his principal case, putting on full display the tactical and rhetorical brilliance for which he had already become famous to his countrymen and notorious to his enemies.

The notes from the argument, which he likely brought with him to the podium that day, have survived as part of Hamilton's papers. As many advocates do today, Hamilton wrote down "questions" and "answers," anticipating the principal lines of attack that would be made against his position. And he used "oversized, elaborate lettering and such visual cues as hand symbols," no doubt to provide easier reference during the course of argument.[16]

Once he rose to make his case, Hamilton quickly framed the terms of the debate. He acknowledged that the Court had the power to strike down a law inconsistent with the Constitution, but reminded the justices that this was a "Power to be exercised with great moderation."[17] He went on to observe that the distinction between direct and indirect taxes was "uncertain and vague," lamenting that the framers had left "so important a point" unaddressed.[18] By highlighting the constitutional ambiguity and asserting the need for judicial deference to Congress, Hamilton deftly created a presumption in favor of the Carriage Act's constitutionality.

Then he went on the attack. Hamilton dispatched his adversary's theories of what constituted a direct or indirect tax with sharply honed hypotheticals. One such theory was that indirect taxes were those that were "ultimately paid by a person different from the one who pays it in the first instance"—for example, an import duty paid by a merchant, who could ultimately pass on the tax's cost through higher prices to consumers as a kind of indirect tax.[19] But what if the merchant failed to sell the goods, or imported them for his own use? Then, Hamilton answered, the tax would "remain . . . upon him who pays it," and, "according to that rule, then, the same tax may be both a *direct* and *indirect* tax, which is an absurdity."[20]

Having undressed his adversary's position, Hamilton made the case for categorizing the carriage tax as indirect. He began by invoking Adam Smith and *The Wealth of Nations*, arguing that direct taxes were primarily those on individuals or on land and its produce. Indirect taxes, in contrast, included those paid "on account of . . . using or consuming goods of a certain kind," and Smith himself listed a "coach-tax" as an example of that category.[21] The Carriage Act, Hamilton reasoned, fell squarely into this latter kind of tax.

Next, Hamilton made an appeal to common sense, posing another hypothetical: What if some states had no carriages, or only a few?[22] If a carriage tax were considered direct—and therefore had to be apportioned among the states by population—its administration would prove disastrous. For a carriage-less state, there would be nothing "upon which its quota could be assessed"; and for a state with only a few carriages, the enormous tax on the few owners would "render it ruinous to [them]."[23] In other words, Hamilton showed that Hylton's position was not only untenable as constitutional law but unworkable as practical matter.

Hamilton ended where he had started: the text of the Constitution. Noting that Article I, Section 8 listed taxes, duties, imposts, and excises separately as powers of Congress, Hamilton considered whether any of these might authorize the Carriage Act. "Taxes" was a general term meant to encompass the others and not especially persuasive on its own. "Duties and imposts" had more particular meaning, but were both tied to importation. This left "excises" as the sole remaining candidate, which Hamilton then eliminated by pointing to the meaning of this term in Britain, the country "from which our Jurisprudence is derived."[24]

As Hamilton went about characterizing the Carriage Act as merely a luxury tax, he also confided: "It so happens, that I once had a Carriage myself, and found it convenient to dispense with it. But my happiness is not in the least diminished."[25] Hamilton wasn't looking for laughs; he was making a point. And he succeeded: Justice Iredell recorded that Hamilton's quip had "affected me extremely."[26] Evidently, Hamilton's line was also a hit in social circles. On February 27, John Adams recounted the story in a letter to Abigail and, ever trying to match his nemesis, added: "I can live as happily without a Carriage as Hamilton."[27]

Hamilton's argument garnered rave reviews. Justice Iredell wrote that Hamilton "spoke with astonishing ability, and in the most pleasing manner, and was listened to with the profoundest attention."[28] The *Gazette of the United States* proclaimed that Hamilton's presentation was "clear, impressive and classical," a breathtaking showcase of "the talents of this great orator and statesman."[29] A future federal judge in the courtroom that day called "Hamiltons Argument . . . the ablest I ever heard."[30] He continued, "[Hamilton] is perfect master of the subject; the Constitution & all political topics connected with it."[31] The *Newport Mercury* characterized Hamilton's argument as "a display of those splendid talents, which have ranked him among the first men of the age."[32] Others lamented that they were "mortified that the Government did not devise ways and means to retain him in office."[33]

As usual, Hamilton's political enemies tried to put their own spin on events. A dour James Madison, for one, wrote to Thomas Jefferson to report that Hamilton "exerted himself as usual"[34] but at best "raise[d] a fog around the subject . . . in a doubtful case."[35] Even then, however, one can't help but hear a hint of begrudging respect. One Boston newspaper reported that "by his eloquence, candor, and law knowledge, [Hamilton] has drawn applause from many who had been in the habit of reviling him."[36]

His power of speech was indeed unimpeachable.[37] In the end, Hamilton's argument carried the day. As was its custom at the time, the Court swiftly delivered a decision. On March 8, the *Philadelphia Gazette* reported, "the Court gave their opinions, unanimously, in favor of the constitutionality of the Carriage Tax."[38]

Typical of the day, the justices issued separate, seriatim opinions, but they agreed on the key holdings. First, the category of direct taxes included only land and capitation taxes.[39] Second, Congress had the power to issue indirect taxes, even if they were not strictly duties, imposts, or excises. To require apportionment for all taxes not neatly fitting into those categories, the justices reasoned, would be to assume the framers intended to create an unmanageable and unfair system.[40] Third, the Carriage Act was a consumption tax, and therefore a permissible indirect tax.[41] In each of these holdings, the justices relied heavily on Hamilton's arguments—at times even following his reasoning line-by-line.

Hylton's influence would extend far beyond the carriage tax. In *Hylton*, the Court first laid the seeds of the doctrine of judicial review, which Chief Justice John Marshall would famously enshrine seven years later in *Marbury v. Madison*. Justice Samuel Chase—though appointed to the Court only weeks before issuing his decision—explicitly recognized this power in his opinion. Although it proved unnecessary to find a law "unconstitutional and void" in *Hylton*, the Court, for the first time, admitted the possibility of doing so.[42]

Hylton would later be invoked in other high-profile disputes before the Court. In *Pollock v. Farmers' Loan & Trust Co.* (1895), decided almost a century after *Hylton,* the Court found that in addition to land and capitation taxes, an income tax also qualified as "direct" and was unconstitutional without apportionment. The Court's decision quoted Hamilton's argument in *Hylton* about consulting British law, and, following his example, found that British law had always considered income taxes direct.[43] The Court's invalidation of the federal income tax in *Pollock* was extremely unpopular and spurred the passage of the Sixteenth Amendment.

The Court again invoked *Hylton*'s reasoning in its 2012 opinion upholding the constitutionality of the Affordable Care Act's individual mandate under the taxing power. In response to claims that the mandate constituted a direct capitation tax, the Court quoted Justice Chase's definition of a direct tax, a construct adopted from Hamilton's argument.[44]

Hamilton was too good not to be asked to argue again before the Court. Just four months after *Hylton*, a prominent Virginia land speculator approached Hamilton after being "informed that you practise in the supreme Court" and asked him to represent him in a land dispute (which would later be resolved by the Supreme Court in the landmark case of *Martin v. Hunter's Lessee*).[45] But Hamilton declined the representation, writing: "Answer in the Negative. It not being my general plan to practice in Supreme Court of U.S."[46]

So it was. Hamilton never again argued before the Supreme Court. As with the rest of his remarkable life, Hamilton's story as a Supreme Court advocate was tragically cut short by a bullet on the morning of July 11, 1804, on the banks of the Hudson River. But whatever was true of the duel that took Hamilton's life that morning, when it came to his one appearance before the Supreme Court, it is clear that Hamilton did not throw away his shot.[47]

5

"NEVER GON' BE PRESIDENT NOW"

Michael Gerhardt

Many conventional mechanisms for holding public leaders accountable for misconduct—gossip, anonymous letters, media coverage, elections, and impeachment—are featured in *Hamilton: An American Musical*. Although dueling has morphed into strident debates on Twitter and media wars, the most potent mechanism for holding public officials accountable—the judgment of history—remains intact. According to one scholar, "To self-conscious, reputation-minded politicians," such as Alexander Hamilton and Aaron Burr, "only one thing could be more volatile than the partisan battles of the 1790s: documenting them in the historical record."[1] Culture shapes the boundaries of social and constitutional mechanisms for holding high-ranking federal officials accountable, but history checks culture. History is always watching, or, as George Washington and the company sing near the end of the first act, "History has its eyes on you."[2]

In life and in the musical, Thomas Jefferson, James Madison, and Burr agreed on little but shared an intense distrust of Hamilton. They further agreed that, in issuing the *Reynolds Pamphlet* to clear his name,

Hamilton, then still the secretary of the Treasury, destroyed his reputation and future political prospects. In the musical, Burr asks, "How does Hamilton, the short-tempered, / protean creator of the Coast Guard, / Founder of the New York Post, / ardently abuse his cab'net post, / destroy his reputation?"[3] Later, Jefferson and Madison answer in glee. "Have you read this?" They joyfully sing, "You ever seen somebody ruin their own life?" They then happily conclude, "Never gon' be president now."[4]

Neither Madison nor Jefferson will sing that same song later for Burr when he self-destructs on a grander scale; instead, Burr summarizes the public's reaction to his misconduct, "Somebody tells me, 'You'd better hide.'"[5] Those who study the history of the Founding era will understand how Hamilton, in exposing his infidelity and paying more than one-third of his yearly income in blackmail money, destroyed himself. By contrast, Burr tried to keep his indiscretions hidden (although he admits to Hamilton at the latter's wedding that he is involved with the wife of a British officer, a woman he will eventually marry after the officer's death in the war), and thus his chicanery is murkier. In the musical, Burr is a scoundrel ("I'm the damn fool that shot him")[6] as he is depicted in history as well as fiction ("[Hamilton] may have been the first one to die, / but I'm the one who paid for it. . . . Now I'm the villain in your history").[7]

The musical shows the many faces of both corruption and redress or the means in America for holding "public men" (in Hamilton's phrase in *The Federalist Papers*)[8] accountable for their corruption. As Larry Lessig of Harvard Law School found in surveying the 325 uses of the term "corruption" in the Founding era, more than half of all cases discussed corruption of institutions, not individuals.[9] The musical reverses that formulation by focusing on corruption within individuals, as reflected in the public's reaction to Hamilton's confession in the "Reynolds Pamphlet," "Alexander Hamilton had a torrid affair. / And he wrote it down right there. . . . Damn!"[10]

The musical shows how corruption as a debasing dependence on illicit factions or self-interest—in individuals or institutions or both—was handled in the Founding era, though it leaves open the question of whether people corrupt in their private life, such as Hamilton, could be trusted in their public life. Not all corruption is on display in the musical, however. That is fitting since corruption is rarely done in the light of day for all to see, though Hamilton managed to do just that. *Hamilton* addresses both the corruption of Alexander Hamilton and Aaron Burr and the ways in which society and the federal government held miscreants responsible for their misconduct.

During Hamilton's all-too-brief life, there were numerous ways to address corruption—or illicit or unethical dependence on self-interest or factional influence. One was social. As we see in the musical, Hamilton's ambition drives him to find ways to rise in society, to become a notable American, and ultimately to serve as a senior aide to General George Washington in 1777 ("his right hand man!"),[11] a delegate to the constitutional convention ("There as a New York junior delegate"),[12] a prominent New York lawyer ("I bet you were quite a lawyer. . . . My defendants got acquitted"),[13] and as the nation's first secretary of Treasury ("Let's go!").[14] Yet, as Hamilton rose, he fell prey to the same forces that had helped his rise, including gossip and intrigue ("Jefferson will pay for his behavior. . . . I'll use the press. / I'll write under a pseudonym, you'll see what / I can do to him").[15] Hamilton became good at using each of these to his advantage, though they are two-edged swords, which can do as much harm to someone's reputation and advancement as any good. Hamilton's unbridled ambition, for that is what it was, led to his demise, leading to his ill-advised consort with a woman, who, with her husband, successfully blackmailed Hamilton ("Dear Sir, I hope this letter finds you in good health, / and in a prosperous enough position to put wealth / in the pockets of people like me: down on their luck. / You see, that was my wife who you decided to . . .").[16] Hamilton's infamous *Reynolds Pamphlet* had the virtue of confessing error, but it also exposed his corruption at the hands of two more sordid characters. Hamilton's fall was not complete until he confronted Burr in their fateful duel. His life was thus bracketed by "one shot," the first sung as an expression of his determination to succeed[17] and later as the bullet fired to end his.[18]

Another means for addressing corruption was political parties, including the newspapers that were their mouthpieces. Jefferson and Madison deceived Washington in founding the first national political party ("Let's show these Federalists who they're up against! . . . Southern motherfuckin'– . . . Democratic-Republicans!"),[19] which drove Washington's Federalists into extinction. Republican newspapers rallied support for their candidates ("You're openly campaigning? . . . That's new. . . . Is there anything you wouldn't do?")[20] while disparaging and undermining their opponents.

Elections were another common means for redressing misconduct. Hamilton never ran for office, but Washington's selection as the nation's first president (and known as "the indispensable man") in 1789 and re-election in 1793 made Hamilton's rise possible. ("It must be nice, it must be nice, to have / Washington on your side!")[21] In the first presidential election held without Washington, the constitutional order nearly broke down. In 1800, Jefferson won the public vote against incumbent John Adams, the only time a president ran against his own vice president. But they ended up deadlocking in the Electoral College because Jefferson's running mate Burr tried to break the tie by lobbying electors against Jefferson. Pursuant to the Constitution, the election was tossed to the House of Representatives.[22] After more than thirty ballots, the House chose Jefferson in a narrow vote. Hamilton influenced some votes, stressing Jefferson was "less dangerous" to America's future than Burr, who, Hamilton declaimed in the musical "Jefferson has beliefs. Burr has none."[23] And in real life, "loves nothing but himself."[24] The tie was broken (the Constitution later amended to preclude similar disasters in the future), but at the cost of inflaming Burr's anger.

Impeachment was the best-known means available in the new Constitution for holding certain "public men" accountable for "their misconduct," as Hamilton described *The Federalist Papers*.[25] However, the "one hundred ton," as one commentator described impeachment,[26] makes no appearance in the musical and for a good reason, since it did not in real life. Neither rumors of misconduct spread by Jefferson, Madison, nor the *Reynolds Pamphlet*, prompted Congress, led by Hamilton's fellow Federalists while he was in the cabinet, to take any action against Hamilton. Instead, the 1800 election drove Hamilton and the Federalists out of office and back to the practice of law and a private life that completed his undoing.

Hamilton features other means for addressing corruption. The most dramatic was dueling, a challenge made to defend one's honor. Weeks before the fateful duel, Burr lost an election for governor of New York. He lost because of his reputation as a scoundrel and, he thought, Hamilton's influencing New York's Federalist leaders to oppose him. Initially, Hamilton tried to undercut Burr (or, in Hamilton's view, tell the truth about his character) through gossip and letters. Gossiping and letter-writing provoke conflict, which provokes violence. ("Careful how you proceed, good man. / Intemperate indeed, good man. / Answer for the accusations I lay at your feet or / prepare to bleed, good man.")[27] Hamilton, in missives to friends about Burr, "attacked his private character, calling him a 'profligate' and a 'voluptuary in the extreme,' a man whose flawed character would drag his followers to ruin."[28] Dueling became the inevitable result of their feud, since "dueling was part of the larger grammar of political combat."[29]

At the musical's end, Burr is running for his life. Though still vice president, Burr was indicted for murder in New Jersey, the locale of the duel. (Alexander and Philip Hamilton declare in the musical, "Everything is legal in New Jersey!",[30] which wasn't true.) Burr became the first vice president to be indicted for a state crime,[31] an indictment that settled the question of whether such a high-ranking official could be indicted for a state felony. Burr did not reach trial. He kept running, eventually returning to Washington in time to preside over the impeachment trial of Samuel Chase, an ardent Federalist whom President Washington had appointed to the Supreme Court.

Burr did not face impeachment, but other political foes of Jefferson and Madison did. Upon taking office, the two realized they had the numbers in Congress to use impeachment to create vacancies in judgeships they could with their own loyalists.[32] The Republicans, led by Jefferson, claimed that judges' partisan decision making justified their impeachment.

One of their first targets was John Marshall, whom Adams had appointed chief justice of the United States while the House was struggling to decide the 1800 presidential election. While presiding over a trial in which the claimants argued that Jefferson and particularly Madison had destroyed their commissions to become judges and therefore deprived them of the offices to which they had been appointed by Adams, Marshall was threatened more than once by surrogates of Jefferson and Madison that if he did not rule as they would like he could expect to be impeached.[33] Marshall stood firm, though he eventually persuaded the Court to rule unanimously that although Jefferson and Madison had broken the law in not delivering the commissions to the claimants, the law granting the Court jurisdiction over the case was unconstitutional and therefore the Court lacked the power to decide the case. Marshall found a way to get rid of the case, without ordering Jefferson and Madison to do anything, but not before he exposed their breaking the law. As Erwin Chemerinsky notes in his chapter in this volume about *McCulloch v. Maryland*, Madison even came to agree with Marshall, at least insofar as Marshall interpreted the Constitution to allow the federal government to establish a national bank.

Supreme Court justice Chase was another target. Chase had been overly partisan as a trial judge in overseeing trials of Republicans for violating the Alien and Sedition Act, which had made it illegal for them to criticize the Adams administration. With Burr on good behavior throughout Chase's trial, the Senate failed to convict and remove Chase.

Next, Republicans came after John Pickering, a Federalist-appointed trial judge, whom Republicans charged with mental instability and drunkenness. Despite pleas from Pickering's son that his father was mentally and physically ill, the House impeached, and the Senate removed him from office.[34] Presiding over Chase's impeachment was one of Burr's last acts as vice president. His last was his resignation from office on March 4, 1805, a reminder that forced resignation was another means for redressing public misconduct.

Burr fled west, where Jefferson claimed he committed treason by conspiring to create an independent country in the center of North America. With the assistance of able counsel including two former attorneys general and the brilliant young lawyer Henry Clay, Burr claimed that he was merely arranging for the purchase of thousands of acres of farmland. At trial, Chief Justice Marshall presided. He found the charges made against Burr by Jefferson lacked the requisite evidence as prescribed in the Constitution to prove treason.

Burr then left Washington but did not find a suitable place to call home in Europe. He returned to New York, where he failed to revive his law practice under a different name. He married, but his wife filed for divorce months later after learning Burr had depleted her finances. Burr died the same day the divorce was granted.

Neither Burr nor Hamilton escaped the judgment of history. Historians have combed the records for years to figure out what Burr was up to in the west, but they cannot agree on the findings. David Stewart, a lawyer and historian, concluded Burr had committed "acts that constituted the crime of treason," but "the moral verdict is less clear" in the context of 1806.[35] He suggests that neither invading Mexico nor supporting secession was considered treason, because of the disputed boundaries of the American Southwest and President Jefferson's suggestions the nation might be split into two different ones. Other historians disagree. Some view Burr as misunderstood,[36] while others consider him evil and still others as both.

Much has changed since Burr and Hamilton died. People remain ambitious and often ruthless in their quest for power, and power can still corrupt. Social media makes both fact-checking and spreading unfounded disparagements easier. Madison's dream after the convention that our federal government would work because of checks and balances and factions keeping each other in check has disintegrated because of several constitutional developments—changing how senators are elected, the rise of political parties, and their control of the Electoral College.

Several mechanisms remain to redress public misconduct. Impeachment remains available, though it also remains difficult if not ineffective because of the constitutional requirements that the House must approve impeachment, and the Senate must approve conviction and removal by at least two-thirds approval.[37] No president has been removed from office for corruption, though the one president who came closest—Richard Nixon—resigned to avoid impeachment, conviction, and removal.[38]

Elections still are available, though they remain imperfect. Most eligible voters do not vote in presidential elections, and outcomes depend on which side has the bigger turnout. Nor is corruption not necessarily a disqualifier for office; many Americans voted for Bill Clinton despite his well-publicized infidelities and for Donald Trump despite news stories about his infidelities and dubious business practices.

The reason why these and other mechanisms for addressing misconduct are flawed is because they are historically and culturally situated. Culture shapes popular sentiments and construction of law. Thus, Clinton's and Trump's extramarital activities were irrelevant because they were not widely considered as disqualifying for election or service in office.

In the musical, it is culture, not government, that sanctions Hamilton. His infidelity and blackmail were enough to ensure he was "never gon' be president now."[39] The same is true for Burr, whose killing of Hamilton and later escapades ended his political career and marked him as a scoundrel for all time. Culture created the conditions that made and broke people. It determined who sat in "The Room Where It Happen[ed]."[40] Culture sanctioned dueling, destructive reporting, racism, sexism, voting restrictions, and ruthless power grabs. As to the ultimate sanction, culture shaped impeachment then, as it continues to do to this day.

HAMILTON

Child Laborer and Truant

Paul M. Secunda

The ten-dollar founding father without a father
got a lot farther by working a lot harder,
by being a lot smarter,
by being a self-starter,
by fourteen, they placed him in charge of a
trading charter

. . .

started workin', clerkin' for his late mother's landlord
tradin' sugar cane and rum and all the things he can't afford.

— "ALEXANDER HAMILTON," *HAMILTON*

In *Hamilton: An American Musical*, the audience learns through song that a group of fellow Caribbean inhabitants sent Alexander Hamilton to the United States based on his amazing skills as the head of a trading charter for a sugar and rum broker and that he learned to read and write through reading voraciously on his own.[1] Although not much of the play concerns Hamilton's life before he came to the colonies to make his fame as a Revolutionary War hero and leader of the new United States government, something stayed with me after listening to the opening song, "Alexander Hamilton." Hamilton worked as a child and did not appear to have attended primary or secondary school. Not only did he work hard as a child, but one is led to believe that his success later in life stemmed both from his early work experiences and from his lack of formal schooling as a child. "Got a lot farther by working a lot harder."[2]

Had Hamilton been born today in any modern, advanced industrial country, he would be barred from working at all prior to age fourteen, and limited in working between the ages of fourteen and seventeen, while required to attend school. If this were Hamilton's reality, would he have been the same "self-starter," who had an insatiable drive to found the U.S. national banking system, the Coast Guard, and the *New York Post*? Would he ever have become the first secretary of the Treasury? Might his tendency "to work a lot harder"[3] been squelched by the "paternalism" associated with modern-day child labor laws and compulsory schooling laws?

Although the question posed here is necessarily hypothetical, had child labor laws and compulsory education laws been in place when Hamilton was a child in the second half of the seventeenth century, he might not have been noticed by his fellow citizens in St. Croix after the calamity of the hurricane hit the island when he was seventeen; he may never have been sent to New York to become a "new man."[4] A Hamilton barred from working at the trading charter and stuck in a conventional school might have well been forced to throw away his shot."[5]

Laws governing employees' compensation and leave include some of the oldest employment legislation in the United States.[6] The primary compensation statute is the federal Fair Labor Standards Act (FLSA),[7] "a major part of the New Deal that still prompts significant political and legal battles. The Act's three pillars—the child labor, minimum wage, and overtime provisions—reflect the Depression-era concerns from which they arose."[8] The FLSA arose from the ashes of the Supreme Court's Lochner era, during which the Court repeatedly invalidated protective workplace legislation.[9] As far as child labor protections, the purposes of the law were two-fold:

> At the outset it should be recalled that the child labor provisions of the law were enacted in the year 1938, and its purposes were both economical and sociological. The entire nation had been affected with a depression that was world-wide. It was desirable to protect adult employees against the competition of minors. Moreover, the Congress was afforded an opportunity by

reason of prevailing conditions to enact a law long agitated [for] and exceedingly desirable to protect children against harmful labor.[10]

Under Section 12 of the FLSA, employers are prohibited from engaging in "oppressive child labor."[11] FLSA regulations define oppressive child labor as any employment of a child who does not meet the minimum age standards—generally sixteen years old for nonagricultural jobs.[12] The Department of Labor (DOL) may allow children between fourteen and sixteen years of age to work certain jobs under specific conditions.[13] The regulations currently allow for them to work in most jobs if the work does not interfere with their schooling or health; the work occurs outside of school hours; and the work does not exceed three hours a day or eighteen hours a week while school is in session, and eight hours a day or forty hours a week while school is not in session.[14] The DOL may also set an eighteen-year-old minimum for jobs it finds to be particularly hazardous.[15] States may, and often do, provide additional protections.[16]

The U.S. child labor prohibitions are well within the mainstream of international child labor standards. For instance, as one of its core conventions,[17] the International Labour Organization (ILO) similarly prohibits most forms of child labor among its signatory countries. In Convention 138,[18] the ILO sets the general minimum age for admission to employment or work at fifteen years (thirteen for light work) and the minimum age for hazardous work at eighteen (sixteen under certain strict conditions).[19] It provides for the possibility of initially setting the general minimum age at fourteen (twelve for light work) where the economy and educational facilities are insufficiently developed.

Interestingly, Saint Kitts and Nevis, where Hamilton was born, is now a signatory to Convention 138.[20] As of June 3, 2005, Saint Kitts and Nevis implemented Convention 138, setting sixteen as the minimum age for working most jobs. St. Croix, which is now part of the United States Virgin Islands, where Hamilton lived with his mother before and after her death, is not a signatory to Convention 138[21] but is bound by U.S. law, including the child labor provisions of the FLSA.[22] Either way, being the head of a trading charter for five months in 1771 at the age of fourteen[23] would now be in violation of both ILO Convention 138 and the FLSA child labor provisions. Hamilton perhaps would not have been allowed to develop the industry associated with "workin', clerkin' for his late mother's landlord, / tradin' sugar cane and rum and all the things he can't afford."[24] The unknown is whether Hamilton would have still "never been satisfied"[25] if he had a more normal childhood, attending formal school and reading what he was assigned to read, as opposed to "scammin' for every book he can get his hands on, / plannin' for the future."[26]

Whereas modern child labor laws would have prevented him from acquiring such positions of leadership in business at the trading post, compulsory education laws would have almost certainly placed him in some form of public schooling.[27] Although such laws are state-based in the United States, they would have applied to Hamilton in the United States Virgin Islands. In all, the combination of child labor laws and compulsory education laws would have kept Hamilton from working and required him to avoid truancy by attending school and keep up with his homework (even after his mother died when he was eleven).

For modern-day citizens of the world, it is gospel that children under the age of fourteen be prevented from working and that those between the ages of fourteen and seventeen be significantly limited in their ability to work. At the same time, children are supposed to attend some type of schooling, at least until they are sixteen or eighteen.[28] Does the story of Alexander Hamilton's childhood challenge our understanding about what is best for children when it comes to school and work?

I think not. As an initial matter, Hamilton was unusual in his resilience ("There would have been nothin' left to do for someone less astute, / he woulda been dead or destitute without a cent of restitution,")[29] surviving on an isolated island first with a single parent and then as an orphan. It was through a good deal of luck (recovering from the illness that killed his mother, surviving the Hurricane that destroyed his town in St. Croix, and then being noticed as exceptional by his fellow citizens) and hard work (both at the job and on his own time) that Hamilton was able to overcome his circumstances and become the hero and scholar[30] portrayed in the musical. It is not far-fetched to say that most children dealt this hand of cards would not have lived to lead such an extraordinary life, let alone survived at all. This tale of overcoming extreme odds is, of course, why *Hamilton* tells such a compelling story.

Like most welfare-oriented laws, child labor laws and compulsory education laws are meant to deal with the majority of cases involving children who without such laws would be forced into a life of difficult labor without any prospect of advancing their education and avoiding the vicious cycle of poverty. We continue to need child labor laws in the United States, where young children of migrant families are picking crops in fields in dangerous conditions and, with few exceptions, school truants do not generally become the leaders of tomorrow. Indeed, truants and kids who drop out of school before high school graduation are far more likely to get involved in illicit activities and spend at least some time in prison or at least struggling to survive.[31]

So hats off to Alexander Hamilton for not only surviving the turmoil of his childhood, but excelling in his role as Revolutionary War hero, scholar, and statesman. Although child labor laws and compulsory education laws might not have been necessary for someone so exceptional as Hamilton, children are far better off living under ILO Convention 138, the FLSA, and state compulsory school attendance law, so that they can focus on their education instead of stressing about the workaday worries that face most adults.

Part 2

"America, You Great Unfinished Symphony"

Hamilton's America — and Ours

Kermit Roosevelt III

Hamilton: An American Musical is a phenomenon.

Part of the triumph is due to the catchy melodies and clever use of rhyme and rhythm. It also helps that *Hamilton*'s musical style is more hip-hop than Hammerstein. But there is something else at work too: *Hamilton* has a political agenda, which it pursues in ways both subtle and audacious. The musical paints a picture of the Founding era that is hospitable to modern values of diversity and inclusivity.

In so doing, it has provoked a backlash, largely from those who share its progressive orientation but question its depiction of the Founding. The criticism is both surprising and understandable. Surprising because *Hamilton* simply continues a persistent trope in American politics, one used by Abraham Lincoln and Martin Luther King: retrojection of current values into the past. And understandable because the critics are right. *Hamilton*'s portrayal of the Founding is anachronistic and inaccurate. So too were Lincoln's and King's.

This conflict leaves us with a dilemma. The way forward, progressives think, is to embrace diversity, inclusiveness, and equality. But America typically moves forward by looking back. It is conventional to argue for contested values via the claim that they are the instantiation or fulfillment of a principle dating back to the Founding. If progressive values were not there at the Founding, is there any alternative to strategic misrepresentation?

There is an alternative. What we need to do is not to distort the Founding, but to recognize that our America is not Founding America, not even its descendant. Our nation was not born in 1776 with independence, as Lincoln argued, or even in 1787 with the constitutional convention. Our America is Reconstruction America, and it was born in 1868.

Hamilton gives us a picture of the Founding Fathers that defies conventional wisdom. Alexander Hamilton, the hero to the extent that the musical provides one, is proud of his immigrant status (which he shares with "America's favorite fighting Frenchman,"[1] the Marquis de Lafayette) and opposed to slavery. Other sympathetic characters, notably John Laurens, also fight slavery. The elimination of slavery, it is suggested several times ("We'll never be free until we end slavery!"),[2] will fulfill the grand aim of the Revolution and the Declaration of Independence (as, perhaps, will the extension of equal rights to women—"I'm 'a compel him to include women in the sequel!").[3] *Hamilton*'s antagonists, primarily James Madison and Thomas Jefferson, are by contrast proslavery ("That's the price we paid for the southern states to participate in our little independence escapade")[4] and anti-immigrant ("This immigrant isn't somebody we chose!")[5]

Those are relatively subtle choices about interpretation, emphasis, and dramatic shading. They are not necessarily historically sound, but they are hardly unprecedented. The present often ascribes its values to the past, both to find normative footing in tradition and to tell a national story of continuity, progress, and success. *Hamilton*'s more audacious move involves the casting: The casting takes a 180-degree turn from stereotyping; virtually without exception, the leading roles, including some Founding Fathers, are played by people of color. Of course, neither Washington, nor Jefferson, nor Madison, were African American. Hamilton himself—typically represented by a Latino actor—was ethnically Scottish.

The effect is quite striking. *Hamilton*'s America is informed by modern values; it sounds like modern America. But even more, it looks like modern America—or if it doesn't, it is because of the overrepresentation of people of color in positions of power. The purpose of this choice, and it's a purpose *Hamilton* achieves brilliantly, is not hard to discern. It is to show modern America an image of the Founding in which we—and particularly people of color—can see ourselves. It "is a story about America then, told by America now,"[6] according to Lin-Manuel Miranda, but it is perhaps more precisely a story about America then told *for* America now. Watching white slaveholders argue about their liberty (and fight against a nation that freed slaves) is alienating. That story of America excludes people of color. But in *Hamilton*'s reimagining, it's people of color who create America.[7]

In both these respects *Hamilton* is inaccurate. Because Alexander Hamilton emigrated from St. Croix as a teen, it is plausible to describe him as an immigrant. However, he qualified for the presidency under the provision that included those who were citizens of the United States when the Constitution was ratified. ("No Person except a natural born Citizen, *or a Citizen of the United States, at the time of the Adoption of this Constitution*, shall be eligible to the Office of President.")[8] But the Marquis de Lafayette was a French nobleman who spent a few years in America assisting the revolutionary forces before returning home to France. Characterizing him as an immigrant—as Miranda does when he has Lafayette and Hamilton sing together ("Immigrants: we get the job done!")[9]—is absurd. *Hamilton* also overstates the antislavery and feminist attitudes of most of its principal characters—notably Hamilton himself and Angelica Schuyler. (John Laurens, by contrast, deserves his abolitionist portrayal.) Historians such as Annette Gordon-Reed[10] and Ishmael Reed[11] have pointed out the inaccuracies; the latter even wrote a play in response.[12]

The criticisms levied against *Hamilton* are sound in their details. But it is hard to imagine that they will have any effect. The move that *Hamilton* makes—locating modern contested values in the past as a way of buttressing their authority—is a staple of American political argument. Consider two other striking examples of the practice: Abraham Lincoln's Gettysburg Address and Martin Luther King's "I Have a Dream" speech.

Lincoln and King appeal to the same text, the Declaration of Independence. The Civil War, Lincoln argues, is a war for the principles of the Declaration, for the idea that all men are created equal. It is a war for

America, for the America created in 1776, a war that will show whether any nation founded on the principles of the Declaration can long endure.

Similarly, King looks back to the Declaration's concept of equality to argue that racial segregation and race-based denial of the right to vote are a betrayal of our Founding ideals. Current practice dishonors the promise of the Declaration. His dream, he says, is that one day we will rise up and live out the full meaning of "all men are created equal."

Like the Declaration of Independence, the Gettysburg Address and the "I Have a Dream" speech are now considered foundational American documents, part of the long American history of working toward the ideals of the Declaration, principles of liberty and equality. Measured on a scale of *Hamilton*'s inaccuracies, they are at the implausible end of the spectrum—somewhere between Lafayette as immigrant and Washington as black.

In the Gettysburg Address, Lincoln is wrong to identify equality as the central ideal of the Declaration. Equality plays a limited and preliminary role in Jefferson's argument. He claims that all men are created equal to deny the divine right of kings and create an account of the source of political authority. All men are equal in the state of nature. Then they create governments and are no longer equal. This is true of insiders, those who form the government: as long as the government is fulfilling the purposes for which it was created, the governed must obey the governors. And it is even more true of outsiders, who remain in a state of nature with respect to the political community of which they are not a part. Jefferson means that they are equal in one sense—they have no duty to obey this government, which to them is foreign. (Having no duty to obey is almost the entirety of what Jefferson means by equal.) But in a more important sense, they are not equal: they have no right to equal treatment by the government they did not create, and no rights that the government is bound to respect. (Equality in these senses is what Lincoln means in the Gettysburg Address.)

Lincoln has performed a daring reinterpretation of the idea of equality—he has moved from Jefferson's equality to Lincoln's equality. From that perspective, he has taken a text that has little relevance and reimagined it to make it central. But he has done something more because the Declaration of Independence does have relevance to the battle of Gettysburg. There were men who fought there for its principles who gave the last full measure of devotion. But they were not the men Lincoln came to honor. They wore gray, not blue; they were the Confederates.

The point of the Declaration is to tell us when people are justified in rejecting political authority. They are justified in doing so when the government starts to threaten the rights it was supposed to protect. The Confederate states joined the Revolution, and later the Union, to protect certain rights of their citizens. High on that list was the right to own slaves. They feared the British might take that right away, and they left the empire. They feared the Republicans might take that right away, and they left the United States. Both times, they explicitly invoked the Declaration of Independence as their justification.

So Lincoln does not just press the Declaration into service in the name of an ideal it does not contain; he erases its central principle, which is political self-determination. He suggests that he and the Union are fighting for the Declaration, when in fact they are fighting against it.

Martin Luther King's move is, in some ways, equally extreme. He suggests that the ideals of the Declaration and the Founders' Constitution are inconsistent with segregation and racially discriminatory disenfranchisement. But this inference is rather obviously untrue. The Declaration says nothing about the duties that the government has to outsiders. In that sense, it is consistent with slavery. The Founders' Constitution is even more consistent with slavery: it recognized and protected the institution in various ways, though without ever using the word. Under the Founders' Constitution, the Supreme Court wrote in *Dred Scott*, black people constituted a class of perpetual, hereditary outsiders. They could not become citizens of the United States; they had "no rights which the white man is bound to respect."[13]

Of course, at the time King spoke, black people were American citizens. The U.S. Constitution no longer countenanced the possibility of a class of perpetual hereditary outsiders. But that inclusion was not because of anything in the Declaration or the Founders' Constitution; it was because of the Fourteenth Amendment. King's speech has an oddity comparable to Lincoln's in that he invokes the Declaration and the Founders' Constitution—texts that do not contain the principles he attributes to them—and ignores the Reconstruction Amendments, which do. State-sponsored racial segregation violates the Fourteenth Amendment;[14] racial discrimination in voting violates the Fifteenth.[15]

What does it mean that two of our greatest, most inspirational documents rely on a radical distortion of the past? Perhaps not much, if there is no alternative. But there is an alternative, as the discussion of King shows. The value of equality that Lincoln championed did not exist in the Constitution when he spoke. But he saw it coming; it was the new birth of freedom he prophesied. And its coming was a revolution, which marked the end of Founding America and the birth of a new nation.

The Reconstruction Amendments inverted the Founding vision of America. Almost all of the Founders saw states as the protectors of liberty. The federal government was the threat. If the federal government became a tyrant, the Founders thought, the state militias would fight it off. That was the structure of the Revolution when the minutemen fought off the redcoats. And it was the structure of the Civil War when the Confederate forces engaged the federal army. But they lost, and the Reconstruction vision, imposed by the Reconstruction Congress and the federal army, was a different one. Now the federal government would intervene to protect people from their own states.

One way of thinking about the scope of the change is to distinguish between two different types of revolutions. The first, which we can call a status quo revolution, does not object in principle to the existing political order. The revolutionaries' complaint is that they are being denied the rights they are due under that order, and they rebel to get what they are due. The American Revolution was of this type; the colonists' basic complaint was that they were being denied their rights as Englishmen.[16] So too was the Southern secession: the Southern states had joined the Union with the understanding that their right to own slaves would be respected and then thought that right was under threat. The second type is what we can call a regime change revolution. It does object to the existing political order. The revolutionaries' complaint is that the existing order is unjust and must be overthrown. Who waged that type of revolution? Abraham Lincoln. The Civil War started as a war for the Union, but it ended as a war for freedom, a war that would overthrow the Constitution that accepted slavery. Reconstruction was a revolution in our political structure, imposed by the victors in war, compelled by military force. It is every bit as radical as the first Revolution. It made a new and different America.

We are Reconstruction America, and we live under the Reconstruction Constitution. The Supreme Court decisions fundamental to our self-understanding—*Brown, Loving, Miranda, Gideon, Roe, Obergefell*[17]—are virtually without exception Fourteenth Amendment cases. The values we think of as fundamentally American—liberty and equality—are Reconstruction values that did not exist in the Declaration and the Founders' Constitution.

And that means something crucially important for the consistent practice of retrojecting modern values into the past, whether by Lincoln, King, or Lin-Manuel Miranda. Yes, it is nice to think that the values we now hold dear existed at the creation of our country. Yes, it is nice to tell a story of that creation that does not show us a group of Founders who are exclusively white and mostly slaveholders. Yes, it is nice to say that opposition to slavery was a big theme of the war that created America. And no, we cannot truthfully say those things about Founding America, the Revolution, and the Declaration of Independence.

But that doesn't mean we have to shade the truth, because our America was not born in that era. Our America is Reconstruction America. Our statement of principles, the Gettysburg Address, puts modern values of liberty and equality front and center. Our Constitution, the Reconstruction Constitution, gives them legal force. And the war that made our nation was a war against slavery, fought in substantial part by African American troops. What we need to do is simply to understand the truth about who we are and where we come from.

Popular culture can help a lot by making this past more accessible, of course. *Hamilton* provides a great example; its flaw is just that it looks to the wrong moment in history. The audiences that thrilled to a hip-hop Hamilton might be just as wowed by the Fourteenth Amendment drafter John Bingham.[18]

Let's go!

Hamilton and Washington at War and a Vision for Federal Power

Elizabeth B. Wydra

As *Hamilton: An American Musical* accurately portrays, much of the force behind our constitutional system of government came from advocates of strong federal power like George Washington and his "right hand man" Alexander Hamilton, who saw firsthand the pitfalls of a weak central government. The result was a vibrant federalist system that empowers the federal government to provide national solutions to national problems. Not ever wanting to see our noble nation barefoot, bloodied, and starving again—for although "as a kid in the Caribbean" he had "wished for a war," his experiences in the real thing showed him the need for unity and direction ("It's the only way to—Rise up!")[1]—Hamilton made sure the federal government established by our enduring Constitution had at least a fraction of the dazzling energy he expended in defending and promoting it.

Narratives of the Founders and activists who portray our Founding vision of a government "small enough to drown in a bathtub"[2] assert our constitutional structure as more of the Jeffersonian, small-government sort. This alternate vision—that the drafters of the Constitution were intent on creating a small, limited government—is frequently championed by conservatives but widely believed by Americans of all political stripes. As Ronald Reagan, perhaps the modern political figure most identified with this constitutional story, once supposedly said, "If more government is the answer, then it was a really stupid question."[3]

Reagan—elected 200 years after the Founding—was not around when our nation's early leaders were considering what sort of government should come after the Revolutionary War was won. As Eliza understood ("The fact that you're alive is a miracle"),[4] that victory was never a sure, or even likely event (note Washington's wonder in "Guns and Ships" when he sings, "If we manage to get this right, / they'll surrender by early light. / The world will never be the same, Alexander . . .").[5] After living and fighting through the limited central government established by the Articles of Confederation, the answer for Alexander Hamilton (and George Washington) to what sort of federal government we needed was indeed more—and more effective—national government. In *Hamilton: The Revolution*, Lin-Manuel Miranda and Jeremy Carter reflect: "It's a very American pastime, this interpreting and discussing. Our musical culture is built on standards, songs meant to be reworked endlessly . . . And it's not just our music: Think of the blood we've spilled looking for the best expression of 'All men created equal' or 'Congress shall make no law.' "[6]

In the mythology around our nation's Founding, we often skip straight from our revolt against a tyrannical monarch ("I will send a fully armed battalion / to remind you of my love!")[7] to the establishment of our federal constitutional system ("I can't stop until I get this plan through Congress")[8] with President Washington standing resolutely as America's first chief executive ("They are asking me to lead. / I'm doing the best I can").[9]

In reality, the rebellious colonies had put together a draft united government before what has become our enduring Constitution. It is important to remember that our Constitution was drafted in 1787—and not without conflict, as the musical portrays in the "Cabinet Battles"—"in Order to form a more perfect Union" that was both more perfect than the British tyranny against which the Founding generation had revolted and the flawed Articles of Confederation under which Americans had lived for a decade since declaring independence.

The Articles of Confederation, adopted by the Second Continental Congress in 1777 and ratified in 1781, established a confederacy built merely on a "firm league of friendship" among thirteen independent states.[10] There was only a single branch of the national government, the Congress, which was made up of state delegations.[11] Under the Articles, Congress had some powers but was given no means to execute those powers. For example, Congress could not directly tax individuals, nor could it enact legislation binding upon them; it had no express power to make laws that would be binding in the states' courts and no general power to establish national courts. Congress could raise money only by making requests to the States, which often fell on deaf ears.

This system created such an ineffectual central government that, according to Washington, it nearly cost Americans victory in the Revolutionary War—it was only because of the "young, scrappy and hungry"[12] troops that the colonies won the battle for independence. Amid several American setbacks during the war, Washington lamented that "unless Congress speaks with a more decisive tone; unless they are vested with powers by the several States competent to the great purposes of War . . . our Cause is lost."[13] In a plea to the state governments, Washington's correspondence, being drafted at that time by Hamilton, cataloged "an extremity of want."[14] Officers outfitted with "indecently defective" clothing, soldiers "almost naked, totally unprepared for the inclemency of the approaching season," with all the reports of officers attempting to procure supplies "gloomy." The letter concludes with the observation that "these circumstances conspire to show the necessity of immediately adopting a plan that will give more energy to the Government." Correspondence from Valley Forge describes the army as "bare foot,"[15] with "not a single hoof of any kind to Slaughter";[16] put plainly, the revolutionary army was "naked and starving"[17] because of the inability of the revolutionary government to provide for their needs. In the musical, Alexander Hamilton expresses the despair succinctly, "Congress writes, 'George, attack the British forces.' / I shoot back, we have resorted to eating our horses."[18]

The necessity of a federal government up to the task of providing for common needs of the new republic was a conviction Washington and Hamilton shared, and it shaped their view of what was required for the government that would eventually be structured in the Constitution. As Washington wrote to Hamilton, he believed that the inability of the central government to address common concerns such as the maintenance of an army could bring disaster: "The sufferings of a complaining army, on the one hand, and the inability of Congress and tardiness of the States on the other, are the forebodings of evil."[19]

In addition to the need for Congress to be able to tax and spend, Hamilton's experience of war under the Articles of Confederation spurred him to think for the first time about a national bank, which he would create as Treasury secretary. Because Congress could not effectively raise money during the war, it resorted to practices, such as overprinting money, that destroyed the young republic's credit. It also meant that many merchants would sell only to the revolutionary army if they had British currency. ("Local merchants deny us equipment, assistance, / they only take British money, so sing a song of sixpence.")[20]

Shortly after the Revolutionary War was won, Washington wrote to Hamilton stating that "no man in the United States is, or can be more deeply impressed with the necessity of a reform in our present Confederation than myself."[21] Washington explained that "unless Congress have powers competent to all general purposes, that the distresses we have encountered, the expences we have incurred, and the blood we have spilt in the course of an Eight years war, will avail us nothing."[22]

Hamilton's dreadful experiences at war under the government, as established by the Articles of Confederation, are dramatically rendered in political writing in multiple sections of the *Federalist Papers*. In the several papers focused on the "insufficiency of the present Confederation," Hamilton writes that "the facts that support this opinion are no longer objects of speculation," placing our country in "almost the last stage of national humiliation."[23] To convince his fellow Americans that a stronger government than that provided for in the Confederation was necessary in this new Constitution, Hamilton went to great lengths in the *Federalist Papers* to render "a full display of the principal defects of the Confederation . . . to show that the evils we experience do not proceed from minute or partial imperfections, but from fundamental errors in the structure of the building."[24]

When considering the architecture of this new constitutional "building," Hamilton and other delegates to the constitutional convention translated their concerns about and experience with ineffective central government into constitutional provisions that would arm the federal government with sufficient power to address the problems and potential of the "new nation"[25] with which babies Philip Hamilton and Theodosia Burr would "come of age."[26] It is perhaps not surprising that the first and one of the most sweeping powers given to Congress in the new Constitution provides the power "to lay and collect Taxes, Duties, Imposts and Excises, to pay the Debts and provide for the common Defense and general Welfare of the United States."[27] As Hamilton explained in the *Federalist Papers*, the power to tax and spend for the common defense and general welfare is "an indispensable ingredient in every Constitution,"[28] though one painfully missing from the Articles of Confederation. Hamilton urged that the Constitution must "embrace a provision for the support of the national civic list; for the payment of the national debts contracted, or that may be contracted; and, in general, for all those matters which will call for disbursements out of the national treasury."[29]

This rapid maturation of the American political project is remarkable— but starving half-naked on the battlefield can provide real motivation to face political reality. Shifting from revolution to statecraft, Hamilton was asking his fellow revolutionaries to grant their new government broad power to tax them. The Articles of Confederation's failure to provide the central government with the power to tax and spend had been a disastrous, if understandable, overreaction to the tyrannical taxes of the British monarch. The new Constitution would remedy that error. As Hamilton wrote in the *Federalist Papers*, a "nation cannot long exist without revenue."[30] As one constitutional scholar observes, "only a decade after they revolted against imperial taxes, Americans were being asked to authorize a sweeping regime of continental taxes, with the decisive difference that these new taxes would be decided on by public servants chosen by the American people themselves—taxation *with* representation."[31]

This zeal for a sufficiently energetic federal government was not simply born from the grumblings of a hungry stomach. Hamilton knew that a properly working government should be shaped not just by the immediate concerns of the people, but flexible enough to face circumstances the nation could not foresee. Hence the need for the Constitution's necessary and proper clause, which provides that Congress shall have the power to make all laws necessary and proper for executing its enumerated powers—such as the power to raise an army, regulate interstate commerce, establish courts, pay the debts of the country—as well as "all other Powers vested by this Constitution in the Government of the United States."[32] In considering how the necessary and proper clause should interact with federal power, then-Treasury secretary Hamilton explained to Washington that "the means by which national exigencies are to be provided for, national inconveniences obviated, national prosperity promoted, are of such infinite variety, extent and complexity, that there must of necessity be great latitude of discretion in the selection and application of those means."[33]

As Erwin Chemerinsky discusses in his contribution to this volume about Chief Justice John Marshall and *McCulloch v. Maryland*, perhaps the greatest example of this broad understanding of the necessary and proper clause was Hamilton's central bank idea, first conceived during the war. His bank bill sparked perhaps the first constitutional crisis, with Madison and Jefferson on one side, worried about what they saw as an ominous expansion of federal power, and Hamilton on the other (with, eventually, "Washington on [his] side").[34]

Although the government has no right "to do merely what it pleases," Hamilton explained the broad discretion given to Congress under the necessary and proper clause. "If the end be clearly comprehended within any of the specified powers, and if the measure have an obvious relation to that end, and is not forbidden by any particular provision of the constitution; it may safely be deemed to come within the compass of the national authority."[35] President Washington agreed with Hamilton's exegesis of the constitutional powers of the federal government, approving the bill to establish a national bank over the objections of other members of his cabinet, including Secretary of State Thomas Jefferson, and hailing Hamilton's vision of federal power.[36]

I agree with Chemerinsky that this vision of federal power, and the words in the Constitution to which it is anchored, is arguably Hamilton's greatest continuing legacy. Because his defense of the constitutionally implied power to create a central bank was so close in time to the creation of the Constitution, Hamilton's definition of federal power has become foundational. His flexible definition has allowed the federal government to respond to a changing world. It served as a model for the enforcement clauses of the post–Civil War amendments—the Thirteenth, Fourteenth, and Fifteenth Amendments that abolished slavery, ensured equal protection, and prohibited racial discrimination in voting—that finally placed the promises of the Declaration of Independence ("'Life, liberty and the pursuit of happiness.' / We fought for these ideals; we shouldn't settle for less. / These are wise words, enterprising men quote 'em. / Don't act surprised, you guys, cuz I wrote 'em.")[37] into our Constitution and gave Congress the power to make them a reality.[38]

9

TWO OATHS

Supporting and Defending the Constitution with Hamilton

Jill I. Goldenziel

Hamilton:	We won the war. What was it all for? Do you support this constitution?
Burr:	Of course.
Hamilton:	Then defend it.
Burr:	And what if you're backing the wrong horse?
Hamilton:	Burr, we studied and we fought and we killed for the notion of a nation we now get to build.

—"NON-STOP," *HAMILTON*

I have the privilege of educating our country's next Alexander Hamiltons. As a prerequisite for doing so, I have taken two oaths to the Constitution: one as an attorney upon admission to the New York Bar, and one upon becoming a professor at Marine Corps University Command and Staff College (CSC). As a civil servant, a lawyer, and a Civilian Marine, I live my two oaths every day as I strive to carry on Hamilton's legacy—and as I use *Hamilton: An American Musical* to teach. Hamilton was a soldier willing to devote his life to supporting and defending the nation and Constitution he helped to build. His ego and peccadillos aside, Hamilton embodies the type of public servant that I want my students to be.

I had no military background when I began my job at CSC. Armed only with a law degree and a PhD, I was charged with teaching Constitutional and International Law, Security Studies, and the Law of War to mid-career military officers. On my first day, I stepped past rifles and cannons in the hallways and into a room of twenty-one crew-cut men in camouflage who would be my new colleagues. Their dialect, known as "Milspeak," was riddled with so many military acronyms that it was unintelligible. Fortunately, one familiar ritual occurred that day. The orientation facilitator held up a pocket Constitution and told new employees to raise our right hands. More than a decade earlier, when entering the New York Bar, I swore to "support the Constitution of the United States." Now, like my students and colleagues, I swore to "defend" it as well.

After my disorienting orientation, with my head spinning, I flipped on the *Hamilton* soundtrack on my commute home. I had a sudden epiphany. *Hamilton* was the key to comprehending my job at CSC. Hamilton was on General George Washington's staff and took command at the Battle of Yorktown; my students are studying to be on high-level staffs and to take battalion command. *Hamilton* taught me what that meant.

Hamilton was also the key to understanding the two oaths I had taken to the Constitution. Most people think of the work of lawyers, civil servants, and military servicemembers as vastly different. However, our oaths to the Constitution, and our work to support and defend it, are two sides of the same coin. As a soldier, lawyer, and civil servant, Alexander Hamilton embodied both oaths and all that they stand for. As a soldier and lawyer, Hamilton shaped the environment in which the Constitution was born. He helped author the Constitution, then supported and defended it as a lawyer and civil servant. Hamilton understood that the Constitution binds the country together, and without it, the Revolutionary War would be for naught. He knew that without a military to protect our Constitution, it could not stand. And without the rights entrenched in our Constitution, our military would have nothing to fight for. For these reasons, *Hamilton* became the key to connecting with my students and colleagues and teaching them about what it means to support and defend the Constitution together.

The Founders placed primacy on ensuring that civil and military officers took an oath of allegiance to the nation and the Constitution. During the Revolutionary War, General Washington ordered that all officers take an oath to the United States. His practice broke from the Roman tradition of swearing an oath to a specific commander. It emphasized that his soldiers would renounce allegiance to the king and "support, maintain, and defend" the new political community. Later, the framers included two articles involving oaths in the bare-bones Constitution. Article VI specifies that senators, representatives, state legislators, and federal and state executive and judicial officers shall take an oath to support the Constitution. The first law of the fledgling U.S. Congress specified that oath's wording: "I, A.B., do solemnly swear or affirm (as the case may be) that I will support the Constitution of the United States." Congress soon created a separate oath for enlisted military personnel.[1] In 1790, Congress made the oath for both officers and enlisted personnel the same:

> I, A.B., do solemnly swear (or affirm) to bear true allegiance to the United States of America, and to serve them honestly and faithfully against all their enemies or opposers whomsoever, and to observe and obey the orders of the President of the United States of America, and the orders of the officers appointed over me according to the articles of war.[2]

Although this oath did not include the Constitution, servicemembers vowed allegiance to the country as a whole, not to a state, nor to a person, reflecting their commitment to the new political community.

The Constitution reentered the oath in 1862, during the Civil War. The "Ironclad Oath" required both civilian and military officers to support and defend the Constitution and swear that they had not borne arms against the United States or held office in the Confederacy.[3] The readdition of the requirement for civil servants and military officers alike to "support and defend" the Constitution, reflects the document's increased importance in holding the nation together during and after the war. The officer's oath was amended in 1868 to remove the "background check" provisions designed to root out supporters of the Confederacy after the war. In 1956, the Oath of Enlistment reinstated the requirement to support and defend the Constitution.[4] In 1966, the oath for civilian and military officers assumed its current form:[5]

> I, A.B., do solemnly swear (or affirm) that I will support and defend the Constitution of the United States against all enemies, foreign and domestic;

that I will bear true faith and allegiance to the same; that I take this obligation freely, without any mental reservation or purpose of evasion; and that
I will well and faithfully discharge the duties of the office on which I am
about to enter. So help me God.

Why these changes in the requirements to support and defend? When
the existence of nation was at risk due to war, the requirement to defend
the Constitution became paramount. The original oath requiring soldiers
to support and defend the United States dated from the Revolutionary
War. After the passage of the Constitution, the first military oath of 1789
required only that servicemembers "support" the Constitution. The active
requirement to "defend" was re-added during the Civil War, when our national existence was again at stake, and when the Constitution was most
at risk of being torn apart. During the bloodiest war in American history,
Congress believed that it was critically important for each servicemember
to affirm that he would take up arms to keep the structure of the nation,
established by the Constitution, from crumbling. In 1868, the "Ironclad
Oath" became mandatory for all military officers and civil servants, requiring that civil servants "defend" the Constitution as well. This, too,
made sense in the Civil War context, when the line between civilians
and servicemembers blurred as untrained civilians took up arms. After
the Civil War, the officers' oath retained the language of supporting and
defending the Constitution itself, in recognition of the Constitution's increased importance to national unity and the fact that so many had given
their lives in defense of the Constitution. The war had agonizingly proven
that without fidelity to the Constitution, the nation itself would not stand.
Around this time, the Thirteenth, Fourteenth, and Fifteenth Amendments
cemented the Constitution's preeminence over state law. Public reverence
for the Constitution as the foundation and embodiment of national unity
began to crystallize into what it is today.

In the military, the oath is more than a formality. Servicemembers
renew their oath at each promotion ceremony to remind them of their
commitment to serve the Constitution above all. Courses on the Constitution are required at all levels of professional military education. *The
Armed Forces Officer*, a foundational text in military education, begins
with a chapter called "The Commission and the Oath."[6] It notes that the
officer's commission is contingent on the oath, but that the oath does not

specify how the officer will support and defend the Constitution.[7] The military officer holds a role different than a civil servant because the public trusts the officer to apply "the disciplined use of legal force"[8] to defend the Constitution, and to offer, if necessary, his or her life in its defense.[9]

Lawyers, often called "officers of the court," have also sworn an oath to the Constitution since Hamilton's day.[10] Although wording varies, most states require lawyers to swear to support the Constitution. Some states also require lawyers to "defend" it.[11] The profession's commitment to the Constitution is reflected in legal education. Almost all U.S. law schools require their students to take a survey course in Constitutional law. The Constitution is a subject on the multistate bar examination required to practice law. Lawyers are extensively trained on how the Constitution is the backbone of our nation's rule of law. The drive to support and defend it motivates lawyers and servicemembers alike.

What do these oaths mean? An oath solemnizes an occasion that might otherwise be seen as ceremonial. By swearing or affirming one's allegiance to the Constitution, the oath-taker pronounces a deep personal commitment to a set of ideals. The words "so help me God" at the end of the oath are meant to reinforce the individual nature of this commitment.[12] They signify that violation of the oath will have personal consequences for the oath-taker, wrought by God or otherwise.

As for "support" and "defend," the definitions are mirror images.[13] The Merriam-Webster dictionary offers six definitions for "support." The most relevant include "to promote the interests or cause of," "to uphold or defend as valid or right: ADVOCATE," "to argue or vote for," "to provide a basis for the existence or subsistence of," "to hold up or serve as a foundation or prop for," and "to keep (something) going."[14] The dictionary also offers five definitions for "defend." These include "to drive danger or attack away," "to maintain or support in the face of argument or hostile criticism," and notably, "to act as an attorney for." These definitions reflect that the Constitution can be supported and defended through words, work, and force alike, and that these are meant to achieve the same ends. Although many lawyers do not swear to "defend" the Constitution, the definitions of "defend" explicitly include both the work of an attorney and protection by force. Full embodiment of the concepts of "support and defend" implies both the use of force and the use of words and nonlethal action. Violence and nonviolence may be necessary to protect the

Constitution but are meant to be used in tandem, by civilian and military professionals working together.

By taking an oath to the Constitution, servicemembers, civil servants, and lawyers pledge themselves to serve the nation as a whole and all for which it stands. Military officers swear allegiance to the rights and ideals entrenched in the constitutional text. Their oath to the Constitution means pledging themselves to a social compact made by "We the people"—a covenant that serves as a higher authority than any individual, even higher than the commander-in-chief. For civil servants, the oath is a reminder that we labor in support of something higher than any specific law, and are required to challenge assignments or duties that would violate the Constitution. The oath reminds lawyers of our profession's commitment to support the Constitution, and our professional obligation to interpret this living document in their work. The Constitution symbolizes the ethical requirements of these professions, and the higher standard to which society holds members of these professions. Military officers, civil servants, and lawyers alike are frequently admonished to "live up to their oaths," especially when misconduct by members of their professions comes to light.[15] Because the oath is mandatory for all members of these professions, the act of oath-taking initiates the oath-taker's membership in a community that is committed to the content of that oath.[16] Servicemembers, public servants, and lawyers often speak of being part of something greater than themselves. The Constitution is a physical and metaphorical embodiment of that "something."

I first understood the full meaning of my oaths from conversations about the Constitution with my military students and colleagues. I have always considered exercising my First Amendment rights and supporting the Constitution through political activism to be a crucial part of my civic duty. So I was surprised to learn that my highly civic-minded military colleagues did not reserve time during election season for campaigning, getting out the vote, and attending rallies as I did. In many respects, the constitutional rights of servicemembers are curtailed so that they can better serve the Constitution. Department of Defense (DoD) regulations prohibit servicemembers from engaging in partisan activity in their capacity as a representative of the Armed Forces and from criticizing the president while in uniform.[17] Servicemembers may privately engage in partisan activities, but must "avoid inferences that their political activities imply or appear to imply official sponsorship, approval, or endorsement."[18] Most servicemembers I know are quiet about their political beliefs while in uniform and often choose not to engage in partisan activities at any time. When I mention politics, some servicemembers walk away. These restrictions serve an important purpose as political tensions among servicemembers could detract from the cohesiveness critical to their mission.[19] And if they are sometimes seen in uniform, the public may view them as representing the military, regardless of how they present themselves in their personal capacity. In my position as a DoD civilian, I have far fewer constraints.[20] I, too, cannot legally engage in partisan activity during duty hours, or portray myself as representing the DoD when engaging in partisan activity at any time. So long as I speak in my personal capacity, however, I can engage in a wider array of political activity when off duty.[21] Doing so is part of my own professional culture as a lawyer, educator, and leader. Talking with servicemembers who have these First Amendment rights restricted made me appreciate my rights even more. Just as important, meaningful conversations with my students and colleagues about what exercising First Amendment rights means for civic duty beautifully manifested how the Constitution can bind together committed Americans with diverse political views.

That first year of teaching, I gave pocket Constitutions to my colleagues and students as holiday gifts. One officer asked for extras so that he could use them as stocking stuffers. We agreed that our rights are a gift. I keep a copy in my classroom, referring to it often to remind my students of our shared oaths. I teach my students about the important constraints the Constitution places on the military's operations within U.S. borders, treatment of U.S. citizens fighting for enemy actors, surveillance of U.S. citizens, and more. Through teaching, I have come to realize that my oath and the officer's oath were not just mirror images but intertwined. While my students and colleagues defend the Constitution with their lives, I support it by exercising my rights and defending those of others to ensure it does not collapse from within. Without their oath to defend the Constitution, my support for it would not be enough for it to stand. Without my oath to support it, they would not have a country to defend—and perhaps not one worth defending. We support and defend the Constitution in ways the other cannot. And as the character of war is becoming ever more complex, it makes sense that we had taken the same oath to be in the fight together.

Long before I arrived at CSC, assigned reading for the mandatory course in Security Studies included the Constitution, the *Federalist Papers*, and Washington's farewell address. To teach them, I introduced twenty-eight military officers to *Hamilton*. Most students thought I was crazy for bringing Broadway into military education—until they heard the music. They told me it was "actually good." Although I could barely comprehend Milspeak, *Hamilton*—and the Constitution—provided a language we could all understand. I used the song "Alexander Hamilton" to have the students meet the author of the *Federalist Papers* and explained how his personal background related to the course material. I played "Non-Stop" to introduce the *Federalist Papers*, and "One Last Time" and "I Know Him" to teach Washington's farewell address. By using *Hamilton* to teach the Constitution, I give servicemembers a lesson they are likely to remember, and to which they might even sing along.

Determined to improve my students' understanding of how the Constitution unites us, I formed and became commander of the faculty's informal Hamilton Operational Planning Team. So far, we have brought groups of students and faculty to visit Montpelier, the home of Hamilton's friend cum nemesis James Madison, for a tour focused on the Constitution and a discussion of the legacy of slavery as we view Madison's slave quarters from the rooms where he authored the Bill of Rights. We have also established a popular trip to Yorktown to tour the battlefield and visit the exhibits on the Constitution at the American Revolution Museum. Hamilton's legacy as a lawyer, soldier, and statesman lives on at Marine Corps University. I am humbled by my responsibility to serve my country by educating our country's next Hamiltons to live up to our oath.

Part 3

"We'll Never Be Truly Free"

Hamilton *and Race*

FINDING CONSTITUTIONAL
REDEMPTION THROUGH *HAMILTON*

Christina Mulligan

An ambiguity about the race of its characters runs through *Hamilton: An American Musical*. *Hamilton*'s audience sees that people of color play the revolutionaries, and the same audience knows that those same historical figures were white. One way to think about these two facts is to understand *Hamilton* as casting people of color in white roles.

Another way to think about *Hamilton*'s diverse cast is to understand the musical as presenting us with an alternate reality in which Alexander Hamilton, George Washington, and their associates were people of color.

The journalist Aja Romano embraces this interpretation, arguing that *Hamilton* is "simultaneously an alternate version of American history and a modern political [alternate universe] in which none of the Founding Fathers are white and everything happens in a blurred temporality that could be modern-day America."[1] The alternate reality illusion is admittedly brittle. Early in the musical, the character John Laurens sings of "sally[ing] in / on a stallion with the first black battalion,"[2] all while sharing the stage with several black actors, including (in the show's original cast) Daveed

Diggs, playing the French Marquis de Lafayette, Leslie Odom Jr. as Aaron Burr, and Okieriete Onaodowan as Irish-born tailor Hercules Mulligan. What would Laurens's battalion look like in this universe? Most easy-to-imagine answers would displace the suspension of disbelief.

Even though it may be difficult to maintain the alternative universe's conceit, it provides a satisfying way of understanding the intentionally ahistorical bits of the show—New York City didn't have a strong claim on being "the greatest city in the world" in the late 1700s, and Burr's admission that he's "a trust fund, baby"[3] makes the audience laugh because it references far-future stereotypes about children who inherit wealth. Historian and law professor Annette Gordon-Reed describes *Hamilton* as historical fiction,[4] but it's even more than that. It's alternative reality historical fiction, intentionally engaging with the historical record and equally concerned with being in dialogue with the present.

Even if we understand *Hamilton* as fiction, it still has a profound effect on how its audience engages with the reality of the Founding era. As history and American culture studies professor Andrew Schocket writes, "When we watch a show, we internalize its messages. That's true even when we're advised that it is a particular interpretation, even when we're told we're watching a fictionalized account, and even when we're informed that parts of it are flat-out wrong."[5] We know that Alexander Hamilton was white, but after watching Lin-Manuel Miranda and his successors play him, we also can't help but feel like, in some inexplicable way, he wasn't.

Daveed Diggs, who originated the roles of Lafayette and Thomas Jefferson in *Hamilton*, describes this phenomenon. "I have to say, the dollar bill looked really wrong after the first workshop. I was like, 'That really should be Chris Jackson [who played George Washington].' "[6] He elsewhere expounds on how Jackson's portrayal affected his relationship to the Founders:

> All of a sudden I have a real connection to this Founding Father who's been the dude on the money for so long. Or, like, you know, some shit about a cherry tree. Having this living, breathing, real, passionate, and supremely virtuosic human being be the stand-in for what that person is in my brain—and that's forever now. Any time I think about George Washington, it's Chris Jackson. And if something similar to that is happening for people

who come see the show, the effect really is profound, because that gives me a type of ownership over the history of this country that I didn't have before.[7]

In *Hamilton: The Revolution*, Diggs describes how *Hamilton* affected his relationship to America despite having "always felt at odds with this country. . . . You can only get pulled over by police for no reason so many times before you say, 'Fuck this.'"[8] He wonders how seeing a black man play Jefferson or Madison or Washington when he was a kid might have changed him. He surmises, "A whole lot of things I just never thought were for me would have seemed possible."[9]

Leslie Odom Jr., the original Aaron Burr, similarly reflects on how the portrayal of these historical figures as people of color affected him: "In the first two minutes of the show, Lin [-Manuel Miranda] steps forward and introduces himself as Alexander Hamilton, and Chris steps forward and says he's George Washington, and you never question it again. When I think about what it would mean to me as a 13-, 14-year old kid, to get this album or see this show—it makes me very emotional."[10]

Commentators differ about whether people of color identifying with the Founders is positive or negative. John McWhorter cheers that "Angelica Schuyler, of all people, will now likely forever be spontaneously imagined as an imperiously lovely black woman like Renée Elise Goldsberry, just as a new generation of kids spontaneously imagine America's president as a pensive black man."[11] But when Patricia Herrera's ten-year-old daughter told her she wanted to dress up like Angelica Schuyler for Halloween, Herrera had a different reaction from McWhorter. "I asked myself, 'How could my beautiful brown-bodied Latina daughter want to be Angelica Schuyler, a slave owner?'"[12] Herrera was concerned with the same phenomenon that struck McWhorter as a positive—that "*Hamilton* may . . . make it difficult for my daughter, and perhaps other youth, to differentiate Angelica Schuyler from Renée Elise Goldsberry, the African-American actress personifying Angelica."[13] Reconsidering her initially positive views on *Hamilton*, Herrera explains: "I realized I had been caught up in a utopian vision of America as a model of diversity, equality and democracy and that it was time for me to wake up from this dream. It wasn't true . . . Miranda gives us permission to imagine the possibilities of multicultural and racial diversity that might have existed in a nation that truly embraced freedom at its birth. But that nation doesn't exist."[14]

McWhorter's applause and Herrera's concern about how *Hamilton*'s audience engages with Schuyler and the other *Hamilton* figures reflect a larger divergence in how Americans understand and relate to the Founding era. At one end sits a cluster of mostly positive views about America's Founding—that it was a moment of great and surprisingly successful political innovation, creating a large and long-lived republic and a national Constitution that is generally considered to have been in force longer than any other.[15] Closely associated with this positive view of America is a style of biographical writing about the Founders, often derogatorily referred to as "Founders chic," a term popularized in a 2001 essay published in *Newsweek*.[16] These works tend to celebrate the Founders, focusing on their personalities and characters.[17] David Waldstreicher and Jeffrey Pasley characterize "the logic of Founders chic" as increasingly "seek[ing] and highlight[ing] antislavery sentiment wherever it can be found."[18] They go on to say that "When well plotted, Federalist antislavery becomes a reason we can still venerate the Founders, or at least some of them."[19]

For others, the fact that Alexander Hamilton was in the New York Manumission Society or that George Washington arranged to free his slaves in his will counts for little when weighed against other Founding-era realities. Many of the Founders owned or traded in slaves, and the framers and ratifiers signed on to a Constitution that not only contemplated the continuation of slavery, but also included provisions like the fugitive slave clause, the three-fifths clause, and the migration or importation clause, which limited the federal government's effective ability to curtail it. The novelist Ishmael Reed, critiquing *Hamilton*, compares slave-holding Founders to kidnapper Ariel Castro. Baffled by black men playing the Founding Fathers on stage, he writes, "Now I have seen everything. Can you imagine Jewish actors in Berlin's theaters taking roles of Goering? Goebbels? Eichmann? Hitler?"[20] Writer Ta-Nehisi Coates draws a further connection between the slavery and racism in the 1700s and the present day: "In America, it is traditional to destroy the black body—it is heritage. . . . There is nothing uniquely evil in these destroyers or even in this moment. The destroyers are merely men enforcing the whims of our country, correctly interpreting its heritage and legacy. This legacy aspires to the shackling of black bodies. It is hard to face this."[21]

At first glance, these competing visions of America suggest that the question of whether we should applaud or recoil from *Hamilton*'s enfranchising effects supervenes on a much more fundamental question: Is America—the political project that extends from the Revolution to today—good? If America is good and becoming better, we should encourage fealty to the project, through *Hamilton* and otherwise. But if America was forever contaminated by the evils of slavery, if it carries these and other flaws with it into the present, then *Hamilton* does a great wrong of tricking its audience members into identifying with their enemy.

But asking whether America is good won't necessarily tell us whether it deserves our fellowship. A more useful question is, can America be redeemed? In his book *Constitutional Redemption*, Jack Balkin sets aside static questions of goodness. "All constitutions are agreements with hell, flawed, imperfect compromises with the political constellation of the moment. . . . The question is whether such a compromise, such a Constitution, can eventually be redeemed over time."[22] Rather than understanding the story of America as a story of progress, decline, futility, or stasis,[23] Balkin argues that America ought to be understood through the lens of redemption, as "a story about the eventual fulfillment of promises made long ago"[24]—specifically, the promises of liberty and equality made in the Declaration of Independence, repeated in the Gettysburg Address, and imperfectly implemented in the Constitution and its amendments. As Americans, our legacy is the project of implementing this vision of liberty and equality, something that the Declaration's author, Thomas Jefferson—who held slaves, fathered children with one of his slaves, Sally Hemings, and clearly articulated his belief in the inferiority of black people in his *Notes on the State of Virginia*[25]—plainly could not and did not do. We will not fully succeed, but we are nonetheless charged with trying. "As the Talmud tells us: you are not required to complete the Great Work; but neither are you free to refrain from it."[26]

Crucial to Balkin's vision is the notion of *we*—the "We the People" that appears at the beginning of the Constitution, that constitutes the America in need of redemption. Culturally and psychologically, the question of who feels part of "We the People" is contingent on each individual's relationship with America. It depends on one's experiences—Daveed Diggs's experience of getting pulled over by police in his car alienated him from America; playing Jefferson and Lafayette brought him closer to it. And whether you can feel part of "We the People" also depends on how others react to you—whether you perceive that other recognizable members of

"We the People" recognize you among them. Recursively, *we* construct who America is. *Hamilton* participates in that construction by "reallocating the ownership of the republic" to people who have historically and unjustly been alienated from it.[27]

In order for America, its Founding, and its Constitution to be redeemed, we have to commit ourselves to the project. And by committing ourselves to the project, we choose to identify with "We the People," a transgenerational "we" that makes us part of the American political project that extends over time.[28] This commitment, or as Balkin would say, fidelity, is a necessary condition for a polity's success. He accurately notes, "A well-designed constitution can fall apart in months without public attachment and support; an imperfect constitution can last for centuries."[29]

Balkin's argument thus unexpectedly reveals a subtle circularity in the question of whether it is good for *Hamilton* to better connect its audience to America. America is in a constant state of becoming. It will become different Americas, depending on whether we, as individuals, choose to commit to it or not. And America's goodness—or, more appropriately, its ability to be redeemed—depends on those decisions to commit to it or not. The act of choosing influences whether it will have been a good decision.

Around the time Washington's farewell song, "One Last Time," was being rewritten, Chris Jackson recalls hearing about the mass shooting by a white supremacist at the Emanuel African Methodist Episcopal church in Charleston, South Carolina. "It stopped me cold," says Jackson. He then adds, "To me, it encapsulated the thought that the struggle continues. The idea is perfect, the execution is not. It's never been perfect."[30]

It's never been perfect. Driving the point home, Jackson explains that he chose to have Washington bow his head in shame at the end of *Hamilton* when Eliza describes her antislavery efforts, as a way of having Washington "accept responsibility for what he did and didn't do."[31]

It won't ever be perfect.

But *we* can still commit to making it more perfect.

Race, Nation, and Patrimony, or, the Stakes of Diversity in *Hamilton*

Anthony Paul Farley

Alexander Hamilton:	"This is the stain on our soul and democracy A land of the free? No it's not, it's hypocrisy To subjugate, dehumanize a race, call 'em property And say we are powerless to stop it, can you not foresee?" — "Cabinet Battle #3," *Hamilton*
John Laurens:	"But we'll never be truly free until those in bondage have the same rights as you and me." — "My Shot," *Hamilton*

Hamilton: An American Musical is a history and a prophesy, a public memory of the America that will be. *Hamilton* asks us to reimagine the Founders, to see them from the inside and illuminate our beginning by our cosmopolitan present. Audre Lorde observed that "poetry is not a luxury."[1] *Hamilton* is an example of what she called "poetry as illumination," poetry as a way to conjure something from nothing, the still "nameless and formless" something that is "about to be birthed, but already felt."[2]

If the twenty-first century were to somehow illuminate the eighteenth, what would we learn about the so-called Founding Fathers, about ourselves, about our inheritance, and about the future and our debt to it?

Hamilton shows us "the land that has never been yet / and yet must be."[3] *Hamilton* presents us to ourselves as if we were fighting for the land where everyone is free, the America that is yet to be.

When Langston Hughes, poet of the Harlem Renaissance, asked us to remember the "America [that] will be!,"[4] he was presenting us with a paradox as a problem and a gift. When Lin-Manuel Miranda wrote *Hamilton*, he followed Hughes's lead, asking, in essence, what if we were all able to call the Founders our forefathers and foremothers? As Richard Primus asks in his chapter in this volume, what if we were all able to imagine ourselves as sisters and brothers? What would it be for America, "the land that has never been yet / And yet must be," to one day be America again? What would it be if we could all say that America "was America to me"?[5]

Seeing and hearing racially diverse actors play the Founders as if their struggles were ours is an invitation to think, or rethink, questions of race, patrimony, filial loyalty, national belonging, capitalism, and future possibilities. We the people are entertained by the "ten-dollar founding father without a father,"[6] but the Founders would not have been at all entertained to see themselves portrayed by blacks or to see their republic claimed by us. The Founders, on seeing us on stage or in the audience *while black*, would deny that we were any part of their heritage and likely kill us if they could not reduce us from the indirect obedience and apparent free-range of wage-slavery to the direct obedience of chattel slavery. "How does the bastard, orphan, son of a whore, / go on and on, / grow into more of a phenomenon?"[7]

Let us go back to the beginning, the first chapter, as sung in *Hamilton*: "Look around, look around at how lucky we are / to be alive right now."[8] What might living eyes have seen in 1776 and 1789? Did slaves see themselves as lucky? "That would be enough."[9] Would being alive, at least in a physical sense, have been enough? Or, was it more like the feelings of Alexander Hamilton: "I imagine death so much it feels more like a memory"?[10]

When Dred Scott, a slave, declared himself a free man and a citizen, he adopted Eliza Hamilton's entreaty to "let me be a part of the narrative / in the story they will write someday. / Let this moment be the first chapter."[11] Scott claimed the rights of a free man and citizen for himself and his family. He argued in U.S. federal court that he, as a slave who had resided in the Missouri Territory, "free" territory under the Missouri Compromise of 1820, was a free man under the "once free, always free" doctrine. Thirty years of precedent supported the idea that owners who took slaves from slave states to free states and territories for extended periods of time lost their right to own the men, women, and children they had taken.

Charles Stewart purchased James Somerset, an enslaved black person, in Boston and brought him back to England in 1769. Somerset freed himself in 1771, only to be recaptured later that year. Stewart's plan to ship the freedom-seeking Somerset to Jamaica and sell him was thwarted by litigation. At the time, *Somerset v. Stewart* was the most important legal decision in the world: "No master ever was allowed here to take a slave by force to be sold abroad because he had deserted from his service, or for any other reason whatever; we cannot say the cause set forth by this return is allowed or approved of by the laws of this kingdom, therefore the black must be discharged."[12] Escape from this ruling that slavery was against "both natural law and the principles of the English Constitution"[13] was the concern in the minds of the Founders when they drafted the new American Founding document.

James Somerset was part of the narrative. His story, a human story from the early beginnings of case reporting, became part of the long story about England, and thus part of our English inheritance. The Somerset case looked back from the eighteenth century to the sixteenth: "In the eleventh of Elizabeth (1569), one Cartwright brought a slave from Russia, and would scourge him, for which he was questioned; and it was resolved, That England was too pure an air for slaves to breath in."[14] The story of England became the story of abolition relied on in the Somerset case. English purity, as the story goes, was seen in the fact that the mere act of breathing its air made one free. American purity could have been measured the same way. Indeed, had the Supreme Court followed the law, it would have been. It matters who tells your story.

Despite the Founding Fathers' proslavery efforts, the abolitionist principle remained, and like Somerset before him, Scott took his shot: "I'm just like my country, / I'm young, scrappy and hungry / and I'm not throwing away my shot."[15] Dred Scott was the only named plaintiff, but his freedom suit was for himself, his wife Harriet, and their children, Eliza and Lizzie. Telling the story of the enslaved Scott family as a story about a family, as a story about Dred and Harriet, parents of Eliza and Lizzie, is itself another story, a story excluded from the law by the Supreme Court. In a 7–2 decision, the United States Supreme Court rejected Scott's freedom suit, as well as any place for Dred, Harriet, Eliza, and young Lizzie Scott in the national narrative.

Dred Scott v. Sandford[16] was the repetition event that tumbled the North and South into the Civil War, bringing the nation back to its constitutive contradiction. Chief Justice Roger B. Taney, writing for the Supreme Court, argued that as neither Scott nor any person descended from Africans, whether slave or free, could be a citizen, Scott's claim of legal standing to bring suit in federal court was invalid. Taney also held that the Ordinance of 1787 could not confer citizenship or freedom on non-whites. Finally, Taney held that the Missouri Compromise was void because Congress did not have the power to grant freedom or citizenship to nonwhite persons in the northern part of the Louisiana Purchase. Jefferson supposed the Missouri Compromise to be the "death knell" of the Union because it enacted a division, with free states on one side and slave states on the other. Slavery, for Jefferson, should not and could not be restricted anywhere if the republic were to survive. Survive? It was dead already. Any nation with slavery was not truly alive. Slavery, to borrow Lorde's language, the "death we are expected to live,"[17] was an end, not a beginning.

Chief Justice Taney told a story, Scott's story, as the story of an object among other objects, not as a member of a class of persons who had ever been or ever could be considered "people of the United States" or "citizens." Both terms, per Taney, describe "the political body who, according to our republican institutions, form the sovereignty and who hold the power and conduct the Government through their representatives."[18] For the Court, the answer to whether blacks could be thought of as "people of the United States," was clear: "We think they are not, and that they are not included, and were not intended to be included, under the word 'citizens' in the Constitution, and can therefore claim none of the rights and privileges which that instrument provides for and secures to citizens of the United States."[19]

Blacks were today, tomorrow, and forever excluded from being considered to have been included within the sovereign that refers to itself in its

Constitution as "we the people" because blacks had been stamped from the beginning as not part of the story. The end was in the beginning. In Taney's words: "They had for more than a century before been regarded as beings of an inferior order, and altogether unfit to associate with the white race either in social or political relations, and so far inferior that they had no rights which the white man was bound to respect."[20] The fixed exclusion of the black from life was both axiomatic, a starting point for rational inquiry, and an everyday observable fact of civilized behavior everywhere: "This opinion was at that time fixed and universal in the civilized portion of the white race. It was regarded as an axiom in morals as well as in politics which no one thought of disputing or supposed to be open to dispute, and men in every grade and position in society daily and habitually acted upon it in their private pursuits, as well as in matters of public concern, without doubting for a moment the correctness of this opinion."[21]

The exclusion of the black from the narrative, from the people gathered together as the sovereign, as Leviathan, was also a matter of inheritance and filial loyalty. "We the people of the United States" would, as Taney explained, be challenging the honor of our forefathers, and therefore our honor, to imagine that our forefathers did not mean what they wrote: "the men who framed this declaration were great men—high in literary acquirements, high in their sense of honor, and incapable of asserting principles inconsistent with those on which they were acting. They perfectly understood the meaning of the language they used, and how it would be understood by others."[22]

"Here, the people rule."[23] Over whom do the people rule? They rule themselves, of course, but that is self-governance, not sovereignty. They rule over the blacks, those who were excluded from the beginning. "The unhappy black race were separated from the white by indelible marks, and laws long before established, and were never thought of or spoken of except as property, and when the claims of the owner or the profit of the trader were supposed to need protection."[24]

The Supreme Court presents itself to history through Chief Justice Taney who presents himself to history as the wisest man in the republic. Taney is so filled with certainty about the answer to the question of liberty that he seems, without any sense of irony, to position himself as philosopher-king to whom we are constrained by logic to say only "yes."

One recalls Plato's Socrates, the wisest man in Athens, encountering Euthyphro, a young man on his way to court to accuse his father of murder. "What is piety?" The young man must know if he plans to accuse his own father of such a crime in open court. We do not find the answer in the dialogue, but we do come to understand that young Euthyphro is certain of things about which he knows nothing, like piety. Euthyphro's well-to-do father, we learn, had ordered one of his workmen to be bound and thrown in a ditch for killing a slave. The workman died in the ditch while Euthyphro's father was awaiting word from the diviner as to how to proceed. Was this action pious or impious? In answering the question of Dred Scott's freedom, who are we, Taney seems to suggest, to accuse our fathers, our forefathers, the Founding Fathers, of impiety? They are the ones, after all, who taught us piety, as was their duty. It was our duty, as our fathers' sons, to learn and follow their teachings. We are stamped from the beginning with our fathers' names and faces, and so were they, and the marks were, to quote Taney, "indelible." We were made into money, made to bow down, made to descend to the permanent death of the commodity form ("ordinary article of merchandise"),[25] stamped from the beginning, coins of the realm.

In the impossibility of the America that yet must be we see and hear the death that we have been made to live. We see the death we have been made to live in the Founders' Constitution and in every repetition since. Looking at our "nameless and formless"[26] selves, spellbound by the musical, not yet living, and yet sensing the possibility that this is the land where every man is free, the land where every man and woman is free. This, then, is the land we see, the yet-to-be future of *Hamilton: An American Musical.*

"The World Turned Upside Down"

Employment Discrimination, Race, and Authenticity in Hamilton

Marcia L. McCormick

I am a huge *Hamilton* fan. I became addicted to the soundtrack when it was first released, not only memorizing all of the songs and parts but also working it into the classes I teach—especially Federal Courts and Employment Discrimination. In Federal Courts, we revisit the writing of the *Federalist Papers*, where Hamilton wrote "the other fifty-one!,"[1] and in every federalism discussion, different parts of "Non-Stop," various "Cabinet Battles"[2] along with the lyrics from "The Room Where It Happens"[3] become good tools to understand the concerns that animated the compromises that were made and just how fragile some of those compromises were. In Employment Discrimination, I use the production to pose hypotheticals, often around the casting call for the first touring company of the musical. Like many of the other contributors to this volume (we have formed a sort of academic fan club), I have listened to it thousands of times by now. Along with *The Hamilton Mixtape* and the various *Hamildrops* that have been subsequently released, the soundtrack is my go-to workout and working music. The musical's history has also been of interest to me as an employment law professor, particularly because of the show's commitment to casting actors of color.

Hamilton: An American Musical debuted off-Broadway in early 2015 and worked something of a revolution in musical theater. Drawing in large part from Ron Chernow's biography of Alexander Hamilton, the musical uses hip-hop, rap, R&B, jazz, and more traditional Broadway-style music to frame the Founding as a story about immigrants building lives for themselves in a new place and in the process, helping to build a new nation. Lin-Manuel Miranda, who wrote the musical, saw echoes of his father, an ambitious self-starter from Puerto Rico who moved to New York City as a young graduate student and became an influential political consultant. He also saw echoes of Tupac Shakur and Christopher Wallace (also known as Biggie Smalls and the Notorious B.I.G.), whose rhetorical talent, social consciousness, and outspokenness were focal points in the East Coast–West Coast hip-hop feud that resulted in the death of both men.[4]

Hip-hop, R&B, and Broadway musicals were the music of Miranda's childhood, so somewhat naturally set the backdrop for this project. He saw hip-hop as one way to bring modern audiences into the story, to see how similar the ambition, imagination, and struggles of the Founding generation were to the ambition, imagination, and struggles of current times.[5] It was also a way to "cram" a lot more words into a manageable time frame to tell the richest story.[6]

Choosing a non-Broadway-style musical framework had consequences. Hip-hop, R&B, and jazz all have roots in the African American experience in the United States, which meant that the casting for *Hamilton* was diverse, and that diversity was a feature, not a bug. Rather than portray the Founding Fathers as elite white men, Miranda wanted more people to see the story of this country's Founding as a story of people like them, as a way to validate an inclusive claim to equal citizenship.

The musical was such a success that it was not long before it was exported to more cities. In May 2016, the producers of *Hamilton* were preparing to assemble a touring company to bring the musical to cities across the country. They sent out an open casting call seeking nonwhite actors to audition, which provided in part: "HAMILTON is holding OPEN AUDITIONS for SINGERS who RAP! Seeking NON-WHITE men and women, ages 20s to 30s for Broadway and upcoming Tours! **No prior theater experience necessary**" The call was controversial for its explicit reference to race and was fairly quickly replaced with a call for singers of "all ethnicities."

Critics of the casting call charged that it was racist and would violate Title VII, the federal law that prohibits race discrimination in employment. Defenders argued that the casting call fell into an "authenticity" exception to the usual antidiscrimination rules and could hardly be said to limit equal employment opportunities for white performers, who dominate the field and have for the history of American theater.

This controversy highlights the fact that theatrical productions are artistic creations and also employment opportunities. These two realities can create tension; artistic vision sometimes runs up against the law designed to regulate and shape the employment relationship to protect workers. Title VII, as one of those laws, may sometimes complicate execution of an artistic vision. The *Hamilton* casting call fits into an uneasy space in Title VII jurisprudence and practice, particularly when we explore what authenticity means for a musical that purposely draws from the musical traditions of communities of color to tell the story of long-dead white men and women who were written out of the narrative.

Title VII has prohibited discrimination on the basis of race, color, national origin, religion, and sex since 1964. The language declares that

it shall be an unlawful employment practice for an employer—

(1) to fail or refuse to hire or to discharge any individual, or otherwise to discriminate against any individual with respect to his compensation, terms, conditions, or privileges of employment, because of such individual's race, color, religion, sex, or national origin; or
(2) to limit, segregate, or classify his employees or applicants for employment in any way which would deprive or tend to deprive any individual of employment opportunities or otherwise adversely affect his status as an employee, because of such individual's race, color, religion, sex, or national origin.[7]

Given this language, the reference to race and color in the casting call for the touring company seems problematic. Because whiteness is a race and defined in part at least loosely by skin color, the advertisement seems to classify applicants by race and color, hinting that applicants of one race and color would not be hired. The advertisement itself would seem to be prohibited: "It shall be an unlawful employment practice for an employer . . . to print or publish . . . any notice or advertisement relating to employment by such an employer . . . indicating any preference, limitation, specification, or discrimination, based on race, color, religion, sex, or national origin."[8]

Title VII does contain some exceptions. It provides, for example, that some classifications or refusals to hire that are based on protected class will be allowed. For example, when the protected class is a "bona fide occupational qualification [BFOQ] reasonably necessary to the normal operation of that particular business or enterprise,"[9] protected class can be relied on as a reason to hire or not hire a person. And in that case, it is also acceptable to tailor an advertisement to fit.[10]

But race and color cannot be bona fide occupational qualifications under Title VII. The statute explicitly only allows that defense for what would otherwise be sex, religion, or national origin discrimination, and the omission of race was intentional.[11] Although national origin can be a BFOQ, it is because national origin includes ethnic heritage and overlaps with our concept of race that the Equal Employment Opportunity Commission (EEOC) has said that the national origin BFOQ will be interpreted narrowly.[12] The drafters of Title VII (using the accepted racially descriptive language of the time) expressly anticipated the issue of casting, and rather than allowing for a BFOQ, opined that "although there is no exemption in Title VII for occupations in which race might be deemed a bona fide job qualification, a director of a play or movie who wished to cast an actor in the role of a Negro, could specify that he wished to hire someone *with the physical appearance* of a Negro."[13] They also suggested that some portion of roles in a theatrical production, particularly background characters or extras, could be chosen by race or color for authenticity's sake even without a BFOQ exception for race.[14]

Despite circumstances that make creating a race-based BFOQ for performances seem like a good idea, neither Congress nor the courts have done so.[15] Still, the entertainment industry regularly uses race-based language in casting calls, and research uncovers no lawsuit challenging this practice,[16] although there have been other kinds of challenges, like union protests and demands for arbitration, public protests, and playwright-imposed limitations when white actors are cast to play nonwhite characters.[17] Perhaps because artistic expression is protected by the First Amendment,[18] actors—and the EEOC—may be hesitant to resort to the courts for a remedy. Because acting is such a competitive profession,[19] actors may be especially hesitant to bring individual claims out of fear of retaliation. This is an area where their interests conflict with the interests of writers and producers, the people who decide who gets work.

One situation where sex, religion, and national origin are sometimes considered a BFOQ is when membership in that class is "necessary for the purpose of authenticity or genuineness, . . . e.g. an actor or actress."[20] This is the rationale put forth to justify race-conscious casting. There are times that race may be irrelevant to casting decisions, but race matters when a theatrical production tells the story of particular people who are known to be members of one race or when the production integrates race into the story. Under those conditions, casting based on race seems not only justified but essential.

Even if the authenticity exception to discrimination were to apply, *Hamilton* sits at an uneasy intersection of this claim. Most of the people portrayed in the musical were white in real life, and so in a sense, a traditional claim to authenticity would seem to require that at least white-appearing actors be cast in those roles. Because the story focuses on these white men rather than on, say, the slaves some of them owned or people of color who also played a role in the Founding generation, the musical has been criticized as reinforcing racial hierarchies and hiding the role that race played in the Founding.[21]

Yet, as the title of this chapter suggests, the world is upside down here,[22] and the authenticity question reversed. The music used to tell the stories of these long-dead white guys comes from a primarily African American cultural tradition. This creates quite a different claim to authenticity; as Miranda noted, "I wanted to write a hip-hop, R&B musical about the life of Alexander Hamilton . . . If it had been an all-white cast, wouldn't you think I messed up?"[23] The medium used to tell this story called for African American performers, in particular, except for one role, the role of King George, whose musical numbers were more Beatles-esque. So if the way of telling the story is what matters for the authenticity claim, then surely *Hamilton* would call for performers of color.

There is a third way that authenticity might matter, and that relates to authorial intent. Miranda intended to use race to say something important about the Founding generation and about this country now.[24] In short, representation matters. Seeing oneself in the role of people who are considered central to America's Founding makes the struggles of that Founding more relatable and puts today's social challenges in context. In addition, seeing oneself in the role of people central to what America has become makes it possible to see oneself as central to American identity today and an important, contributing participant in creating its future.

Outside of the authenticity exception, it seems important to consider employment opportunities on the basis of race in the performing industry writ large. On the one hand, the casting call could be interpreted to be the inverse of the "help wanted, white only" advertisements that characterized the Jim Crow era and which Title VII was designed to prohibit. On the other hand, the United States has had no similar Jim Crow–type history where white people have been systematically and structurally excluded from employment opportunity. In fact, the opposite is true. The casting call was issued when calls for greater diversity in entertainment work were spawning a movement, most publicly through #OscarsSoWhite, a hashtag campaign started by April Reign, managing editor of *Broadway Black*.[25] In 2016, Broadway was having a diverse season, but that was in large part because of *Hamilton* and several other shows that featured African American performers.[26]

Given the lack of diversity in the entertainment industry, a better framing for the casting call was that it was an affirmative action effort. One of the reasons Miranda has written the musicals he has is to create works that give performers of color parts to play that they would not otherwise have.[27] In other words, *Hamilton* is one important mechanism that is being used to remedy and prevent industry-wide discrimination in casting.

Race-based affirmative action does not violate Title VII, at least as long as the purpose of an affirmative action measure is to provide opportunities for historically underrepresented groups in occupations that have been closed to them and where the measure doesn't unnecessarily interfere with the interests of white employees.[28] *Hamilton* and the traveling company casting call fit this definition well. The lack of opportunity for performers of color is well-documented. And one musical hardly makes a dent in the overall opportunities for white performers. In addition, the casting call could be framed as encouragement for nonwhite performers to audition. It does not bar white performers, but is a more robust version of common affirmative action statements in job postings—that applicants from underrepresented groups were encouraged to apply. Moreover, other behind-the-scenes jobs connected with *Hamilton* offer many opportunities for white applicants to work on the musical.[29]

The musical offers us many gifts—from the historical framing, to the musical allusions, to the hip-hop sampling and homages, to the commentary on race, identity, and citizenship. That using race to tell a historical story about government and American society can also create lessons and spark discussion and debate in popular culture about race and opportunities in modern America is just one more.

Look around[30]—and look at the *Hamilton* stage. How lucky we are to be alive right now![31]

HAMILTON AND THE POWER OF RACIAL FABLES IN EXAMINING THE U.S. CONSTITUTION

Danielle Holley-Walker

As I teach my first-year course in Legislation and Regulation, we often wade into the origins and structure of the United States Constitution. We examine Article I powers of the legislature and Article II powers of the executive branch. In the classroom of a historically black law school, there is skepticism about the Founding Fathers and their vision of the American democracy. My students don't believe that the Founding Fathers, many of them slaveholders, have a lot of credibility to define what should be the bedrock values of our multiracial democracy.

In my classroom, *Hamilton: An American Musical* provides an opportunity for a useful thought experiment as we think about the Constitution, as well as a window to reexamine the values of America's Founding documents. What if the drafters of the original Constitution and portions of the *Federalist Papers* had been people of color? What would the Constitution have been if—as in the musical—women of color had been directly involved in influencing its drafting and meaning?

In *Hamilton*, Lin-Manuel Miranda creates a fictionalized version of the Founding of the United States and the drafting of the original Constitution, one that casts people of racial and ethnic minority backgrounds as the Founders and their families. Miranda does not explicitly state that the multiethnic casting of *Hamilton* was done to make the audience reflect on fundamental U.S. constitutional values and the way that white supremacy was a cornerstone of the American democratic experiment. But what is clear is that Miranda sees the multiethnic casting of *Hamilton* as critical to its musical and artistic integrity. In interviews, he objected to the idea that white actors would be cast in *Hamilton* in the roles that were originated by Latinx and black actors. Miranda specifically stated that "Authorial intent wins. Period"[1] when asked about the future casting of *Hamilton*. He made clear in 2015 that "Eventually, acting editions of the text will include language that specifies the author's casting intentions. 'I will find the right language to make sure that the beautiful thing that people love about our show and allows them identification with the show is preserved when this goes out into the world.' "[2]

Miranda's commitment to the concept of multiethnic casting is important because, even today, many African Americans and people of color (like my law students) challenge the relevance of the Constitution in protecting their civil rights because of the flaws and contradictions ("The constitution's a mess. . . . So it needs amendments. . . . It's full of contradictions. . . . So is independence.")[3] in the original document as to issues of race. By casting Founders as members of racial and ethnic minority groups, the audience is invited to reexamine the origins of America without the taint of white supremacy and racism, to focus on the aspirational values of the Constitution, such as freedom, justice, and equality for all persons. In doing so, *Hamilton* becomes a powerful allegory for viewing the Constitution as a modern document.

Through this allegorical approach, *Hamilton* follows the tradition of racial fables: fictional stories or allegories that use the story to examine racial discrimination. These literary and scholarly writings reimagine the role of racial and ethnic minorities in the drafting and interpretation of the United States Constitution. In literature, racial fables include renowned works like *Native Son*, *Beloved*, and *Invisible Man*; in legal scholarship, they appear most prominently in the work of critical race theorists. As the esteemed academic Derrick Bell explains racial fables,

> In order to appraise the contradictions and inconsistencies that pervade the all too real world of racial oppression, [we use] the tools not only of reason

but of unreason, of fantasy . . . [A]s Professor Kim Crenshaw has put it, "allegory offers a method of discourse that allows us to critique legal norms in an ironically contextualized way. Through the allegory, we can discuss legal doctrine in a way that does not replicate the abstractions of legal discourse. It provides therefore a more rich engaging, and suggestive way of reaching the truth."[4]

Sounds like *Hamilton*, right? Whether or not Lin-Manuel Miranda knew of Bell's work or the history of racial fables, he undertook a very similar project in *Hamilton* through casting, conceptualizing, writing, and composing the musical.

Miranda employs the fable construct early in the musical, in "My Shot." The notion of rising up and throwing off the bonds of oppression takes on a particularized meaning when performed by a cast of black and Latinx performers. The revolutionaries of Hamilton's period meant to throw off the oppression of King George and England. When Alexander Hamilton and the ensemble sing the refrain, I immediately think of slave rebellion, the civil rights era protest movement, and the protests at Stonewall for LGBTQ rights.

> This is not a moment, it's the movement
> where all the hungriest brothers with something to prove went?
> Foes oppose us, we take an honest stand,
> we roll like Moses, claimin' our promised land.
> And? If we win our independence?
> 'Zat a guarantee of freedom for our descendants?
> . . .
> We're gonna rise up! Time to take a shot!
> We're gonna rise up! Rise up!
> Time to take a shot!
> Rise up! Rise up!
> Time to take a shot![5]

The song continues to discuss slavery explicitly, through the voice of John Laurens, a soldier in the Revolutionary War, a close aide to George Washington, and an abolitionist. He advocated recruiting black soldiers to fight for the colonists and then freeing the slaves as a reward. The John Laurens plot in *Hamilton* is small, but it speaks to the issue of slavery.

("But we'll never be truly free / until those in bondage have the same rights as you and me, / you and I. Do or die. Wait till I sally in / on a stallion with the first black battalion.")[6]

Laurens dies for the cause. In the musical, Eliza Hamilton reads her husband a letter containing the news that Laurens was killed in a gunfight that occurred while Laurens was recruiting troops for an all-black regiment. When Laurens died, the black recruits are returned to their masters, not set free as Laurens had wanted. The John Laurens subplot emphasizes the hypocrisy of a country founded on principles of freedom and equality, while also relying on an economy built on slavery.

In addition to his allegorical treatment of slavery, Miranda highlights the treatment of immigrants, one of the most pressing issues in modern American society. Hamilton was an immigrant in the sense that he was raised on the Caribbean island of St. Croix, but the lyrics in "Washington On Your Side" ("Oh! / This immigrant [Hamilton] isn't somebody we chose. / Oh! / This immigrant's keeping us all on our toes. / Oh! / Let's show these Federalists who they're up against!")[7] make us reflect on our country's current debate on immigration, which centers mostly around the immigration for people from Mexico and Central America. Through his casting choice, Miranda is able to reframe Alexander Hamilton's biography as one that touches on current American legal and policy debates.

But does the racial fable succeed? There's no settled answer. Critics have had their own opinions about the meaning of *Hamilton*'s multiethnic casting. Many, like Spencer Kornhaber in *The Atlantic*, argue that the casting makes the story of the early days of America and the formation of our government more relatable and universal. "*Hamilton* is not, by the common definition, colorblind. It does not merely allow for some of the Founding Fathers to be played by people of color. It insists that all of them be. This insistence is part of the play's message that Alexander Hamilton's journey from destitute immigrant to influential statesman is universal and replicable (and comparable to the life stories of many of the rappers who inspired *Hamilton*'s music)."[8] Kornhaber quotes President Barack Obama, who hosted the cast at the White House when the musical was still in workshop form. "With a cast as diverse as America itself, including the outstandingly talented women, the show reminds us that this nation was built by more than just a few great men—and that it is an inheritance that belongs to all of us."[9]

Other reviewers disagree with the common understanding that *Hamilton* is a work of racially progressive politics. Some, like the historian Lyra Monteiro, "wonder why no historical people of color find a place in *Hamilton*'s narrative."[10] Monteiro considers, "Is this the history that we most want black and brown youth to connect with—one in which black lives so clearly do not matter?"[11]

Monteiro criticizes *Hamilton* for distorting the historical record. For example, the lyrics of *Hamilton* suggest that Alexander Hamilton was antislavery, but Monteiro points out that Hamilton worked on a slave ship in the Caribbean, and there is no proof that he opposed slavery. She argues that it is likely Hamilton was not a slave owner only because he was poor. ("Before the Revolution, the dude had no money, so of course he didn't own slaves. It wasn't a moral achievement, just an economic reality.")[12] Monteiro points out that the Schuyler family owned slaves, and that although Thomas Jefferson is one of the most notorious slave owners in America, this fact is hardly mentioned in the musical.[13]

Critics also point out that Alexander Hamilton's relationship to and views on slavery were more complicated than indicated by the musical. As one put it, "Hamilton's biographers praise him for being a public abolitionist, but his position on slavery is more complex . . . Careful research indicates that Hamilton detested the institution of slavery with fervor, but whenever the issue of slavery came into conflict with Hamilton's central political tenet of property rights, his belief in the promotion of American interests, or his own personal ambition, Hamilton allowed these motivations to override his aversion to slavery."[14]

Even some cast members struggled with the portrayal of slave owners by black and Latinx actors without an overt explanation or reconciliation. Christopher Jackson, who played George Washington in the original production, has said: "I spent a lot of time and a lot of angst trying to figure out how I reconcile being in this [slave owner's] skin . . . As a black man, I just couldn't put it together."[15] But this paradox is exactly why *Hamilton* becomes a powerful racial fable, even if its creator's intent was softer, more general, more benign. The musical allows us to imagine America's first president as an African American. The legal and sociopolitical implications of that choice are obvious. If Washington was African American, it is hard to believe that he—or the American public—would have tolerated slavery. The body politic that would elect an African American as president would not tolerate slavery, although some may argue that the body politic that elected Obama also elected Donald Trump.

Hamilton is a powerful teaching tool for lawyers, law students, and the general public to contemplate the way that our Constitution would look if it were drafted today in our modern, dynamic, multiethnic country, while we still face complex issues like continuing racial and gender discrimination, xenophobia, and religious bigotry. In creating a story in the tradition of a racial fable, Lin-Manuel Miranda confidently presents this alternative reality as one in which our new America would be built firmly on the purest versions of the bedrock American principles, including freedom and equality.

Part 4

"I'm 'a Compel Him to Include Women in the Sequel"

On Women's Rights, Legal Change, and Incomplete Sequels

Eloise Pasachoff

Angelica:	You want a revolution? I want a revelation
	So listen to my declaration:
Angelica/Eliza/Peggy:	"We hold these truths to be self-evident
	That all men are created equal"
Angelica:	And when I meet Thomas Jefferson,
	I'm 'a compel him to include women in the sequel!

— "The Schuyler Sisters," Hamilton

The Belmont-Paul Women's Equality National Monument—a museum located in the former home of the National Women's Party, which brought us the constitutional right for women to vote via the Nineteenth Amendment—sits about a mile from the campus of the Georgetown University Law Center, where I am a professor. During orientation week in August, I typically lead a tour of first-year students there. While waiting for the tour, we pass through the small gift shop, which carries a variety of feminist merchandise. There is a replica of a tea set that says "Votes for Women," which suffragist and socialite Alva Belmont used with all of her guests, never content to let a moment pass without making her life's mission clear. There are buttons and magnets that say "Alice Paul: American Revolutionary," describing the lawyer and PhD-educated Quaker founder of the

National Women's Party. There are Ruth Bader Ginsburg-themed mugs and T-shirts, including the ever-popular "You can't spell 'TRUTH' without 'RUTH.'" There is notepaper inscribed "Feminist with a To-Do List." And there are copies of the Declaration of Sentiments, the document debated and signed in Seneca Falls at the first women's rights convention in America, which opens with this then-radical statement, modeled after the Declaration of Independence: "We hold these truths to be self-evident; that all men *and women* are created equal."

If she were to look around this room, Angelica Schuyler would be proud. The 1848 Declaration of Sentiments may have come three decades after her death, and it may have been drafted by Elizabeth Cady Stanton rather than Thomas Jefferson, but here, at last, women are included in the sequel. The life and work of Belmont, Paul, Ginsburg, and more are further testament to that accomplishment.

Yet the story of the American women's movement, as reflected on the walls of the Belmont-Paul Museum, is not a straightforward one of ever-increasing rights on the nation's path to a more perfect union. It is not a sequel that neatly wraps everything up in victory with the addition of women to the concept of equality. Instead, it is an uncomfortable story of partial successes and continued exclusion.

After all, the Seneca Falls Declaration explains without shame, in racist terms, the claimed injustice of "the most ignorant and degraded men, both natives and foreigners," getting formal rights that (white) women have been denied. The Belmont-Paul Museum includes an exhibit on the efforts of the African American journalist Ida B. Wells to walk alongside the delegation of white women from her home state of Illinois in the 1913 march for suffrage down Pennsylvania Avenue—the first Women's March on Washington. Denied the right to do so, Wells slipped into the delegation along the way without formal permission. (As the caption on the display explains, "You can't spell 'FORMIDABLE' without 'IDA.'") A further exhibit on ratification illustrates that the Nineteenth Amendment barely survived ratification, coming down to one man's vote in the Tennessee statehouse to break the tie (and only after a note from his mother urged him to do so). The tour through the Belmont-Paul Museum concludes with an exhibit on the failed ratification of the Equal Rights Amendment, the final hurrah of the National Women's Party before it transformed itself from a political into an educational organization.

Students sometimes come to law school to learn "The Law" as though it is a final and complete product equivalent to justice. Upon learning about a legal doctrine with which they agree, they assume that that ends the matter. Upon learning about one with which they disagree, they assume that changing it will achieve the outcome they want. And they also often assume that the law is synonymous with the Constitution, whose meaning is pronounced from on high by the Supreme Court.

The Belmont-Paul Museum and *Hamilton* both help reorient their thinking. The work of law is ongoing. It is the product of people working through many different governmental and nongovernmental institutions and structures. It is often flawed. And it will always be incomplete.

In this way, Angelica Schuyler's yearning for inclusion in "the sequel" is oversimplistic, because no one sequel can fully effectuate equality. The purchase from the Belmont-Paul gift shop that best meets Schuyler's desires isn't the replica of the Declaration of Sentiments, but the "Feminist with a To-Do List" notepaper.

So what should a feminist with a to-do list take from *Hamilton* and the Belmont-Paul Museum? As *Hamilton*'s characters were well aware, the law is not just a monolithic giver or taker of rights. Instead, students who care about women's rights need to be aware of the roles played by Congress, the president, state and local lawmakers, the courts, and the public. Together, these many different actors can expand rights—but they can also undo many of the victories Angelica Schuyler would have wanted.

Hamilton: I have to get my plan through Congress.[1]

When Hamilton wants to establish a national bank, it is Congress he needs to convince. As Jefferson and Madison taunt Hamilton, "You're gonna need congressional approval / and you don't have the votes."[2] Similarly, the National Women's Party kept careful notes on each member of Congress to track their opinions about suffrage, and for a long time their opinions were overwhelmingly negative. Congress is an important player in the struggle for women's rights, and it is critical to learn how it operates.

Women may have won the right to vote in the Nineteenth Amendment, but it was not until the 1964 Civil Rights Act that employers were prohibited from discriminating on the basis of sex (as well as race, color, national origin, or religion) in Title VII of that act. It was not until the passage of

Title IX in 1972 that educational institutions receiving federal funding were prohibited from discriminating on the basis of sex. It was not until 1993 that the Family and Medical Leave Act created an opportunity for guaranteed leave for men and women to deal with certain kinds of familial or health-related responsibilities. And, as Rosa Frazier discusses in her chapter in this volume, it was not until 1994 that the Violence Against Women Act brought a coordinated federal response to domestic violence.

However, notice how these laws are incomplete. There are many domains outside work and publicly funded schools with no explicit federal prohibition against sex discrimination. For its part, the Family and Medical Leave Act guarantees unpaid, not paid, leave, and more women than men take advantage of it, undercutting the law's gender-neutral effectiveness. The Violence Against Women Act is under jeopardy during each reauthorization over how expansive its coverage will be and how much funding will be available under it. That is because congressional actions are not set in stone but are subject to renegotiation over time.

The bottom line? Congress is important, but no one law can provide a sufficiently permanent sequel. The work is ongoing.

Washington: Remember, my decision on this matter is not subject to congressional approval. The only person you have to convince is me.[3]

A feminist with a to-do list also can take from *Hamilton* and the Belmont-Paul Museum the importance of executive authority. It was President George Washington, not Congress, who had the authority to decide whether to stay neutral in the conflict between France and England in 1793 or give aid to the French in exchange for their support in the Revolutionary War, ultimately rejecting Jefferson's argument ("Revolution is messy but now is the time to stand.") in favor of Hamilton's. ("We signed a treaty with a King whose head is now in a basket.")[4] Similarly, it was President Woodrow Wilson who the members of the National Women's Party sought to influence when they marched on Washington the day before his inauguration in 1913, and again four years later when they began the first public picket of the White House, with signs demanding "MR. PRESIDENT HOW LONG MUST WOMEN WAIT FOR LIBERTY?" and "MR. PRESIDENT WHAT WILL YOU DO FOR WOMAN SUFFRAGE?"

Consider examples of executive action in the women's movement. Title IX has a strong association with women's sports, but nothing in the text of the statute mentions athletics. It is only through the executive process of drafting regulations to implement Title IX in the 1970s that the focus on equity in athletics came about. The Obama administration's use of Title IX to address sexual harassment and violence on campuses was also a product of executive action.

As to employment opportunities, the Equal Employment Opportunity Commission issued decisions during the Obama administration interpreting "sex" in Title VII to include sexual orientation and gender identity. After all, the EEOC held, it is illegal under Title VII to discriminate on the basis of sex stereotypes, and discrimination on the basis of sexual orientation and gender identity relies on underlying assumptions of what it means to be a "real" man or woman. Other executive agencies, including the Department of Education and the Department of Health and Human Services, followed suit.

Executive action on feminist issues may also come from surprising places. For example, a significant guidance document on the administration of federal grants issued by the Office of Management and Budget in 2013 includes several provisions on the use of federal funding explicitly designed to make it easier for women to have careers in the sciences.[5]

Executive actions are as changeable as the chief executive—and *Hamilton* shows us just how much the government changed from President Washington to President Adams to President Jefferson. President Donald Trump's administration has undone many of the Obama administration's initiatives on gender issues, including those on campus sexual assault, sexual orientation, and gender identity. With executive action, just as with congressional action, no victory is ever complete, and one sequel is not enough. The feminist with a to-do list remains busy.

Hamilton: A series of essays, anonymously published, defending the document to the public.[6]

When Hamilton asked for Aaron Burr's help in drafting what became the *Federalist Papers*, he was trying to shape public opinion about the new Constitution so that the New York State Legislature would ratify it. ("My client needs a strong defense. You're the solution," he implores.

When Burr asks, "Who's your client?" Hamilton responds, "The new U.S. Constitution?")[7] The Belmont-Paul Museum contains a room dedicated to the ratification of the Nineteenth Amendment in the state legislatures. A feminist with a to-do list should understand the importance of state legislatures, and other state and local lawmaking authorities such as state agencies and city councils, as important levers for action.

Some of this action might seek to improve upon limits at the federal level. For example, various state and local civil rights laws explicitly include sexual orientation and gender identity status among the characteristics on which it is illegal to discriminate. Other state and local laws provide paid family leave.

Some state and local action for the feminist with a to-do list might be defensive. Working against state and local laws restricting women's access to health care options is one such example. Opposing state and local laws that seek to codify the permissibility of discrimination on the basis of sexual orientation and gender identity is another.

State and local actions are as incomplete as federal ones are, and for the additional reason that state and local protections have jurisdictional limitations that national protections do not. Yet state and local actions can provide a wider berth for action at times, sometimes even providing better circumstances that set an example for later federal action to follow. Either way, the feminist with a to-do list needs to know that, as with congressional and executive action, the state and local arena requires more than one sequel to get equality.

Hamilton: Gentlemen of the jury, . . . Are you aware that we're making hist'ry?[8]

For all of the lawyers around the eponymous Hamilton—Burr, Jefferson, Adams, Jay—there is little mention of courts in the musical. In some ways, this is not surprising. The federal courts were not busy during the Founding era as compared with our own; it was not until the Supreme Court's 1803 decision in *Marbury v. Madison* that the principle of judicial review, under which the Supreme Court has the authority to declare Acts of Congress unconstitutional, became institutionalized. The feminist with a to-do list at the Belmont-Paul Museum can similarly observe the absence of courts from the story told there, as the National Women's Party was instead pursuing legal change through the other branches of federal, state, and local governments.

The dearth of courts in *Hamilton* and the Belmont-Paul Museum is noteworthy for the many students who come to law school thinking that the way to make legal change is through argument in courts. The importance of Congress, the executive branch, and state and local governments should be evident.

To highlight the importance of these other institutions is not to discount the role of courts in the women's movement. Many scholars believe that the Supreme Court's interpretation of the Fourteenth Amendment's equal protection clause—largely through the efforts of then-advocate, now-justice Ruth Bader Ginsburg—has brought about everything that the Equal Rights Amendment would have made explicit. The Court has, in some instances, expansively interpreted the meaning of sex discrimination under antidiscrimination laws like Title VII and Title IX. Meanwhile, courts all over the country hear individual lawsuits brought under these laws.

But none of these legal victories for the women's movement provides a fulsome sequel. The Court's commitment to *stare decisis*—that is, standing by its previously decided cases—varies, sometimes by era, sometimes by issue, sometimes by justice. The resolution of new issues to come before the Court depends on which justices are on the Court at the time. Congress sometimes overturns a statutory interpretation decision by revising the statute in question. And any victory in an individual antidiscrimination case must still be implemented and enforced, which is often difficult. Either way, a judicial decision that effectively includes women in the sequel can't mark the end of equality efforts for the feminist with a to-do list.

Laurens:	Raise a glass to the four of us.
Hamilton/Laurens/Mulligan/Lafayette:	Tomorrow there'll be more of us.[9]

Hamilton may have worked non-stop, but even he couldn't accomplish all of his goals himself. It took a movement to make it happen, both before and after the war ("this is not a moment, it's the movement").[10] Similarly, photograph after photograph in the Belmont-Paul Museum reflects the masses of women marching together and engaging in other forms of nonviolent resistance in their long campaign for the Nineteenth Amendment and thereafter. The feminist with a to-do list should note the importance of collective action in producing legal and social change.

None of the laws granting women rights would have come into existence without the women's movement's actions, which resulted in political pressure, changes in the composition of elected officials, and a shift in baseline societal expectations. Even changes in the Supreme Court's doctrine are not immune from the effects of collective action. For example, the Supreme Court's equal protection jurisprudence was born as part of the crucible of public debate about the Equal Rights Amendment, while the Court's gay marriage decision came out of a decades-long movement that first resulted in state and local political change as a result of activists' actions.

But winning is easy; governing is harder.[11] That is, winning looks easy in retrospect from the position of needing to implement a victory, which requires perpetual collective action. A social movement that achieves some success cannot fold up shop.

Eliza: And when my time is up, have I done enough?[12]

When my students and I leave the Belmont-Paul Museum at the end of our orientation tour, the mood is typically some combination of sober and exhilarated—sober at the weight of historical struggle and contemporary challenges, and exhilarated about getting involved in all the unfinished business. There's a million things we haven't done,[13] after all.

Eliza has the last word in *Hamilton* as she describes her accomplishments during the fifty years she lives after her husband's death. She asks the question that the feminist with a to-do list ought to carry with her throughout her career. It's not Jefferson's "What did I miss?"[14] but rather, in effect, "What else can I do?" Rather than *looking* for a mind at work,[15] I hope that my students will use their own minds to work from sequel to sequel, recognizing that the work will never be done.

Here's to the feminists with a to-do list!

When Your Job Is to Marry Rich

Marriage as a Market in Hamilton

Kimberly Mutcherson

> Marriage is a social invention, unique to humans.
> —Stephanie Coontz, Marriage, a History

Certain realms of life exist in which market language gets a bad name, including the world of marriage. As Rosa Frazier explains in her chapter about Maria Reynolds in this volume, modern U.S. society rejects the idea of marriage as a market transaction in favor of romcoms, romance novels, and modern retellings of fairy tales that always have a happy ending. But civil marriage as a romantic endeavor, rather than a transaction, was invented, not preordained. For women of many stripes, marriage has long been contested territory in which the humanity of women was compromised at best and denigrated at worst. Though *Hamilton*'s creator, Lin-Manuel Miranda, took much creative license in his telling of the life of Alexander Hamilton, there is historical accuracy in the depiction of Angelica Schuyler's understanding of her obligation to marry well for the benefit of her family. Her story arc reveals how marriage worked (and still works for some), but also how marriage historically and presently is an institution experienced differently across gender, race, class, and status.

For white women in the eighteenth century, marriage was sometimes a way to gain social status, but at the expense of being legally subsumed within a husband's identity. For black enslaved women, legal marriage was not even an option in most cases and did not mean much legally, even when allowed. In any case, marital unions functioned to reinforce white male power and privilege, leaving women with few options to forge their own paths in the world. Particularly salient in this context, and in our modern one, is the demand to recognize the intersectional nature of women's experiences such that it is not only impossible, but also dangerous, to speak of women as a monolith. Instead, progress demands that as we look backward and forward, we are attuned to how structural forces shape women's experiences and the different ways that law must be reformed to accrue to the benefit of many women and not just those with race or class privilege.

Angelica Schuyler laments that she is "a girl in a world in which [her] only job is to marry rich,"[1] reminding us of the long history of marriage not as a love-filled union between equals, but as a means of conferring power, citizenship, and worth. Her initial meeting with Hamilton has all the hallmarks of the timeworn trope of love at first sight. Angelica sings that Hamilton sets her "heart aflame, ev'ry part aflame."[2] She longs for life with a man with whom she can "match wits"[3] and who is on her level, but Angelica knows that she cannot give in to her heart and pursue a relationship with a man who is "penniless"[4] and "flying by the seat of his pants,"[5] thus accepting that she will live a life of regret during which she "will never be satisfied."[6]

Particularly for marginalized groups of the time, marriage carried significant weight. As the eldest child of a rich man who had no sons, Angelica Schuyler's character, as reimagined by Lin-Manuel Miranda, well understood her place in the world. Angelica believes that she must marry rich for the sake of her family, which leads her to reject the strong attraction between her and Alexander Hamilton and leave him to woo her sister, Eliza. In her era, parties did not enter marriage solely for the benefit of the individuals who married. Rather, marriage was "a way of raising capital, constructing political alliances, organizing the division of labor by age and gender, and deciding what claim, if any, children had on their parents, and what rights parents had in their children."[7] When women who grew up in families with property married, those marriages were an "economic investment" in that they involved exchanging dowries, bride wealth, or monetary tributes.[8]

The Alexander Hamilton and Schuyler sisters' triangle (or square if one includes Peggy) fits well with the narrative of life for women of Angelica's stature in the years immediately preceding and after the American Revolution. It was late in the eighteenth century that marriage for love and based on choice became a cultural expectation, and then only in Western Europe and North America.[9] A woman marrying for wealth might in modern parlance be given the pejorative title of gold digger—a woman who wanted a man only for his money. But, for white women of Angelica Schuyler's time, marriage was the primary, and for some, only means of acquiring or maintaining societal and economic status. White women could not reasonably aspire to lucrative careers as their ability to find and maintain work that paid significant amounts of money was circumscribed by limited access to education and explicit bans from careers that were reserved for men.[10] For most women of the time, "finding a husband was the most important investment they could make in their economic future."[11]

Given Angelica's reported intelligence, quick wit, and logical ability, she might have pursued a career in law given the chance. Unfortunately for her, well into the nineteenth century, the legal profession excluded women from being admitted to practice law. In an 1873 case, *Bradwell v. Illinois*, Myra Bradwell appealed the decision of the Illinois State Supreme Court that denied her a license to practice law in part because she was a married woman and, as a consequence, "would be bound neither by her express contracts nor by those implied contracts which it is the policy of the law to create between attorney and client."[12] This inability to contract arose from the law of the time, imported from England, which took the position that upon marriage, a woman's identity was subsumed within her husband's identity. The legal union meant that the wife would basically cease to exist as an independent individual even as her husband's independence remained firmly intact.[13] By the rules of coverture—the name for this dissolution of a woman's legal identity upon marriage—a married woman was her husband's dependent, like a minor child.[14] In most circumstances, she could not own property in her name, sign contracts, or keep her earnings if she had any. It was not until 1848 that married women in New York gained the right to own property in their name.[15] The law assumed a wife's consent to sex within her marriage. If she got divorced, any children to whom a woman had given birth during the marriage would generally be placed in the custody of the child's father, who was also the primary beneficiary of any wages from the child's labor.[16] Thus, for men marriage "symbolized the acquisition of a leadership role," whereas "for women, it was a lateral move from the dependent role of daughter to that of wife."[17]

This vision of dependent womanhood, more specifically white womanhood, found voice in a U.S. Supreme Court opinion in *Bradwell v. Illinois*, authored by Justice Bradley, who explained the natural order of the world from his perspective when it came to women's roles. He wrote:

> The civil law, as well as nature herself, has always recognized a wide difference in the respective spheres and destinies of man and woman. Man is, or should be, woman's protector and defender. The natural and proper timidity and delicacy which belongs to the female sex evidently unfits it for many of the occupations of civil life. The Constitution of the family organization, which is founded in the divine ordinance as well as in the nature of things, indicates the domestic sphere as that which properly belongs to the domain and functions of womanhood. The harmony, not to say identity, of interest and views which belong, or should belong, to the family institution is repugnant to the idea of a woman adopting a distinct and independent career from that of her husband. . . . It is true that many women are unmarried and not affected by any of the duties, complications, and incapacities arising out of the married state, but these are exceptions to the general rule. The paramount destiny and mission of woman are to fulfill the noble and benign offices of wife and mother. This is the law of the Creator. And the rules of civil society.

The law, as Bradley's opinion makes clear, was simply a reflection of the natural proclivities of women versus men. To legislate otherwise, Justice Bradley implies, would be to violate the tenets of faith and those of civilized societies. It is no surprise, then, that marriage remained a legal constraint for women for centuries.

Justice Bradley's writing applies to white women for the most part; the lives of black women at this time in U.S. history were decidedly different from those of their white counterparts. Had Renée Elise Goldsberry, the actress who originated the role of Angelica Schuyler, lived as a black woman during the period of the Revolutionary War, her life would have been remarkably different than that of the woman whom she portrayed on stage in the twenty-first century. The idea that marriage and domesticity were the proper roles for black women was anathema in an era in which marriage law racialized and circumscribed access to marriage. For black women who were enslaved, and therefore considered legal property, marriage to a man who was also a slave offered no protection from sexual abuse by their masters, from being sold away from their husband or children, or a respite from difficult back-breaking work in exchange for fulfilling the "noble and benign offices of wife and mother."[18] For these women, marriage might have been rooted in love or affection, but it did not bring with it any legal benefits.

That the law excluded black women from marriage and later forbade any women of color to legally marry white men exemplifies how marriage law worked to mark the fullness or lack thereof of citizenship and humanity for nonwhites in the eighteenth century. If marriage was something to which women should aspire, the fact that the law forbade some women to marry reinforced the low status of those women. If slave owners were not bound to respect the marriage vows that enslaved people made to each other, it was because the status of being a slave was inextricably tied to a denial of legal personhood. Although marriage might not have offered white women great solace, it was a status to which many black women could not even aspire.

For the thousands of free blacks who lived in America, especially in Northern states, marriage was an option that many of them took advantage of.[19] The free women who married free men still assumed the legal disabilities attendant to any woman who married during this time period such that marriage brought with it the erasure of a woman's legal identity.

Relationships, of course, existed between slaveowners and female slaves that have created controversy about when, if ever, it is possible to imagine a loving union between a woman and the man who legally owns her and therefore can treat her as he would any other piece of his property.[20] Annette Gordon-Reed wrote a prize-winning book about Thomas Jefferson and Sally Hemings, the woman he enslaved and with whom he had a decades-long relationship and seven children. When posed the question of whether theirs was a relationship of love, even though marriage was forbidden to them by law, Reed concludes, "Strong emotions that two individuals may have had cannot mitigate the problem of slavery or

Jefferson's specific role as a slave owner."[21] In other words, even if two people love each other, and it's not clear that this was the case for Hemmings and Jefferson, that reality does not relieve a slave owner from moral culpability for the horror of holding human beings as chattel.

The irony is that in the centuries after slavery ended and marriage rights finally extended to black Americans as a whole, the right to marry, and the failure of many black people to avail themselves of that right, was turned against an entire community. This turn was exemplified by the 1965 Moynihan Report, which presented the lower marriage rate and higher rate of births outside of marriage for black families as part of a persistent pattern that kept low-income black Americans living in chaotic and violent communities.[22] In no small measure, this pathology was perceived as a problem by Senator Daniel Patrick Moynihan and his ilk because it reflected that many poor black families were headed by women. This, though not intrinsically bad, morphed into "pathology" by virtue of being "out of line with the rest of the American society, [which] seriously retards the progress of the group as a whole, and imposes a crushing burden on the Negro male and, in consequence, on a great many Negro women as well."[23] Thus, marriage became a tool with which to punish communities that did not fit presumed norms of marriage as a male-dominated institution meant to bring financial stability to families and decrease dependence on government support.

Based on these beliefs in the widespread benefits of marriage and the social inadequacy of those who did not marry, lawmakers began decades-long attempts to encourage (require) marriage and to punish low-income people who failed to fall into line. Welfare caps that refused to raise public benefits when a woman already on public assistance gave birth to another child,[24] attempts to force or coerce poor women of color, especially black women, to use long-acting forms of birth control; and sterilization abuse across the country, but particularly in the South and Puerto Rico,[25] made clear that procreation without marriage, and the presumed stability and financial independence that it would bring, was an affront to government policy.

Centuries separate us from Angelica Schuyler's experience of marriage and Renée Elise Goldsberry's understanding and expectations of marriage no doubt differ from the character she portrayed. By law, marriage in America is no longer reserved for opposite-sex couples. Marital rape is now a crime. States may no longer forbid marriages between white people and people of color. Women remain independent people even within a marriage and can own property and sign contracts. Divorce may be pursued on a no-fault basis. The power of marriage, and its myths, remains strong within U.S. society, even as many people no longer consider marriage to be a requirement of a happy life. Books and articles have proliferated about the decline of marriage in American society[26] and about the race and class implications of that decline.[27]

The real Angelica Schuyler married John Baker Church in 1777 when she was twenty-one years old. Church was a member of the British Parliament who managed to amass a fortune during the Revolutionary War by selling supplies to the American and French armies.[28] Perhaps fearing her father's disapproval of the marriage because of her future husband's wartime activities, Angelica and John eloped.[29] She eventually gave birth to eight children, several of whom died young. Thus, Angelica fulfilled her job of marrying rich, but she did so in a way that created a bit of historical intrigue, and she did not do so happily. In the song "Congratulations," which did not make it to the stage in *Hamilton*, Angelica tells Hamilton that she "languished in a loveless marriage," reinforcing that her marriage was a transaction and not a personal triumph.

In stark contrast to Angelica, Goldsberry married in 2002 and gave birth to her first child at the age of thirty-eight.[30] She describes her marriage as one "based in mutual support and true partnership."[31] For Goldsberry, marriage offered something different than the gilded cage it represented to women of means in the late eighteenth century.

By 2002, marriage in the United States was no longer premised on solidifying power and did not automatically force women into a subordinate position. Even so, marriage continues to be a site of fluctuation that is deeply intertwined with law. As Coontz explained, "For centuries, marriage did much of the work that markets and governments do today. It organized the production and distribution of goods and people. It set up political, economic and military alliances. It coordinated the division of labor by gender and age. It orchestrated people's personal rights and obligation in everything from sexual relations to the inheritance of property."[32]

The purpose of marriage and characteristics of those who marry have shifted; yet the institution remains controversial and its origins as a form of patriarchal oppression have not been forgotten. When Angelica sings in *Hamilton* that she will compel Thomas Jefferson to "include women in the sequel,"[33] she perhaps imagines in some fashion the United States in which we now live where many women pursue greatness without being legally yoked to a man. A world in which parties to a marriage can enter into this legally sanctioned union of their own will and exit it with some measure of ease, and in which women remain full legal persons, is no doubt progress of a certain kind. This is not at all to say that marriage in the modern United States is without its drawbacks, and the fact that increasing equality for women seems to play a role in declining marriage rates is important. But there is no doubt that many more women—like Goldsberry—are poised to find satisfaction in marriage in the twenty-first century than was true in the eighteenth.

"Love" Triangles

Romance or Domestic Violence?

Rosa Frazier

As a romance novelist, I can find romance in almost every story. And romance plays an essential role in *Hamilton: An American Musical*; through Hamilton's eyes, we get a romantic view of war, marriage, and the process of establishing a new nation. Even the Constitution is sexy and stimulating. It almost feels like a love triangle: one between Alexander, Eliza, and the brand-new United States.

The romance novelist in me is also drawn to the love triangle between Angelica, Eliza, and Alexander, one full of heat, drama, and intrigue. It starts with an attraction between Alexander and his future sister-in-law, Angelica Schuyler; when he's introduced to his wife Eliza, their mutual attraction is also undeniable. The visuals in the musical help define the relationships. Eliza's blue dress represents unwavering loyalty to her husband. Angelica, wearing the demure peach to symbolize virginity, demonstrates fidelity to Alexander and Eliza. Peggy Schuyler wears a yellow dress for friendship—platonic and familial, painting the picture that Alexander has no physical attraction to her. In due course, in the stuff of romance novels, peachy Angelica makes way for the marriage between her true-blue little sister and Alexander—a sacrifice that gives way to a close friendship maintained through their correspondence.

The show has a third love triangle, which is less romantic and more disturbing. As a former clinical law professor working with victims of domestic violence, I view the last "love" triangle—the one between Alexander, Maria, and James—differently. Maria Reynolds is initially painted as virtuously and distinguished as the Schuyler sisters. On the *Hamilton* stage, Maria wears a dark red dress in stark contrast to the cool pastels of Eliza, Angelica, and Peggy—literary symbolism at its finest. Red is fiery, seductive, passionate—hot emotions that can lead to danger and violence. As soon as Maria, clad in red, sets foot on stage, the audience knows she is a seductress. Even if they know nothing about the story, as soon as they see Maria's red dress, the audience expects the worst to come. Yet, as powerful as the red imagery might be, I see Maria not as a dangerous foe but as a woman living during a time when she had no power or control over her life and circumstances.

The first two love triangles and the conflicts inherent to them play out throughout Act I. There is little time to consider the larger significance of these relationships, especially that the emotional affair between Alexander and Angelica portends the former's penchant for seeking comfort in women other than his wife.

Then, in Act II, just when we believe that Alexander has achieved success as the first Treasury secretary and is content with his wife and children, we learn of his infidelity. This is a type of conflict that many romance novels introduce as a hurdle for the hero and the heroine to overcome on their journey to their Happily Ever After or, as it is known in the industry, HEA. Seeing Alexander and Eliza overcoming infidelity would satisfy the romantic trope of "second chance at love." If they could get past the affair, then we're confident they could survive any other obstacle.

On the *Hamilton* stage, the story of Maria and Alexander's affair starts with Hamilton rapping/singing, "Say No To This":

Longing for Angelica.
Missing my wife.
That's when Miss Maria Reynolds walked into my life . . .

In turn, Maria sings:

> My husband's doin' me wrong
> beatin' me, cheating' me, mistreatin' me . . .
> Suddenly he's up and gone.
> I don't have the means to go on.[1]

Hamilton sings about his dilemma: vacillating between accepting Maria's tempting offer to enter her home and remaining faithful to his wife. In a Hamilton Mixtape of remixed songs not heard on stage, R&B singer Jill Scott sings, "Say Yes To This" in a longer response to Hamilton's "Say No To This." The lyrics paint a different picture than the historical accounts of Maria's participation in the scandal.

> Ooh, everybody round here wants me
> I think you can, and you should
> We could be so happy, baby
> I'll be your ever-lovin' woman
> You'll be me ever-lovin' man . . .
> You can have my loyalty and all of my affection[2]

"Say Yes To This" portrays Maria as being in love with Alexander, offering herself as a lover, friend, and confidant during a lonely period in his life—so how could Alexander possibly turn her down? It was a temptation most men couldn't resist, especially in a romance novel.[3]

When Maria's husband, James Reynolds, discovers the infidelity and confronts Alexander, he gives the latter "permission" to continue the affair. The affair has new strings attached; Alexander has to pay Reynolds a weekly fee to continue consorting with Maria. Alexander Hamilton, with all the upbeat rhymes and frenetic dances, glosses over the crimes also committed against Maria. In a word, one that is heavily used in our present time, Maria is *trafficked* by her husband.

Connecting what we know from *Hamilton*'s limited recounting of Maria's story with other historical information, we can see that Maria was a victim of abuse. Male privilege—accompanied closely by misogyny—was the typical way of life in 1791. Once Maria and James married, James had the legal right and societal encouragement to make all decisions for his family; he was legally permitted to coerce and threaten Maria to do anything he wanted, even if it were otherwise illegal. James isolated Maria from her family and friends when he moved her from her birthplace of New York City to Philadelphia, where she had no family and no friends. When James abandoned her, she had no resources to support herself and their young daughter, Susan. In that same vein, we can presume that James used Susan as a pawn to control Maria. As an uneducated woman in 1791, Maria would not have been able to support her child without financial assistance. This fact would have forced her to stay with James despite his control and abuse. James likely also economically abused Maria by using her to make money while not allowing her to keep it or even benefit from the funds acquired through his blackmail. We don't know, for example, if James took the thirty dollars when Alexander first gave it to her.

James Reynolds exclusively held power and control over Maria during a time when women had no recourse for divorce, alimony and child support, restraining orders, and other social services to assist them as single parents. The Power and Control Wheel created by The National Center on Domestic and Sexual Violence illustrates all the ways, even with our limited knowledge of Maria's victimization, James might have abused his wife.

If the federal Violence Against Women Act (VAWA) of 1994 had been available to Maria in 1791, she would have had the benefit of a rape shield law,[4] community violence prevention programs, protections from eviction because of domestic violence or stalking, support from victim assistance services, legal aid for survivors of domestic violence. The act provides around $500 million toward investigation and prosecution of violent crimes against women.[5] Congress has twice reauthorized this statute, with 2012's reauthorization extending the act's protection to same-sex couples, and adding provisions that allow undocumented individuals who are victims of domestic violence to claim temporary visas to remain in the United States.

As the director of the Domestic Violence Immigration Clinic at The University of Wisconsin Law School in Madison from 2009 to 2013, I modeled our work on VAWA principles. Six law students per academic year helped me serve over two hundred victims of violence whose experiences ranged from domestic abuse, childhood sexual and physical abuse and neglect, sexual assault, and labor trafficking with humanitarian relief. We helped to obtain restraining orders, assisted in training of law

enforcement on VAWA, and prepared immigration applications; if necessary, we represented clients in Immigration Court in Chicago, Illinois. When we couldn't represent the client for restraining orders or divorces, we referred her to our colleagues in the Family Court Clinic in our department. It was a wonderful cooperation between service providers.

If Maria Reynolds had walked into our office instead of Alexander Hamilton's study, we would have interviewed her, using the Power and Control Wheel, to assess whether she had been abused and to determine the types of abuse she'd suffered. We would have explored the services needed to help her overcome her victimization, and the service providers who'd best aid her toward independence. We would have sought a restraining order against James. If she preferred to return to New York, a restraining order granted by another state would have been enforced in her new state, thanks to the full faith and credit clause. The local domestic violence advocates would have taught her safety measures against James's future threats. Other social services programs would have helped her get back on her feet, a far better alternative to her only choice at the time—seeking the assistance of men such as Aaron Burr.[6] In the end, it was Burr who aided her in 1793—two years after her affair with Alexander but four years before the *Reynolds Pamphlet* was published—in successfully petitioning for a divorce from Reynolds.

Maria does not make another appearance in *Hamilton* after the black-mail scene. In real life, however, after the *Reynolds Pamphlet* scandal, Maria Reynolds found her HEA. Like many abused women, Maria was able to rebuild her life and find love again. She married a doctor and became an active member of a church.[7] Unfortunately, not everyone is lucky in love. Maria's daughter Susan married and divorced many times. I hope that Susan didn't experience abuse from her husbands after observing the same of her parents; given the vicious cycle of domestic violence and the customs of the time, she was more than likely a victim herself.

Romances are an escape, a way to live vicariously through a fictional character's journey to love. I strive to write romances where my heroines are strong and independent; they want but do not need a romantic partner, someone to walk with together through a precarious path riddled with burrs and cracks and crevices because that journey in real life is winding and circular and hilly. But my romantic-novelist self is always informed by my advocate self, wondering whether what looks like love is dependence, what looks like a relationship is an example of power and control. *Hamilton* gives us insight into the fact that love triangles might be mechanisms for abuse. After all, in the end? It all ends in a duel.

Part 5

"Immigrants, We Get the Job Done"

Hamilton's Dissent to the Travel Ban

Neal Katyal

> You know, and it gets into this whole issue of border security
> you know, who's gonna say that the borders are secure?
> We've got the House and the Senate debating this issue,
> and it's, it's really astonishing that in a country founded
> by immigrants,
> "immigrant" has somehow become a bad word.
>
> —K'naan, Snow Tha Project, Riz MC, and Residente

Three days after Donald Trump won the 2016 election, I heard these opening words on the soon-to-be-released *Hamilton Mixtape*. The track, titled "Immigrants (We Get the Job Done),"[1] takes its name from a celebrated lyric in *Hamilton*.[2] When I heard it that day, my first thoughts were, "This can't be right. It's not happening." But. It. Did.

The song was prophetic—the writers understood that President Trump wasn't going to depart from his campaign rhetoric. Trump had, after all, lambasted immigrants throughout his hate-filled campaign. On December 7, 2015, he called for a "total and complete shutdown of Muslims entering the United States."[3] A few months later, he explained: "I think Islam hates us . . . [W]e can't allow people coming into this country who have this hatred of the United States . . . [a]nd of people that are not Muslim." Trump justified his position by comparing it to President Franklin Roosevelt's placement of Japanese-Americans in internment camps during

World War II, stating, "[Roosevelt] did the same thing."[4] On another occasion he asserted that "we're having problems with the Muslims, and we're having problems with Muslims coming into the country." A few days after becoming president, on January 27, 2017, President Trump signed Executive Order No. 13769, titled "Protecting the Nation from Foreign Terrorist Entry into the United States."[5] As he signed it, he read the title, looked up, and said: "We all know what that means."

We all did know what it meant. The order imposed an immediate, ninety-day ban on entry by nationals of seven overwhelmingly Muslim countries. It also suspended the U.S. Refugee Admissions Program for 120 days and lowered the cap on annual refugee admissions. The suspension included a carve-out for refugees who were "religious minorit[ies]" in their home countries. In an interview on the day the order was signed, President Trump explained that this exception was designed to "help" Christians, asserting that in the past "if you were a Muslim [refugee] you could come in, but if you were a Christian, it was almost impossible."

On behalf of the State of Hawaii and others, I challenged this travel ban in federal court. The Ninth Circuit Court of Appeals struck down this first version. Trump later retooled it a bit, and it was struck down yet again. After the president issued yet another version of the ban, we challenged it again. We won again in the federal trial and appeals courts but lost 5–4 in the Supreme Court. It was grueling work, involving dozens of people and many sleepless nights. And it was a heartbreaking loss.

It's fair to say that *Hamilton* was the soundtrack to our work for those 500 or so days, and "Immigrants (We Get the Job Done)" the deepest source of comfort on the worst of those caffeine-filled evenings. I walked into the Supreme Court to argue the case on April 25, 2018, iPhone headphones jammed in my ears, listening to that song, as well as to "My Shot." Lin-Manuel Miranda was riding with his wife, Vanessa Nadal, and my family in a separate car—they were separate because I had to have bodyguards just to walk into the Court, the same court that I had entered hundreds of times before without incident.

When the Supreme Court issues a decision—especially in a close vote like this one—the justices who disagree will often pen a written opinion—a "dissent." In the travel ban case, four justices joined strong dissents, but the most vicious was written by Justice Sotomayor, who lambasted the five justices in the majority for turning America's back on freedom and its traditions. It was full of fire, concrete evidence, and commentary on the president's discriminatory public statements and policies, and it eviscerated her colleagues' formal, largely textual legal reasoning.

But in my mind "Immigrants (We Get the Job Done)," and *Hamilton* as a whole, can be understood as an even stronger dissent to the Supreme Court majority opinion in *Trump v. Hawaii*. The musical follows Alexander Hamilton's rise from being just "another immigrant, comin' up from the bottom,"[6] to his status as General George Washington's "right hand man."[7] Not too shabby for "a bastard, orphan, son of a whore and a / Scotsman, dropped in the middle of a forgotten / spot in the Caribbean."[8]

Grit explained Hamilton's "rise to the top."[9] In the opening act, the audience is instructed that "the ten-dollar founding father without a father / got a lot farther by working a lot harder, / by being a lot smarter, / by being a self-starter."[10] And, in one of the most repeated verses in the musical, Hamilton proclaims,

Hey yo, I'm just like my country,
I'm young, scrappy and hungry,
and I'm not throwing away my shot![11]

His toil does not go unnoticed. "Maaaaan, the man is non-stop!"—expresses some heavy praise from Hamilton's rival (and ultimate executioner) Aaron Burr.[12] Nor does his success go unquestioned. During a bout of infighting for control over President Washington's cabinet, Madison, Burr, and Jefferson scoff: "This immigrant isn't somebody we chose. . . . This immigrant's keeping us all on our toes."[13] Later in the musical, Burr doubles down on this xenophobia by leveling accusations at Hamilton, whom he calls "an immigrant embezzling our government funds."[14] But in the end, "America forgot him."[15] James Madison quips in the last scene: "He took our country from bankruptcy to prosperity. I hate to admit it, but he doesn't get enough credit for all the credit he gave us."[16]

In writing *Hamilton*, Miranda understood the way in which our Founders celebrated, and did not demonize, immigration. In the song "The Schuyler Sisters," Angelica Schuyler—Hamilton's admirer—takes pride in "reading *Common Sense* by Thomas Paine."[17] Interspersed in this famous 1776 pamphlet encouraging the colonists to fight for independence were various moral and political observations.[18] Paine tellingly reflected: "This new World hath been the asylum for the persecuted lovers of civil and religious liberty from every part of Europe."[19] That America is a nation of immigrants was a recognition also shared by *Hamilton* characters Thomas Jefferson and James Madison during their lifetimes. Jefferson once famously advocated for "a right which nature has given to all men, of departing from the country in which chance, not choice, has placed them."[20] And Madison echoed these sentiments, defending immigration on the grounds that it is "always from places where living is more difficult to places where it is less difficult," so "the happiness of the emigrant is promoted by the change."[21]

"Immigrants (We Get the Job Done)" beautifully captures many of these points, both in verse and in the video (coincidentally released the week before the Supreme Court upheld the third travel ban). One Spanish-language verse reads, "We packed our entire house in one suitcase / With a pick, a shovel / And a rake / We built you a castle."[22] Another verse describes immigrant labor as "The ink you print on your dollar bill, oil you spill / Thin red lines on the flag you hoist when you kill."[23] The chorus, meanwhile, remains resolute: "Immigrants, we get the job done / Look how far I come."[24] And the video's through-line strikes hard at every turn; just like Alexander Hamilton's service to the fledgling republic, the labor of these modern-day immigrants is also forgotten. "With they pitchforks," they do the "rich chores," all "done by the people that get ignored."[25] They are "America's ghost writers, the credit's only borrowed."[26]

The video, for its part, is replete with images of immigrant verve and unrequited labor. Migrant workers pick citrus fruits and butcher meat.[27] A man rescues a child from the rubble of a war zone.[28] A dark, jolting train is thick with Immigration and Customs Enforcement Agents dragging out passengers.[29] And hunched brown and black bodies stitch together American flags.[30] At one point in the music video, Riz Ahmed—a British Pakistani rapper[31]—seems to critique the Trump administration's travel ban directly. From the depths of a flickering subway car,[32] he raps: "Who these 'fugees, what did they do for me / But contribute new dreams / Taxes and tools, swagger and food to eat."[33] It is no surprise that Miranda called the song a "musical counterweight" to the "xenophobia and vilification of immigrants" dominating the election cycle.[34] It reaffirms my long-standing belief that immigrants are often the people in America who cherish their freedoms and opportunities the most.

I am a deep believer in the power of art to bring people together. And I think what Miranda has done with *Hamilton* captures the essence of America and immigration far more than any dry Supreme Court opinion in the United States Reports. It is not an exaggeration to say that Miranda's work helps pave the way toward reconceptualizing (or restoring) our political system and reminding us of the dignity and promise of America at its best. As one report put it, "Lin-Manuel Miranda's inspiring *Hamilton* lyrics are rising up throughout this current political moment, appearing on countless protest signs all over the world":[35] "*History has its eyes on you*"; "*You want a revolution? I want a revelation*"; "*Immigrants, we get the job done.*"[36] Miranda even said, "I keep seeing 'Immigrants, We Get the Job Done' on placards at every march, at every protest. I can't tell you what that does to me as a writer to see a line [I wrote]. And what it means for the conversation, in this moment in history."[37]

I have no doubt that conversation is sorely needed at this fraught moment. The travel ban is only one track in the Trump administration's anti-immigration playbook. The attempt to terminate the Deferred Action for Childhood Arrivals program (DACA) is a particularly egregious new front.[38] The Trump administration is—horrifically—now engaged in forcibly ripping parents away from their children at the southern border.[39] They have also recently announced that victims of domestic and gang violence no longer deserve asylum.[40] As I write these words, I am preparing to argue the challenge against President Trump's sanctuary city policy, which cuts off federal funds for local policing unless cities agree to carry out Trump's draconian immigration policies. (You can guess what I'm listening to as I pen this.)[41]

This is not our nation's first go-round with exclusionary rhetoric. Taking to Twitter to express it might be new, but xenophobia and nationalism are hardly of recent vintage. Some examples come to mind. The bar to citizenship imposed by the Chinese Exclusion Act of 1882.[42] National origin quotas for the "undesirables" of Eastern and Southern Europe codified by the Immigration Act of 1924.[43] And, of course, the detainment of Japanese-Americans during World War II upheld by the Supreme Court in *Korematsu*.[44]

It is also not the first time that works of art like *Hamilton* and "Immigrants (We Get the Job Done)" have inspired national engagement on morally infused topics. Take, for example, nineteenth-century art and poetry, which highlighted the plight of female slaves.[45] Hiram Powers's famous sculpture *Greek Slave* of a beautiful woman in chains was used by many abolitionist newspapers to deplore the sexual subordination of female slaves.[46] Also drawing popular attention to the rape of slaves was Henry Wadsworth Longfellow's poem "The Quadroon Girl," which described how a planter, "whose passions gave [his female slave] life, / Whose blood ran in her veins," sold his daughter to a slave trader to "be his slave and paramour."[47] And an early antislavery novel documented the harrowing experiences of Cassy, a slave: "She started up;—but he caught her in his arms, and dragged her towards the bed. . . . [S]he looked him in the face, as well as her tears would allow her . . . 'Master-Father,' she cried, 'what is it you would have of your own daughter?' "[48]

Art at its best can inspire public vigilance and debate, a much-needed antidote to political fear-mongering that even the most independent branch—the judiciary—cannot subdue. Mexican-American rapper Snow Tha Product described her role in "Immigrants (We Get the Job Done)" as a chance to urge the public to "be woke."[49] She shared the following popular Spanish-language saying with NBC news: "*Camarón que se duerme se lo lleva la corriente*—the shrimp that falls asleep will be swept away by the current."[50]

We won't fall asleep.

We can't.

History has its eyes on us.[51]

18

HAMILTON AND THE LIMITS OF CONTEMPORARY IMMIGRATION NARRATIVES

Anil Kalhan

"Cool, they flee war zones, but the problem ain't ours
Even if our bombs landed on them like the Mayflower."
Buckingham Palace or Capitol Hill
Blood of my ancestors had that all built

It's the ink you print on your dollar bill, oil you spill
Thin red line on the flag you hoist when you kill
But still we just say "look how far I come."

—K'NAAN, SNOW THA PROJECT, RIZ MC, AND RESIDENTE

Lin-Manuel Miranda and the other creators of *Hamilton: An American Musical* have often described the show as "a story about America then, told by America now."[1] The musical's code-switching reimagination of eighteenth-century political history through the lens of inclusive, contemporary values has garnered acclaim for foregrounding the centrality of immigration to the American experience. But "America now," like "America then," is "a nation of *both* nativists *and* immigrants."[2] Informed by immigration history, what might the opposite approach—a story about immigration in "America now," told by "America then"—look like and reveal?

Consider, for example, the musical's biggest applause line, when Hamilton and Lafayette proclaim, "Immigrants: we get the job done!"[3] With a boost from the track bearing that same name on the bestselling tie-in album, *The Hamilton Mixtape*, the line might be the show's most widely known—highlighting, as Miranda has stated, "that many people who contribute to the prosperity of this nation aren't born here."[4] Read in light of *Hamilton*'s larger themes, the line could be understood as a broad affirmation of the full range of immigrants' contributions to society—large and small, tangible and intangible, visible and hidden.

When read against the status-based, hierarchical practices of Hamilton's own era, however, that same line might carry a rather different meaning. Eighteenth-century authorities selectively welcomed migration and settlement by white Protestants seen as desirable, but simultaneously subjected those deemed undesirable to marginalization, exploitation, exclusion, and removal. A story about immigrants "getting the job done" told by "America then" accordingly might be understood as a qualified, instrumental affirmation—one that similarly values only immigrants deemed desirable, and then, too, in narrowly defined economic terms.

This circumscribed interpretation of Hamilton's celebration of immigrants who "get the job done," resting on a dichotomy between desirable and undesirable immigrants, is not exclusively the product of antiquated eighteenth-century values. To the contrary, contemporary discourse about immigration, which *Hamilton* reflects and incorporates, carries analogous distinctions between "good immigrants" and "bad immigrants." The persistence and reinforcement of such distinctions obscure the full range of principles embodied in immigration policy—including, for example, family unity, humanitarian protection, human rights, and the rule of law—and hinder efforts to affirm that immigrants should be treated with dignity on an expansive, egalitarian basis, regardless of their perceived "worthiness" in immigration law or political discourse.

> All you Black folks, you must go
> All you Mexicans, you must go
> And all you poor folks, you must go
> Muslims and gays
> Boy, we hate your ways
> So all you bad folks, you must go.[5]

The coexistence of these inclusive and restrictive tendencies may be seen throughout the contentious period following Barack Obama's inauguration as president. On August 6, 2015, for example—the same evening that *Hamilton* officially opened on Broadway—seventeen candidates participated in the first Republican Party debates of the 2016 presidential campaign. In contrast to the tone presented in *Hamilton*, the Republican candidates largely fell in line with the trajectory of Donald Trump's nascent campaign, which intertwined openly racist attacks on immigrants, Muslims, and people of color with the more implicit, "dog-whistle" appeals that long since had become conventional in Republican campaigns. Ultimately, the Republican candidates largely embraced Trump's anti-immigration agenda. The handful who offered qualifications, that evening or later, did so gingerly, equivocally, and with low energy.[6]

That evening's divergent messages reflected contestation over race and immigration that shifted greatly during the six years in which *Hamilton* was written and developed. Shortly before Miranda's White House performance of his work-in-progress in 2009, Obama administration officials signaled their desire to make comprehensive immigration reform a top legislative priority, to provide millions of undocumented immigrants a pathway to legalization and better align the immigration system with contemporary needs. However, the administration's first term was simultaneously marked by considerable severity in its immigration policing, detention, and deportation practices—evidently based in part on an assessment that demonstrating "toughness" on enforcement was politically necessary to achieve success in the administration's legislative reform agenda—and steadily growing hostility toward immigrants and people of color in political discourse.

Although the Senate passed sweeping, bipartisan reform legislation four years later, in 2013—exactly one month before the first workshop performance of *Hamilton* at Vassar—legislative reform ran aground in the Republican-controlled House of Representatives. Parallel administrative reforms, which sought to establish formalized immigration enforcement priorities and temper the severity of the administration's first-term enforcement practices, also faced Republican resistance. In 2012, Obama administration officials announced the Deferred Action for Childhood Arrivals (DACA) initiative, which permitted certain undocumented immigrant youths to seek deferral of their potential deportation—falling well short of legalization, but still providing a limited reprieve—and to apply for work authorization. Two years later, the administration built upon DACA to extend analogous opportunities to many more individuals—which, controversially, Obama characterized as part of an effort to direct immigration enforcement activities toward "felons, not families." Both initiatives faced Republican lawsuits, and the latter initiative was blocked in 2015—one day before *Hamilton* officially opened at the Public Theater—by a judge with a proclivity for the kind of rhetoric used by Trump and other anti-immigration politicians.[7]

Since 2017, when Trump and his allies claimed the presidency, immigration politics, policy, and law have hurtled in exceedingly racist and xenophobic directions. High-profile initiatives have banned Muslims from entering the country; slashed refugee admissions and other humanitarian protections; expanded detention and immigration policing; rescinded DACA; and blocked individuals from seeking asylum, including by criminally prosecuting asylum-seekers and forcibly separating their families. Less visible changes to day-to-day immigration law administration have erected an invisible wall of dozens of barriers for immigrants seeking to enter or remain. At the same time, the crackdown also has triggered widespread mobilization in support of immigrants' rights, which *Hamilton* sometimes has been invoked to support. Importantly, although the Trump-Pence administration's initiatives genuinely constitute major shifts from previous administrations, both Republican and Democratic, they also have been facilitated by laws, institutions, and practices inherited from those same Janus-faced predecessors.[8]

> Now we're nomads
> That stay in one place
> Not a country
> Not a face
> Standing out but still like ghosts
> Long-term guests
> Ungracious hosts
> Re-written history
> A sleepy slavery.[9]

"Janus-faced" does not describe the narratives on immigration presented in *Hamilton*. Consistent with the characterization in Ron Chernow's biography, Miranda depicts Hamilton as a particular kind of "immigrant": one who came "up from the bottom" by "working a lot harder, by being a lot smarter, by being a self-starter."[10] This portrait of an "immigrant striver"—"hard-working, ambitious, desperate to prove himself," and "the prototype for millions of men and women who followed him, and continue to arrive today"—recurs throughout the musical.[11] *Hamilton* connects this portrayal to broader conceptions of New York ("In New York you can be a new man.") and America ("I'm just like my country, I'm young, scrappy and hungry," and "A place where even orphan immigrants can leave their fingerprints and rise up.") as open, egalitarian places characterized by social mobility.[12] Hamilton's background as an "immigrant" is not lost on his antagonists, who repeatedly use that term to describe him, albeit as an epithet. At one point, his rivals (Burr, Jefferson, Madison) even insult him in a xenophobic manner that, aside from being rendered in Jamaican patois, would be recognizable to members of immigrant communities today: "Ya best g'wan run back where ya come from."[13] However, coming from his less sympathetically portrayed antagonists, these expressions of xenophobia only reinforce the musical's sympathetic depiction of Hamilton as an archetypical immigrant success story.

At a time when the Trump-Pence presidency has literally scrubbed the idea of the United States as a "nation of immigrants" from official descriptions, *Hamilton* delivers a powerful clapback—an affirmation, in Miranda's words, that immigrants are the "renewable life-blood of our country."[14] And yet, the musical's narratives, like the "nation of immigrants" idea itself, are also noteworthy for what they minimize and obscure about immigration history.

Migrants arrived in eighteenth-century America in large numbers. But as a white, male British subject arriving in freedom—and as a student, with wealthy patrons bankrolling his elite education—Hamilton hardly was typical. The overwhelming majority of colonial-era migrants arrived in America in unfree statuses, whether as slaves, indentured servants, or persons transported following criminal convictions. A minority of eighteenth-century migrants were British; between one-third and one-half were African slaves. Unlike Hamilton, most did not remain in larger cities but instead proceeded to colonial outposts—reflecting an intimate but often-neglected relationship in American history between immigration and settler colonialism. As Aaron Fogleman describes, not only did colonial migrants enter a world "characterized by a hierarchy of ranks and degrees of dependency," but in varying degrees migration itself helped to create that hierarchical social structure.[15]

As Elizabeth Keyes notes in her contribution to this volume, no centralized "immigration law" regime existed as such. However, in a disaggregated manner, colonial authorities adapted existing British legal principles as a set of migration and membership principles. These principles functioned as mechanisms to both encourage and restrict migration and membership in the polity, and later became the foundation for immigration and citizenship policies in the United States after independence.

On the one hand, to promote inhabitation and development of conquered territories—something regarded both before and after independence as critical to the political, economic, and military success of the settler colonial project—authorities created incentives to encourage migration by those European Protestants who were regarded, in racial, ethnic, religious, and class-based terms, as distinctively capable of performing higher forms of work associated with land ownership and productive control and, therefore, worthy of full membership in the polity. These incentives included relaxation of naturalization requirements, land grants, cash bounties, tax exemptions, and expansions of political and other rights. At the same time, because settler ideology simultaneously presumed a need for dependent groups to perform lesser, degraded forms of labor, authorities also periodically acted to facilitate migration by members of subordinated groups, including slaves forcibly brought from Africa and indentured servants from Europe, on terms relegating them to second-class and outsider statuses.[16]

On the other hand, authorities instituted measures to exclude, remove, and impose other legal disabilities on persons deemed undesirable, including the poor, persons with criminal convictions, and Catholics. These mostly local measures adapted status-based legal regimes from Britain that restricted territorial presence and mobility for both British and non-British subjects alike. As Kunal Parker emphasizes, individuals subject to these provisions "might come from across the ocean, from relatively nearby, or from nowhere at all."[17] Authorities also manipulated rules governing British subjecthood to exclude and remove Native Americans and African Americans, both enslaved and free, from membership in the polity—effectively, in many cases, rendering them "foreign" and subject to exclusion, removal, and other legal disabilities akin to those faced by non-British subjects. Women faced many of these same legal disabilities as well.[18]

Contrary to what Hamilton's atypical experience might suggest, the migration and membership principles that emerged from his era were complex and multifaceted—simultaneously welcoming and exclusionary, egalitarian and hierarchical, integrative and expatriating, emancipatory and dispossessive. Although the centuries since then have obviously seen enormous changes, these dichotomies have endured or resurfaced in various forms.[19]

Conventional understandings of immigration history often overlook these dualities. As Julian Lim and Maddalena Marinari describe, by dividing immigration history too categorically into sharply defined periods of "inclusion" and "exclusion," those interpretations miss the ways in which immigration and citizenship in the United States have "always been simultaneously open *and* closed."[20] Exclusion and inclusion, they emphasize, have "always occurred in tandem," and "a preoccupation with the racial makeup of the immigrants and U.S. society has remained constant."[21]

La circunstancia me limita
No puedo ir pa' college
Porque no tengo mi green card
. . .
Ya no soy el mismo joven inocente
América me convirtió en delincuente.[22]

Today, these kinds of dichotomies take a variety of forms. As in earlier periods, for example, some immigration law provisions distinguish between desirable and undesirable immigrants in economic terms. Some immigrant admissions criteria emphasize employment opportunities, skills, achievements, and wealth, while other provisions—directly tracing their origins to eighteenth-century laws targeting the poor—render individuals inadmissible if officials believe that they are likely to become a "public charge" (meaning dependent on the government for subsistence) and deportable if officials conclude that they have become a "public charge" after admission.[23]

These kinds of distinctions can easily be reinforced by the very narratives that seek to affirm immigrants' contributions to society. For example, in the course of proposing to slash legal immigration in half, Trump and his allies have urged that immigrant admissions criteria emphasize education, skills, and English-language proficiency to a greater extent. Simultaneously, they have sought to significantly expand the definition of the "public charge" removal grounds, which could reduce immigration from poor countries and inhibit immigrants from accessing social services. Narratives that affirm immigrants primarily in terms of their economic achievements and contributions—or, as *Hamilton*'s John Laurens might put it, whether they can get "a lot farther by working a lot harder, by being a lot smarter, by being a self-starter"—may not offer particularly strong responses to these kinds of proposals.[24] To the contrary, they might indirectly and comfortably reinforce the premises of such proposals.

The risks of reinforcing these kinds of dichotomies similarly may be seen in the prevailing discourse about undocumented immigrant youths. During the 2000s, when seeking to build support for immigration reform in a political climate of pervasive hostility toward immigrants, advocates self-consciously crafted public representations of undocumented youths designed to avoid stigmas associated with undocumented immigrants. These representations instead emphasized qualities that presented undocumented youths in sympathetic terms to build political support for their legalization—for example, their high levels of assimilation into U.S. society, English-language proficiency, and identification with American values; their "exceptional" qualities making them among the "best and brightest" of their generation; and their "legal innocence" in migrating to the United States "through no fault of their own," having been brought by their parents as young people. The name of the bill introduced to provide qualifying undocumented immigrant youth with legal status was itself formulated with an acronym, the DREAM Act, intended to directly connect these representations to widely recognized conceptions of the "American dream."[25]

These strategies of depicting undocumented youths as "good immigrants"—indeed, as "model Americans"—have contributed to qualified successes in garnering political support for proposals such as the DREAM Act, DACA, and various state and local initiatives. However, they also have created a dilemma. Indirectly and sometimes directly, these strategies can marginalize those undocumented immigrants who do not fit the constructed representations. Such individuals—including those who are less integrated, who have arrived more recently, who came to the country as adults (including undocumented youths' own parents), who do not have exceptional and superlative achievements, or who previously have committed crimes—thereby risk being constructed as "bad immigrants" and being deemed less "deserving" of legalization and dignified treatment. Efforts to disassociate immigrants from persons convicted of crimes, such as Obama's emphasis on deporting "felons, not families," carry similar risks of deepening the marginalization of both immigrants and U.S. citizens with criminal convictions.[26]

Especially since 2010, as undocumented youths have projected their own voices into political discourse to a much greater extent, they have sought to bring more nuance into these representations, in part to avoid the risk of further marginalizing other immigrant groups. However, especially since more simplistic representations nevertheless endure in political and media discourse, these dilemmas persist. To the extent that these distinctions sharpen the lines between those deemed worthy of legalization and those who are not, they risk deepening the marginalization of those falling on the "wrong" sides of those lines even further.[27]

En tu sonrisa yo veo una guerrilla
Una aventura, un movimiento
Tu lenguaje, tu acento
Yo quiero descubrir lo que ya estaba descubierto.[28]

Since 2017, even as xenophobia has been ascendant among political and judicial elites, polls have steadily indicated that majorities of Americans largely oppose the Trump-Pence anti-immigration agenda and continue to hold positive views about immigration—slightly more positive views, in fact, than before Trump became president. In this context, *Hamilton*'s themes celebrating immigration, diversity, and the ideals of the American Revolution have been frequently and forcefully invoked in opposition to the anti-immigrant crackdown, including by the show's cast, crew, and creators themselves.[29]

These invocations replicate a version of the dilemma with which undocumented immigrant youths have wrestled. The musical's themes resonate powerfully with broad segments of society, and in a climate in which political and judicial elites have been hostile to the claims of immigrants, that resonance offers an important potential resource to intervene constructively in political and legal contestation over immigration. At the same time, the limitations inherent in those themes may, in some in-stances, themselves risk reinforcing the very lines being drawn to exclude and marginalize particular groups of immigrants. Ultimately, *Hamilton* itself might be an "unfinished symphony"[30] with respect to its narratives on immigration, one challenging its audiences to "rise up"[31] by developing more nuanced and expansive narratives that seek to move beyond perva-sive, but perilous distinctions in contemporary discourse between "good immigrants" and "bad immigrants."

Hamilton's Immigrant Story Today

Elizabeth Keyes

Juan and Sandra.[1] Seeds in the garden planted so long ago by another immigrant who was young, scrappy, and hungry.[2] *Hamilton* is their story. The musical tells a specific story about a specific man in a specific era. It also conveys a timeless story of immigration, dreaming, and possibility, and captures some of the story of my clients, Juan and Sandra. Except for this: their stories take place under today's harsh immigration laws and broken immigration systems, which are the "damn fools"[3] of their stories. Instead of an America where "even orphan immigrants can leave their fingerprints and rise up,"[4] we have an America that treats immigrants with contempt; with jail; with life in the shadows; with the hope of political accommodation dashed when leaders respond to the worst voices of fear, and not to the call of Hamilton's legacy.

Hamilton has extraordinary resonance for immigrants and, even before the 2016 presidential election, for immigration lawyers like me who see in our clients the promise of America. From the first song asking us to spot Alexander Hamilton, "another immigrant, comin' up from the bottom,"[5] Hamilton is an immigrant story, featuring the ambitious young person with little more than a "top-notch brain,"[6] who makes his way here and thrives in a land full of opportunity for anyone bold enough to seize it. I managed to see *Hamilton* before the cast album came out, and it became impossible to get a ticket. Watching that night in 2015, I felt my heart soar with deep gratitude and recognition. Here was the achingly familiar story of an immigrant who refused to be defined by the disdain he received, and a story told with unabashed pride and glory and power.

The power is all the greater for being performed by a diverse cast, many of whom have their own recent family stories of immigration.[7] Others descend from enslaved Americans whose story is one of forced migration, a story in the background of the musical, with nods from Laurens and Eliza in particular. With all these backgrounds, the cast and musicians imbue each performance with love and respect for immigrants that leaps off the stage, an energy that mirrors what I feel for Juan, Sandra, and so many of my clients who so seldom feel the love and respect from anyone.

Hamilton's story is possible because of the laws of his day. No immigration law prevented him from arriving in the United States in the early 1770s. He was a British subject who could travel freely among all parts of the world that Britain controlled. When he and Lafayette came to colonial America, there was no such thing as being "undocumented" or immigrating without authorization because there were no immigration laws to break and no visas to acquire. States had some rules about who could arrive, and sometimes charged fees on arriving passengers, but that was about it until the late nineteenth century, when our country started excluding Asians, then poor people, then LGBT people, and so on.[8] Once here, Hamilton could study without needing a Social Security number to register for classes, he could work without needing a work permit, he could join the military without proving his lawful status. He had challenges aplenty, but immigration law was not one.

In his era, Hamilton could and did lay immediate claim to his new country, shifting from loyal, royal British subject to American as easily as he breathed. Ron Chernow, in the biography that inspired Lin-Manuel Miranda to create *Hamilton*, writes: "Few immigrants have renounced their past more unequivocally or adopted their new country more wholeheartedly. 'I am neither merchant nor farmer,' he now wrote, just a year and a half after leaving St. Croix. 'I address you because I wish well to my country.' "[9] "My" country.

Hamilton quickly rose to become General George Washington's chief aide-de-camp in 1777; Chernow evokes his "rapid metamorphosis into a full-blooded American": "The Continental Army was a national institution and helped make Hamilton the optimal person to articulate a vision of American nationalism, his vision sharpened by the immigrant's special love for his new country."[10]

How does someone with the "immigrant's special love" metamorphose into an American today? Loving is easy, young man. Metamorphosis is harder.[11] First, for the Burrs and Schuylers of the world, wealthy and educated with the right connections and degrees, legal migration is still possible—albeit full of strange delays and bureaucratic frustrations. But let's talk about the world's Hamiltons.

For a few, who already have green cards or unusual language skills, valiant military service offers a possible path. Margaret Stock, a MacArthur genius award recipient like Lin-Manuel Miranda, kept this idea alive when she worked with the Pentagon to create a rapid path to citizenship for lawful immigrants providing valuable military service to the nation.[12] One of those immigrants, a woman originally from Haiti, took my immigration law class recently. Dag, she amazed and astonished.[13] Seeing her occasionally in her National Guard uniform packed an emotional punch. She is one of Hamilton's heirs, certainly.

Then there's the lottery, and by that I don't mean the contest to win tickets to *Hamilton*, but something much more life-changing. America has a green card lottery for would-be Hamiltons who come from countries underrepresented in our mix of immigrants. Anyone with a high school diploma and a dream can apply, and some lucky few win each year.[14] Just as Hamilton boarded a ship from St. Croix with a letter of introduction and not much else, just as Irish and Chinese, then Russian and Italian migrants set sail with nothing more than hope and energy, these green card winners arrive with no family connections or job offers, but trusting the American Dream. Sadly, the lottery, the legacy of the American immigration story, is the piece of our immigration system most likely to be cut if and when immigration reform happens.

For others, like Sandra, the path to America is not through luck and education, but through abuse, qualifying some for our tortured asylum system. Sandra faced death threats from both the gangs in her Salvadoran neighborhood and from her ex-partner, her son's dad. She and her son made their way to the United States in 2015, where they were separated and detained—in different states—in *hieleras*, the freezing cells run by Customs and Border Patrol at the border. Upon release and, months later, reunification, they applied for asylum in immigration court. While Sandra was waiting, she got a work permit,[15] and this high school–educated woman in her thirties found work in construction. Her teenage son enrolled in school and learned English at a pace equal to Lafayette's rap (although I admittedly have not heard Sandra's son rap). Their day in court came relatively quickly: in two years.[16] If Sandra had applied from inside the border, to one of the ten asylum offices scattered around the country, she would probably still be waiting, due to extraordinary backlogs at those offices.

Sandra and her son won their cases in early 2018. Why? Partly because her case was in Baltimore, where asylum-seekers have a fighting chance, and not Atlanta or Charlotte, where they do not.[17] Partly, also, because she found a lawyer. In 2015, Sandra could not afford an attorney, and she was among thousands of asylum-seekers overwhelming the capacity of nonprofits.

My clinic was stretched thin, but in a stroke of uncanny luck for Sandra, we found a way. April Guevarra, a law student, provided expert legal support on the case as my research assistant. Maybe Sandra would have won without April's and my help, but statistics show that it is unlikely. When the current president pushes for immigration laws based on "merit," he means people with advanced degrees or deep pockets, not people like Sandra and her son. But when I think of "merit," I think of someone able to start with nothing, and do honest and necessary labor, and build a good life for her and her son, and now their rambunctious dog, too. When you knock Sandra down, she "get[s] the fuck back up again."[18] And that's our American story: built on the experiences and contributions of people just like Sandra.

For too many others, metamorphosis is simply impossible. That is where Juan's story differs from Hamilton's. Yet Juan's story is probably my favorite of all, and I have to hope that there are many chapters of his story yet to be written.

Juan came to the United States from Bolivia in his late teens, with a high school education, intent on getting further. Literally the day after he arrived, he started loading and unloading trucks at a nearby hardware store, earning the precious dollars he needed to go to school. He hasn't stopped working since, but he also managed to put himself through community college and then transfer to the University of Baltimore. No big deal? Well, he graduated from there summa cum laude, while studying in a second language and working full-time. Young, scrappy, hungry . . . you see it, right?[19]

Being a non-stop[20] person, Juan applied to graduate school and went to a prestigious one on the scholarship he earned from being so danged studious. He now organizes undocumented youth, bringing his capacious intellect to one of the hardest challenges of all: fixing our broken immigration system in ways that respect human dignity. Like Hamilton, there are a million things he hasn't done, but just you wait.[21] I expect him to reinvent the world one day.

But unlike A. Ham claiming citizenship in his new country, Juan cannot. He did not qualify for DACA, and there is no line he can stand in for any other status. Sometimes I wonder, do people think "getting legal" is like getting your license, and you just have to stand in the right line for a while? Because that is not remotely how immigration works. Even in a straightforward case with a family or employer sponsor, the lines can take years or decades.

And the line disappears for any of a multitude of reasons—from committing small drug offenses to entering illegally in the first place.[22] The merger of criminal justice and immigration removal systems makes it treacherously easy to be deported for even minor infractions. Nowhere is this more true than for people of color living in communities that are overpoliced, or for those who accept guilty pleas for crimes they may not have committed, just to get out of jail or stop a terrifying process before it gets worse. I could go on, but let me just note the deep, sometimes painful, beauty in the immigrant story being told as passionately and evocatively as it is by the richly diverse case of *Hamilton*, when our enforcement policies target so many people who look like that cast.

Imagine America if Hamilton had not been admitted because, in 1774, he lacked proof of his merit, with all his contributions still to be in the future. Imagine if he had been deported for lacking papers or for, say, dueling. It doesn't matter if everything is "legal in New Jersey"[23] if the federal law makes dueling a deportable offense. Wouldn't a judge look at all his contributions, though, weigh the equities, and let him stay, you ask? No. We rarely balance equities in immigration. There is a widespread myth that when people who have lived here long enough, and contributed a lot, end up before an immigration judge, the judge can simply let them stay and give them status. Not true.[24]

So under today's laws, we would have lost a man who—by the time of his engagement to Eliza Schuyler in 1780—even Hamilton's future father-in-law recognized as American, a mere seven or so years since he first set foot on our shores. Philip Schuyler told Eliza that Hamilton was "the ornament of his country."[25]

Juan, too, is an ornament of his new country, as is Sandra, as are the DREAMers who are reinventing our idea of citizenship by claiming their American-ness so forcefully, as are the people who come, as immigrants have since our country's beginnings, for safety or for opportunity. In this, and in their project of redefining what America is, and who Americans are, they are Hamilton's heirs. They are the seeds he planted in a garden[26] 250 years ago when he walked off that boat in New York.

If we could see them as Hamilton's heirs, that would be enough.[27] And if we could reform our laws to let them be the Americans in law that they already are in their hearts, that, too, would be enough.

Hopefully, it's only a matter of time.[28]

Part 6

"The Ten Duel Commandments"

Hamilton, Hip-Hop, and the Culture of Dueling in America

Glenn Harlan Reynolds

On July 11, 1804, Alexander Hamilton died at the hands of sitting vice president Aaron Burr in a duel conducted outside Weehawken, New Jersey.[1] Hamilton's famous end hangs over the entire *Hamilton: An American Musical*.

Most fans of *Hamilton* are probably vaguely familiar with the custom of dueling, though many may not realize that, at the time of Hamilton's death, it was a relatively recent import to North America. It caught on with amazing speed and completeness. Dueling existed as a class-privileged method of protecting reputational capital, supported by a body of custom that functioned outside of, and in many ways superior to, law. A party who was insulted could issue a challenge that, if he was of sufficient rank, could not be ignored by the challenged party without ostracism and social and possibly financial ruin.

In the early nineteenth century, partly as a reaction to the Hamilton–Burr duel, an antidueling movement sprang up, which stressed libel law and other alternatives in preference to duels, and which altered some state constitutions to provide that duelists and their seconds would be ineligible for public office.[2] This movement also led to restrictions on weapons carriage that remain relevant in Second Amendment law to this day, as the antidueling movement tried to reduce the availability of handguns, an effort noted by Clayton Cramer in his *Concealed Weapon Laws of the Early Republic*.[3] Yet vestiges of the custom of dueling occasionally surface, including one famous event during the 2004 presidential election, when Democratic senator Zell Miller of Georgia threatened to challenge television pundit Chris Matthews to a duel, and its most significant survivor can perhaps be found in honor-linked violence among young people living in certain urban settings. For example, Annie Sweeney describes how gang members in Chicago use "Facebook to challenge rivals or signal disrespect," which often precedes gun violence.[4]

As William Oliver Stevens notes in his magisterial *Pistols at Ten Paces: The Story of the Code of Honor in America*,[5] during the Revolutionary War, the practice of dueling rapidly caught on in the colonies. It wasn't until the last quarter of the eighteenth century that dueling became *de rigeur* in North America, as a combination of colonist sons returning from education at Eton and Oxford, and British and Continental military men over for the war, brought the culture of duels and dueling with them. Although the criminal law made no exception for duels, public opinion meant that duelists were almost never charged with murder and, if they were, were almost never convicted—even Burr, who was indicted in both New York and New Jersey for the murder of Hamilton, was not tried, much less convicted. The code of dueling existed, by common consent, outside the otherwise applicable rules of society, under its own strictures and conventions. In a surprisingly short time, dueling went from something largely alien to American culture to a fixture.

At the time of Hamilton's duel, and for nearly one hundred years thereafter, dueling was a custom limited to the gentry; despite America's formally classless character, a gentleman was under no obligation to respond to a challenge from those viewed as low class (though an aggrieved lower-class challenger might respond by simply gunning the "offender" down with no further ado; honor-based violence of a less structured kind was so common that the formalities of the duel were often defended as a civilizing influence). Certain words or phrases carried special weight: "The language of insult between gentlemen usually required a specific term, unmistakably from the lips of the insulter, such as *rascal, coward, liar, scoundrel* to bring things to the brink of gunfire."[6] And while words could be cured by an apology or reconciliation, which a duelists' seconds were honor-bound to seek, a blow generally could not be addressed except by violence.

The use of large-caliber smoothbore firearms, usually at short range, meant that the fatality rate for American duels was considerably higher than that on the Continent. A duel with swords could be stopped at "first blood," something far less practical when gunfire was being exchanged. In general, the giving and receiving of challenges was in deadly earnest. Social pressure in favor of the dueling code was so strong that failing to give a challenge when insulted, or failing to accept a challenge when received, was unthinkable. One who failed to go along with the code was likely to be stigmatized as a coward, a stigma that carried real-world consequences. Not only was a man with such a reputation likely to face additional, and worse, insults, such a reputation meant social exclusion, with serious consequences for one's marriage prospects or those of one's children, and often had financial implications as well. As Joanne Freeman observes, " 'Character assassination' set the tone of political debate; to destroy a man's character was to destroy his reputation, and to destroy his reputation was to crush the very foundations of his public career."[7]

Sometimes the two duelists were reluctant participants, swept along by social pressure that they were unable to resist, even together. To modern ears this sounds absurd, but the custom of dueling was widely accepted and had many defenders. On the one hand, it was held to promote courage, which in a sense it did, as the social pressures meant that one might face death at any time. Simply to function as a member of polite society thus required a degree of courage that few display today.

In addition, the custom took hold at a time when third-party sources of reputational capital, ranging from credit rating agencies, to a "neutral" press, to political parties, were weak or nonexistent, and libel suits were rare and disfavored, making individual reputations vital. Defending one's reputation under such conditions was serious business, serious enough that defense might extend to lethal force. On the other hand, many defended the formalities of dueling as a restraint on violence. With on-the-spot violence in response to perceived slights being astoundingly common by modern standards, many saw the dueling code as a civilizing influence: it imposed a cooling-off period, and seconds were charged with seeking a reconciliation. ("Your last chance to negotiate. / Send in your seconds, see if they can set the record straight.")[8] Such reconciliations often happened, and the argument was that without the code, thoughtless violence would be more common, and more deadly.

By the time of the Hamilton–Burr duel, the dueling code had taken hold, both on the elites themselves and on society in general. This gave the whole affair a momentum of its own, eventually claiming Hamilton's life and, despite his short-term dueling victory, Burr's political career. (As fellow duelist Andrew Jackson told Burr later, Hamilton dead was a more formidable political adversary than Hamilton alive.)[9]

As such affairs go, the Hamilton–Burr duel would have to be categorized as rather optional. There was no face-to-face encounter, no episode of Hamilton calling Burr names in front of witnesses, no disrespectful blow. Instead, the duel was built up out of Burr's outrage and insecurity at having lost the New York governor's race, and of Hamilton's feeling that he could not disregard the challenge without losing face and thus political support.

As Benjamin Barton explains in his chapter in this volume, the "insult" of which Burr complained came via the ambiguous words of a third party, Charles Cooper, who in a piece of correspondence published in a Federalists newspaper assured his correspondent that he "could detail . . . a still more despicable opinion which General Hamilton had expressed of Mr. Burr." As Joanne Freeman notes, "Though Cooper only hinted at a personal insult, Burr seized on this remark as a provocation for an affair of honor and demanded an explanation from Hamilton."[10]

But there was more to it than personal honor. Dueling, Freeman maintains, was a part of the overall political system at the time. "[To] early national politicians, duels were demonstrations of manner, not marksmanship; they were intricate games of dare and counter-dare, ritualized displays of bravery, military prowess, and, above all, willingness to sacrifice one's life for one's honor. . . . Politicians considered themselves engaged in an affair of honor from the first 'notice' of an insult to the final acknowledgment of 'satisfaction,' a process that sometimes took weeks or even months."[11]

With political parties still in their infancy, politics remained highly individualized, revolving around leaders with strong personalities. It was not uncommon to see a losing party's representative, or a supporter, challenge a member of the winning party. By doing so, the loser removed some of the stain of defeat, and reestablished himself as a contender, one willing to fight and take risks. On most occasions this was accomplished without actual bloodshed.

Such exchanges between politicians were far more strategic than the run-of-the-mill challenge and response. Freeman notes that between 1795 and 1807 sixteen such affairs of honor took place in New York City, "most of them heretofore unrecognized because they did not result in a challenge or the exchange of fire."[12] She continues: "These duels did not result from a sudden flare of temper; politicians timed them strategically, sometimes provoked them deliberately."

Yet they were not wholly artificial, either. Although we associate the phrase "the personal is political" with the 1960s, it would not have seemed strange to leaders of the early Republic. With parties still too weak to offer a meaningful institutional imprimatur, politicians had to resort to what today is called "personal branding." Among other things, that meant demonstrating to their supporters important traits of firmness, integrity, and manliness. In modern parlance, this was a form of "expensive signaling." The willingness to risk death or crippling in a duel was a demonstration that a politician genuinely possessed these characteristics, rather than manufacturing a convincing-but-false simulacrum thereof.

Freeman's description of the times sounds unexpectedly like the present: "Without the anonymity and formal alliances offered by membership in an institutionalized party, political interaction revolved around the identities and aspirations of individual politicians. Factional alliances and personal friendships were often indistinguishable. An attack on a political measure was an attack on an individual, and an attack on an individual demanded a personal defense. A politician's private identity and his public office were thus inseparably linked."[13] When the personal is political, and when personal slurs must be answered with violence or at least the serious threat thereof, then political disputes are particularly likely to turn into causes for a duel. That is what happened with Hamilton and Burr.

Thus, Burr's challenge—which persisted after much back-and-forth among the pair's seconds—left Hamilton in an awkward spot. The details are well described elsewhere, but the upshot was, as Freeman notes, that Burr thought he could repair his wounded reputation, redeem his honor, and possibly subject Hamilton to dishonor, via a duel. A failure to challenge would have cost Burr political support, as his own followers lost faith in his character as a "man of the sword."[14]

In the end, the duel had to take place, with Hamilton composing a long and lawyerly defense of his participation in a ritual that, he said, he generally disapproved of. But at the core, Hamilton's reasons for participating were the same as Burr's. Had he backed down, he would have ended his political career (which, according to the musical's Jefferson, Madison, and Burr, he'd already largely done with the *Reynolds Pamphlet*: "Never gon' be President now.")[15] As Lin-Manuel Miranda and Jeremy McCarter put it in *Hamilton: The Revolution*, "He had to go to Weehawken, and he had to hold a loaded gun, but he didn't have to fire it at Aaron Burr."[16] Thus, when John Quincy Adams, many years later, put down the cause of Hamilton's assent to the duel as "AMBITION,"[17] he wasn't entirely wrong.

As Fleming also notes, with regard to Adams's characterization, "There is some truth in this reduction, but it is inadequate as an explanation of why General Hamilton chose to risk his life." Hamilton was torn between his vision of himself as a soldier, past and future, and his growing and, to Fleming, genuine Christian faith. "Anyone who has given some thought to the journey of the human soul can summon compassion for this divided, tormented man. Hamilton was, like most of us, absorbed, even obsessed with the things of this world. Faith had invaded his soul without warning."[18] Miranda has Hamilton sing about this conversion, "I take the children to church on Sunday, / a sign of the cross at the door, / and I pray. / That never used to happen before."[19]

Ultimately, it was the world that won, as it so often does, although the musical's Burr wonders whether that was true. ("I should've known / the world was wide enough for both Hamilton and me.")[20] Despite his faith, Hamilton was no doubt correct that his future prospects would have been dim had he declined the duel. In a world where courage was viewed as the supreme virtue, and political power was reserved for "men of the sword," Hamilton would have had to abandon all hope of a secular career had he followed his Christian instincts. Some might view such a withdrawal from a sinful world as virtuous, but Hamilton was a politician, not a monk. When things came to a point, he couldn't abandon his constituency, or let his constituency abandon him. To be seen as a man of the sword, he was forced to be a man of the sword. (As a friend told Gouverneur Morris upon Hamilton's death, "If we were truly brave, we would not accept a challenge. But we are all cowards.")[21]

The problem with "expensive signaling" is the flipside of its virtue: that it is expensive. When you have a tattoo inscribed on your face to demonstrate your commitment to your group, it is a convincing signal because it imposes immediate real-world costs in terms of employment and associations. Likewise, when you live by the dueling code, your signaling as a man of the sword is credible because you place your life at genuine risk: expensive signaling, indeed. In Hamilton's case, the price of this signaling turned out to be his life. In Burr's case, it turned out to be his political career. Though both politicians thought that they had to go ahead with the duel in order to maintain their political viability, both wound up losing it: in Hamilton's case because he was dead, and in Burr's case because he had killed Hamilton. ("Death doesn't discriminate / between the sinners and the saints, / it takes and it takes and it takes. / History obliterates. / In every picture it paints, / it paints me with all my mistakes.")[22]

At the time, many politicians went on to successful careers after killing an adversary in a duel. Brockholst Livingston, then a judge on the New York Court of Appeals, the state's highest court, had six years earlier killed Federalist James Jones. Burr perhaps anticipated a similar reaction. Instead, the reaction was "grief and rage at Vice President Burr."[23] There was even talk of burning Burr's townhouse, and sending another mob to do the same to his country estate at Richmond Hill. ("When Alexander aimed / at the sky, / he may have been the first one to die, / but I'm the one who paid for it.")[24] Despite a public letter from both Hamilton and Burr's seconds, concluding that "We conceive it proper to add that the conduct of the parties in that interview was perfectly proper as suited to the occasion,"[25] public sentiment grew angrier. Newspapers that had been friendly to Burr denounced him in no modest terms. Even the anti-Hamilton newspaperman James Cheetham wrote that this "national loss [was] the inevitable and deplorable effect of a long premeditated and predetermined system of hostility on the part of Mr. Burr and his confidential advisers."[26]

The extent of anger over Hamilton's death seemed to surprise everyone, even Hamilton's friends, for Hamilton "had never been a popular figure with the masses."[27] Although Burr and Hamilton may have regarded each other as politicians, to the public they—and particularly Hamilton—were Founders, which by 1804 was taking on a deeper meaning. To see a

Founder gunned down, particularly on such an attenuated claim of insult, was more than the public was able to bear.

After Hamilton's death, America saw the first stirrings of an antidueling movement. Though some (including Benjamin Franklin) had opposed the custom from its introduction, post-Hamilton serious voices spoke for its eradication. Yale president Timothy Dwight sermonized against dueling, calling it a sin. So did a preacher named Lyman Beecher, father to Henry Ward Beecher, calling for good Christians to refuse to vote for a man who had ever participated in a duel. According to Beecher, America's very egalitarianism made dueling more of a curse: "In Europe, only gentry pretend to the code. Here, where every man is as good as another, each feels it his duty to defend his honor at the point of a pistol."[28]

Beecher also commented on the involvement of lawmakers in dueling. As Stevens writes:

> Although the [dueling] code was outlawed by the statute books of New York and New Jersey, there were not a few meetings in the first decade of the century, as we have seen in an earlier chapter. How little weight the existing law had on the consciences of gentlemen is indicated by the legal eminence of the principals and seconds concerned in this story. Burr and Hamilton were the most prominent lawyers of the state . . . To these distinguished gentlemen of the law, an anti-dueling proviso had no more influence than the Prohibition Amendment had on their successors in a later age. [The seconds] prided themselves on the fact that everything had been done according to the most correct procedure.[29]

Efforts to encourage the use of libel law in place of duels—covered at more length in Ben Barton's chapter—faced an uphill battle. Honor was not a quality that could be repaired through the legal system. For a man to turn to the legal system to repair his honor, perhaps by filing a libel or slander suit, was akin to a man admitting that he was unable to protect himself. It was an admission of both weakness and cowardice. A libel suit also carried the message that the plaintiff was one who thought his honor could be repaired by monetary damages.[30]

Some vestiges survived. As late as the time when I was in high school during the Carter presidency, the notion that an insult might be answered by a ritualized fistfight out behind the gym still had some currency (I myself engaged in a few such), and any aficionado of classic cinema knows that in the mid-twentieth century even sophisticated adult characters played by actors like Cary Grant might engage in fisticuffs if sufficiently provoked. And the first modern Olympics had a dueling pistols event, where competitors shot each other with wax bullets from ten paces while wearing protective gear. It was discontinued after 1912, though a poll taken in 2000 showed that 32 percent of respondents favored bringing it back.[31] And although in the 2004 presidential election, Senator Zell Miller (D-Ga) issued a dueling challenge—or perhaps more accurately, threatened to do so—to MSNBC host Chris Matthews,[32] nowadays, this custom is essentially extinct.

While a vestige of this culture persists in certain settings in which perceptions of "disrespect" can lead to physical violence, it seems unlikely that dueling will spread to the political class of today, though the latter offers plenty of cause for concern. The differences with Hamilton's era are many, but in some ways the similarities are growing: As trust in institutions like political parties, news media organizations, and government declines, politics seems to be becoming more personal, as it was in the early days of the Republic. Though this may not lead to a resurgence of the politically oriented dueling that claimed Hamilton's life and Burr's career, it may lead to new manifestations of the need for politicians to prove themselves to their followers, and for followers to wage war on behalf of their chosen leaders. Perhaps the social media wars of today are an example of that phenomenon.[33]

If so, they represent an improvement. Social media combat among U.S. politicians occasionally ends careers but generally doesn't cost lives. And our current political class seems far more comfortable with living a consequence-free life than that of earlier ages. Looking at the state of politics today, that may represent the best argument in favor of the custom of dueling, with all its flaws.

ALEXANDER HAMILTON, CITIZEN-PROTECTOR?

Jody Madeira

Lin-Manuel Miranda and the producers of *Hamilton: An American Musical* intended the production to provide powerful social commentary on contemporary politics and culture. Though firearms and the Second Amendment are not explicitly integral to *Hamilton*'s core themes, they are still woven into the fabric of the Founding Fathers' story.

Throughout American history, firearms and their various uses have had profound social, cultural, political, and even moral implications for citizens. Americans have lived different models of what it means to be a citizen through firearm access, ownership, and carry; behavioral norms have changed with time and context. As in Revolutionary War–era America, some argue that today's guns are "tools of citizenship," "gun politics is about what it means to be a good American," and "gun ownership is a civic virtue, a hallmark of American self-reliance and duty."[1]

Much of the musical emphasizes that Hamilton is "not throwing away [his] shot!"[2] In her book *Citizen-Protectors: The Everyday Politics of Guns in an Age of Decline*, Jennifer Carlson argues that "the everyday practice of gun carry sustains a model of citizenship—the citizen-protector—that celebrates the protection of self and others as an everyday civic duty that is particularly compelling in contexts where alternative ways of asserting masculinity (such as being the sole financial provider for one's family) are eroding and the state's capacity to protect (through policing, for example) appears precarious."[3] Citizen-protectors "use firearms to actively assert their authority and relevance by embracing the duty to protect themselves and police others."[4] According to the citizen-protector model, protecting oneself is a moral duty.

Alexander Hamilton is a citizen-protector among other citizen-protectors. Miranda has emphasized that *Hamilton* is about "an underlying belief in stories, and their power to change the world."[5] The musical leaves the audience with important questions: Did Hamilton need firearms to succeed as a citizen-protector? How do firearms fit into the *Hamilton* story? Are these instruments even Hamilton's most effective weapon?

The Alexander Hamilton of *Hamilton* fame certainly has a weapon of choice, but it is rhetoric, not firearms. Though he meets death at the end of Aaron Burr's dueling pistol, Hamilton's fatal course is charted by words, not bullets; in the grand tradition of hip-hop, he engages mostly in verbal duels, not physical ones. To the Alexander Hamilton of the musical (and to other Founding Father characters), words are tools to engineer creation and opportunity, not wreak destruction and misfortune. Hamilton boasts that he is a master of words ("My power of speech: unimpeachable")[6] even as he admits he can say too much ("Sometimes I get over excited, shoot off at the mouth").[7] Hamilton seeks to use nonviolent means to realize his goals, particularly learning, speaking, and writing. ("I'm past patiently waitin'. I'm passionately / smashin' every expectation, / every action's an act of creation!")[8]

Historical evidence suggests that the actual Alexander Hamilton envisioned that Americans would be armed; in *Federalist 29*, he wrote, an "army can never be formidable to the liberties of the people while there is a large body of citizens, little if any inferior to them in discipline and the use of arms, who stand ready to defend their rights and those of their fellow-citizens."[9] In the Founding Fathers' time, firearms were a critical implement.

Revolutionary citizens—usually male heads of households—owned at least one firearm for household protection against opponents, intruders, and wild animals; one had to fend for oneself in matters of personal protection because there were no states, let alone state apparatus for law enforcement or emergency services. Some states required that indentured freedmen receive a gun as freedom dues (because men could not set up their households without firearms),[10] that men carry firearms to church to protect congregations,[11] and that firearms be made available for inspection at public musters.[12] In revolutionary New York, there was not a right to bear arms as such; rather, male citizens had a "duty" to be prepared and willing to defend the state in times of war, and to pursue felons under the "hue and cry." Thus, the militia had to be always "armed and disciplined, and in readiness for service." In addition, a statute passed in 1787 stated that a citizen could not be "constrained to arm himself, or to go out of this state" unless the state legislature decreed.[13]

General George Washington required that soldiers enlisting in the Continental Army bring their own firearms, and he and other commanders credited the army's good marksmanship to Americans' skill and experience with these weapons (particularly in hunting).[14] Certainly, individuals could serve as citizen-protectors through military service, reaffirming their commitments to and sacrifices for American citizenship. In this context, firearms and the militant citizen-protectors who wielded them were critical to nation-building. When the Declaration of Independence fell on deaf British ears, muskets were the only means for wresting independence from an ineffectual and distant nation-state that overtly harmed and could not protect (or did not care to protect) its colonies.

But once revolutionary battles are won, as *Hamilton* tells the story, those who use firearms rather than words to protect personal honor engage in a fool's errand and become citizen-saboteurs who embark on campaigns to destroy their comrades as well as themselves. Such destructive actions undo one's capacities to protect and provide, whether the goal is to build a nation or a family. Overwhelmingly, firearms (in the musical, especially, dueling pistols) undermine, rather than preserve, legacies, and create division and confrontation—in contrast to the firearms that unified a new nation through revolutionary means. Dueling pistols both mark failures (of compromise) and fail their marks, escalating interpersonal conflicts into bloodshed. Defending one's honor at the price of one's life may be a romantic choice, but it is scarcely a practical one for a man whose legacy as citizen-protector is predicated upon being in "the room where it happens."[15]

Hamilton does not rely on a firearm to get ahead in prerevolutionary New York City. ("These New York City streets get colder, I shoulder / ev'ry burden, ev'ry disadvantage / I have learned to manage, I don't have a gun to brandish, / I walk these streets famished.")[16] As a new émigré, Hamilton continuously seeks opportunities, vowing, "I am not throwing away my shot."[17] In contrast stands King George III, who is honest about his intentions when he warns in the song "You'll Be Back": "Cuz when push comes to shove, / I will kill your friends and family to remind you of my love."[18] Thus, Hamilton initially offers different skills to the revolutionary effort than military prowess; he is a citizen-protector of the first order, but one who convinces others through verse, not violence. This ambition to create and protect his legacy as citizen-protector drives much of the musical's action.

Hamilton's commitment to the power of words does not stop him from occasionally expressing sour grapes with his wordsmithing role. He longs for a more militant glory; as he states in "Right Hand Man": "As a kid in the Caribbean I wished for a war / I knew that I was poor, / I knew it was the only way to– [Hamilton/Burr/Laurens/Mulligan/Lafayette] Rise up!"[19] Indeed, many of Hamilton's compatriots, such as Jefferson and Washington, had extensive gun collections.[20] When he hires Hamilton as his aide-de-camp, Washington (the grandfather of all American citizen-protectors) empathizes with these militant ambitions ("It's alright, you want to fight, you've got a hunger. / I was just like you when I was younger. / Head full of fantasies of dyin' like a martyr?").[21] But Washington's plans for Hamilton keep him out of action (and out of danger) for some time; as Burr notes in "A Winter's Ball": "Washington hires Hamilton right on sight, / But Hamilton still wants to fight, not write."[22]

In the musical's version of history, Hamilton's first brush with violence comes not in the Revolutionary War but in his friend John Laurens's duel with fellow patriot Charles Lee. Hamilton wants to defend Washington's honor after Lee insults the General, but Washington orders him not to take part in such activities. Instead, Laurens steps up to "demand satisfaction" (another word, like "shot," that invites considerable entendre during the show).[23]

It is through the Laurens–Lee duel that Hamilton first learns the "code duello,"[24] which in the musical takes the form of "Ten Duel Commandments." From its first introduction, Hamilton's comrades speak of dueling as a senseless practice. ("Can we agree that duels are dumb and immature? / [Hamilton:] Sure. But your man has to answer for his words, Burr. / [Burr:] With his life? We both know that's absurd, sir.")[25]

Practically speaking, it is far from certain that either duelist must die. As the company sings, "Most disputes die, and no one shoots."[26] Several of the "Ten Duel Commandments" require the parties to attempt to resolve their conflict without violence. After Laurens duels Lee, Washington takes Hamilton to task ("You solve nothing, you aggravate our allies to the south. . . . Watch your tone. / I am not a maiden in need of defending, I am grown").[27] This condemnation of dueling with weapons lodges in viewers' minds for the remainder of the show. This story has a clear moral: dueling—at least the physical kind—is something that harms, not protects. That message questions the traditional role of a citizen-protector and asks whether, as Hamilton has the opportunity to fight with weapons, violence is the tool for peace and protection.

At the Battle of Yorktown, Hamilton finally gets his shot, trading his position as Washington's aide-de-camp for a role as a fully masculine, militarized American citizen-protector ("weapon in my hand, a command, and my men with me").[28] Hamilton is so adamant that no man among his troops usurps the citizen-protector role before the battle begins that he prepares for his sneak attack by ordering his men to remove the bullets from their guns.

By now, Hamilton has matured enough to know that martyrdom is no longer a viable option; others, including his pregnant wife, Eliza, are counting on him to come home. ("Then I remember my Eliza's expecting me. . . / not only that, my Eliza's expecting, / We gotta go, gotta get the job done, / gotta start a new nation, gotta meet my son!")[29] Here, Hamilton exemplifies the more traditional citizen-protector role, taking that one crucial shot at surprising the British. After the Americans prove victorious at Yorktown, the combatants lower their weapons to the stage, signifying that the time for violence has passed and the time for nation-building, including constitutional ratification, is at hand. This bloodshed was necessary to accomplish something for future generations ("You will come of age with our young nation. / We'll bleed and fight for you, we'll make it right for you. / If we lay a strong enough foundation / we'll pass it on to you, we'll give the world to you, and you'll blow us all away.")[30]

Following the Revolutionary War, Hamilton emerges fully into his role as wordsmithing citizen-protector and devotes his full attention to the fight for constitutional ratification. Burr asks him in "Non-Stop," "Why do you write like you're running out of time? . . . / Ev'ry day you fight, like you're running out of time."[31] Hamilton, for his part, begs Burr for his help with the ratification project ("Burr, we studied and we fought and we killed / for this notion of a nation we now get to build.")[32] Burr refuses to openly support the new Constitution, however, and Hamilton embarks on his first battle as rhetorical citizen-protector, writing the majority of the essays in the *Federalist Papers*—a mammoth accomplishment in the new post-Revolution war of words that is nation-building.

Hamilton remains obsessed with his legacy as citizen-protector throughout this period. ("God help and forgive me, / I wanna build something that's gonna / outlive me.")[33] Thomas Jefferson, recently returned from France, forms a dislike to both Hamilton and his ideas, and references firearms in yearning for his political demise. ("Somebody gimme some dirt on this vacuous mass so we can at last unmask him. / I'll pull the trigger on him, someone load the gun and cock it.")[34] Jefferson's fear of Hamilton stems from his rhetorical prowess, not his martial mastery. ("Hamilton's a host unto himself. As long as he can hold a pen, he's a threat.")[35]

Alas, even the most respected citizen-protectors such as Washington must eventually pass their torches to younger firebrands. When Washington decides to step down from the presidency, Hamilton writes Washington's final words. When John Adams succeeds Washington as president and fires Hamilton from his cabinet position, Hamilton is no longer in the "room where it happens," and his legacy is endangered. Reflecting back on his achievements in "Hurricane," Hamilton recalls how writing has been indelibly linked with the course of his life:

I wrote my way out of hell.
I wrote my way to revolution.
I was louder than the crack in the bell.
I wrote Eliza love letters until she fell.
I wrote about The Constitution and defended it well.
And in the face of ignorance and resistance,

I wrote financial systems into existence.
And when my prayers to God were met with indifference,
I picked up a pen, I wrote my own deliverance.[36]

These statements haunt audiences for the remainder of the musical, as Hamilton's words retrace the path to his last moments: reputational damage, then two duels, followed by two deaths. First comes the *Reynolds Pamphlet*. Hamilton has so obsessively pursued the citizen-protector role that he is willing to sacrifice his personal reputation to save the reputations of his party and the Treasury Department. Heartbroken and enraged, Eliza burns the letters that Hamilton wrote to her—in effect destroying his legacy as a husband.

Hamilton and Eliza are still at odds at the time the second duel in the musical is fought. Hamilton's son, Philip, duels George Eacker for disparaging Hamilton in a Fourth of July speech. ("He disparaged my father's legacy in front of a crowd. / I can't have that, I'm making my father proud.")[37] Philip seeks advice from his father, who advises him to delope, or throw away his first shot. ("Stand there like a man until Eacker is in front of you. / When the time comes, fire your weapon in the air. / This will put an end to the whole affair.")[38] After Philip worries that this strategy will result in his own death, Hamilton confidently reassures him, stating, "No. He'll follow suit if he's truly a man of honor. / To take someone's life, that is something you can't shake."[39] Philip departs with Hamilton's dueling pistols, and his father's wish "Make me proud, son."[40] Alas, Philip is mortally wounded when Eacker fires early. In "Stay Alive," Hamilton witnesses his son's death, living a painful reminder of Washington's cautionary words that dueling is unnecessary and unwise. The death of his son undoes Hamilton's competency to continue acting as citizen-protector; for self-preservation, he retreats from public life.

Hamilton meets his end in a third and final duel. This time, Burr is the instigator; now vice president under Jefferson, Burr takes issue with Hamilton's public remarks that he is groundless and commits to no beliefs: "Now you call me 'amoral,' / a 'dangerous disgrace,' / if you've got something to say, / name a time and place, / face to face."[41] Hamilton refuses to retract his words, and ultimately agrees to duel Burr. ("[Burr:] Then stand, Alexander. / Weehawken. Dawn. / Guns. Drawn. / [Hamilton:] You're on.")[42] It appears that Hamilton's consciousness of his role as citizen-protector persuaded him that his participation in the duel was necessary. Trapped between irrelevancy and possible death, Hamilton elects to participate in the duel but throws away his actual shot, and dies when Burr does not.

And so what story can we learn from the history of dueling, from America's story as well as Hamilton's? A new American revolution is at hand: a struggle to increase firearms' accessibility and cultural acceptability. As in Hamilton's time, firearms might seem like an attractive means to wrest one's independence back from an ineffectual state that cannot protect, and to deter a state that would act tyrannically. But instead of furthering goals of national independence as in the revolutionary era, firearms now mark and confirm individual freedom. Their presence might seem to speak louder than words, more strident even than the text of the Second Amendment—and they are increasingly attractive to those who want to "talk back" to the government.

In contemporary America, gun carriers who opt into the citizen-protector role walk in different shoes than Hamilton's boots. They carry for many reasons—to feel safer, protect themselves and others, show support for Second Amendment rights, demonstrate that others like them can carry with impunity, and thwart or prevent crime. Enacting the right to bear arms has become more important than winning it.

Contemporary citizen-protectors may believe that they are under attack from federal and state governments, which they regard as ineffectual (or even dangerous, if these bodies enact "gun control" laws). If government is in disarray and police cannot protect, they reason, then everyone should be his own soldier or law enforcement officer. For citizen-protectors, firearms help individuals mobilize to secure their lives and liberties against feared governmental or criminal incursions, in the process reinforcing foundational American frameworks that are now crumbling.

Through grassroots and lobbying efforts, these citizen-protector perspectives are rapidly becoming etched into state and federal legal and regulatory frameworks. Governments are in effect subsidizing these activities, shielding firearms and their owners from many adverse types of expression, including those that are allegedly discriminatory. For example, states like Florida have passed laws forbidding physicians from asking patients about firearms ownership or access without medical necessity.[43] Indiana enacted a measure that forbids employers from asking employees about these same issues without a public safety exception, but with a penalty of treble punitive damages plus attorneys' fees.[44] The "guns everywhere" ideology can go strongest, fastest by silencing dissent.

Contemporary battles over the Second Amendment and the right to bear arms continue to rage on. These issues are not at the heart of the action in *Hamilton*; however, the musical has harnessed these differences to make powerful statements, both in production and in response to contemporary events. For example, although the *Hamilton* ensemble usually uses prop muskets when performing the song "Yorktown" (with the cast setting them down immediately after the battle is won), the producers adapted the choreography to eliminate prop guns when performing at the 70th Tony Awards on June 12, 2016.[45] Lin-Manuel Miranda and his friend, Ben Platt, used the music of *Hamilton* and *Dear Evan Hansen* to advocate for gun control at the March for Our Lives in March 2018. After the event, Miranda said, "In the wake of Parkland, I was awestruck by the strength and leadership of the students and their ability to speak truth to power. In the midst of their grief, they mobilized the youth of our nation and created a movement. This is their moment. Not just for themselves, but for all of us."[46] The Parkland students, in other words, were citizen-protectors. Their dueling weapon? Words.

Thus, we are confronted by two types of citizen-protectors, one proffering words and the other proffering armed readiness. Each claims to represent the Founding Fathers' legacy, but they are on a collision course with one another. As of now, it's unclear which one will be most prominent in America's story.

We Will Never Be Satisfied

Hamilton and Jefferson's Duel Over Constitutional Meaning

Ian Millhiser

Jefferson: " 'Life, liberty and the pursuit of happiness.'
We fought for these ideals; we shouldn't settle for less."
—"Cabinet Battle #1," *Hamilton*

Hamilton: "We need bold strokes."
—"Cabinet Battle #1," *Hamilton*

Angelica: "My dearest Alexander,
You must get through to Jefferson.
Sit down with him and compromise,
don't stop 'til you agree."
—"Take a Break," *Hamilton*

Part of the genius of *Hamilton: An American Musical* is Lin-Manuel Miranda's decision to cast Thomas Jefferson, if not necessarily in the role as the villain, very much in the role as the adversary. Hamilton and Jefferson do not duel each other with pistols, but they duel with philosophy, fighting each other's conception of the role of the Constitution in the Founding and governing of America. As Burr tells the audience about how Jefferson affected Hamilton's influence in a common understanding of the

Constitution, "Someone came along to resist him. Pissed him off until we had a two-party system."[1]

In the musical, Jefferson's first encounter with Hamilton is an argument over two different economic models. Jefferson is agrarian, aristocratic, and feudal—hence Hamilton's quip that the South's "debts are paid cuz you don't pay for labor."[2] Hamilton not only envisioned something much closer to a modern market economy, he also understood that healthy markets require government institutions that nurture and regulate those markets.

As Erwin Chemerinsky and Mehrsa Baradaran explain in-depth in their contributions to this volume, though Hamilton's plan to "establish a national bank"[3] is mentioned only briefly in the musical, it was both the centerpiece of his financial plan and the focal point of what is arguably the most important constitutional dispute in American history. Jefferson and Hamilton's dispute over this bank didn't simply determine what kind of economy we would have, it also determined what kind of Constitution we would have.

Within his lifetime, Jefferson was the victor in his political struggle with Alexander Hamilton. Jefferson became president, while Hamilton's Federalist Party faded into irrelevance. Yet it is Hamilton's vision—cosmopolitan and capitalist, centralized and urbanized—that dominates America today.

This battle between the Jeffersonian and Hamiltonian visions has always been at the heart of American politics ("we are engaged in a battle for our nation's very soul").[4] The fact that the argument between Jefferson and Hamilton about the proper way to read the Constitution remains ongoing more than two hundred years after it began suggests that the New Deal settlement of this debate was correct. The debate will not be resolved in a way that satisfies all parties by citations to the Constitution's text, history, and structure. The best course of action is to leave to the voters the question of how we should be governed.

The primary disagreement between Jefferson and Hamilton concerned whether the Constitution lays out which *ends* Congress may lawfully pursue, or whether the enumerated powers also place strict limits on the *means* Congress may use to achieve a legitimate end. This debate ("Head-first into a political abyss!")[5] began with Hamilton's bank ("Hamilton's new financial plan is nothing less / than government control").[6]

For Hamilton, the "only question" facing President George Washington, who ultimately would decide to sign the bank bill or veto it based on whether he agreed with Jefferson or Hamilton, was "whether the means to be employed . . . has a natural relation to any of the acknowledged objects or lawful ends of the government."[7] "It is incident to a general sovereign or legislative power to regulate a thing," Hamilton explained, to also be permitted to "employ all the means which relate to its regulation to the best and greatest advantage."[8]

Jefferson devoted the bulk of his argument against the bank to a narrow interpretation of Congress's necessary and proper power. "The Constitution," Jefferson wrote, "allows only the means which are 'necessary,' not those which are merely 'convenient' for effecting the enumerated powers."[9]

Hamilton's vision was ultimately embraced by the Supreme Court. "Let the end be legitimate," Chief Justice John Marshall famously wrote, in an opinion upholding Hamilton's bank, "let it be within the scope of the Constitution, and all means which are appropriate, which are plainly adapted to that end, which are not prohibited, but consist with the letter and spirit of the Constitution, are Constitutional."[10] These words were little more than a restatement of the argument Hamilton offered in his own defense of the bank bill.

Five years later, Marshall offered a similarly Hamiltonian understanding of the Constitution's commerce clause in *Gibbons v. Ogden*: "The sovereignty of Congress, though limited to specified objects, is plenary as to those objects."[11] The Constitution defines the ends Congress may lawfully pursue, but the choice of how to achieve those ends was left to the legislature's discretion. It follows that, if Congress could regulate commerce among the several states, then it could do so by using a bank to establish a national currency.

Although Jefferson's understanding of the Constitution suffered an early defeat, it has not truly been laid to rest. Consider, for example, Jefferson's argument that the power to charter a bank does not fall squarely within Congress's power to regulate interstate commerce. "He who erects a bank," Jefferson claimed, "creates a subject of commerce in its bills, so does he who makes a bushel of wheat, or digs a dollar out of the mines." Nevertheless, "neither of these persons regulates commerce thereby," Jefferson claimed, because to "make a thing which may be bought and sold, is not to prescribe regulations for buying and selling."[12]

It's the sort of argument that, if lifted from its historical context, could just as easily have landed in a brief opposing the Affordable Care Act in 2012. The provision of Obamacare requiring most Americans to carry health insurance or pay higher income taxes, Chief Justice John Roberts wrote, was beyond Congress's power to regulate commerce because it "[did] not regulate existing commercial activity," but instead "compel[ed] individuals to become active in commerce by producing a product."[13] *National Federation of Independent Business (NFIB) v. Sebelius'* conclusion that the commerce clause distinguishes between regulations of "activity and inactivity"[14] was a novel addition to the United States Reports.[15] But it was not without precedent. To the contrary, *NFIB's* reading of the commerce clause closely resembles the reading Jefferson offered in his opinion labeling Hamilton's bank unconstitutional.

The commerce clause was not the only subject for constitutional debate. If anything, Jefferson took an even narrower view of the spending clause than he did of Congress's regulatory power. He embraced a view closely associated with his friend and ally James Madison—that "the grant of power to tax and spend for the general national welfare must be confined to the enumerated legislative fields committed to the Congress."[16] Congress, in Jefferson and Madison's view, may raise and spend money pursuant to the exercise of its other enumerated powers; they did not believe the spending power to be an independent grant of authority to tax and spend to "provide for the common defense and general welfare of the United States."[17]

For modern audiences, Jefferson's reading of Congress's regulatory and spending powers is largely a road not taken. But they are hardly a historic relic. To the contrary, presidents, justices, and other high officials frequently relied on Jefferson's narrow vision of the Constitution to attack federal legislation throughout American history. The Jeffersonian vision animated President Andrew Jackson's 1832 veto of legislation rechartering the national bank.[18] It drove President James Buchanan's decision to veto land-grant colleges.[19] And it influenced much of the constitution of the traitorous Confederate states, which placed strict, Jeffersonian limits on the Confederate congress's spending power and its power to regulate commerce.[20] Jefferson's vision is likely to see a revival as the Supreme Court lurches to the right.

Consider a largely forgotten—yet shockingly relevant—work of political analysis from another century. "Two great parties have always divided the people of this country," an obscure Illinois lawyer named Melville Fuller wrote in 1883. "The object of the one," Fuller claimed, "has been to confine the action of the general government within limits marked out in the Constitution; and of the other, to give the general government great powers and a wider field for their exercise."[21] One of these parties, Fuller went on, "believes that that is the best government that governs least." The other "that government should exercise the functions belonging to Divine Providence." And where did these parties come from? "The leader and type of one school of thought and politics was Thomas Jefferson; and Alexander Hamilton was the leader and type of the other."[22]

Had Fuller remained a lawyer in private practice, these musings would be little more than the argument of one partisan for Jefferson's (and Madison's) vision. ("So he's doubled the size of the government. / Wasn't the trouble with much our previous government size?")[23]

But Fuller also had a friend in a high place. After Grover Cleveland became president in 1885, Fuller made a habit of visiting his friend at the White House while the Jeffersonian lawyer was in Washington to argue before the Supreme Court.[24] When the chief justiceship became vacant in 1888, Cleveland gave the job to his friend—and the Fuller Court became one of the most powerful champions for Jeffersonianism in American history.

Though Chief Justice Fuller was an avowed Jeffersonian, the constitutional arguments he and his Court used to limit federal power took a somewhat different form than the ones Jefferson himself deployed against Hamilton. This was likely due to one of the most important constitutional developments in American history—the construction of a national railroad system.

Before the age of railroads, a traveler going from the east coast of the United States to the west coast had to spend nearly four months on a ship. After the completion of the transcontinental railroad, the same trip from one ocean to the other required only six days.[25] The railroads also transformed our nation's economy. Before the railroads, a farmer in Iowa was likely to sell his crops in a local market to customers in his own state. After, the same crops would travel to one of several central railroad hubs, and then potentially to anywhere in the nation or even overseas.[26]

This new interconnected economy placed the Constitution's text at war with the framers' original expectations of how it would function. After the railroads, no discernible barrier existed between commerce entirely within one state and commerce among the several states. Thus, as a textual matter, the railroads massively expanded the constitutional authority of a Congress empowered to "regulate commerce . . . among the several states."[27] The Supreme Court resisted this conclusion for much of the late nineteenth and early twentieth centuries—largely based on a distinction that many modern-day Jeffersonians associate with Alexander Hamilton.[28]

Jefferson warned that Hamilton's construction of the necessary and proper power "would swallow up all the delegated powers, and reduce the whole to one power."[29] Indeed, this structural turn reared its head in a much more recent case—*NFIB v. Sebelius*. There, once again, Jeffersonian justices argued that federal power must be restricted because upholding the Affordable Care Act would "extend federal power to virtually all human activity."[30]

Twentieth-century Hamiltonians grounded their theory of the Constitution much more closely in its text. In 1941, in *United States v. Darby*, the Supreme Court held that "the power of Congress over interstate commerce 'is complete in itself, may be exercised to its utmost extent, and acknowledges no limitations other than are prescribed in the Constitution.' "[31] The Court laid out the textual basis for the modern rule that Congress may "regulate intrastate activities where they have a substantial effect on interstate commerce."[32] The power to regulate the production of goods that travel in interstate commerce flows from the commerce clause itself, while the power to regulate goods that are sold in-state flows from a Hamiltonian reading of the necessary and proper clause.

For most of the years following, it seemed likely that this settlement would stick. Both parties embraced a limited role for the judiciary. ("You have to find a compromise!")[33] They agreed that fundamental questions about what kind of government the United States should have are best hashed out by elected officials and not by judges. President Richard Nixon pledged to appoint judges who would not behave as "super-legislators with a free hand to impose their social and political viewpoints upon the American people."[34] President Ronald Reagan promised judges who will exercise "judicial restraint."[35] President George W. Bush railed against judges who "give into temptation and make law instead of interpreting."

He added that "such judicial lawlessness is a threat to our democracy, and it needs to stop."[36]

This constitutional truce was as much a monument to Hamilton's vision as our modern capitalist economy. Unlike the Jeffersonians, who insist their preferred system of government is mandated by the Constitution, Hamilton's vision is far more modest. Jefferson and Madison's musical taunt against Hamilton—"you don't have the votes"[37]—remains a powerful one. Hamilton's vision merely permits a robust federal government.

The seemingly perpetual struggle between Hamilton's and Jefferson's interpretation of the Constitution suggests that this conflict will not be resolved by legal arguments. It may very well be unresolvable. There is no one correct way to read a document as vague as the Constitution of the United States.

This is why it is wise to leave this choice up to the people, rather than having the courts declare one side an eternal victor. If the people want a Jeffersonian government, let them elect Jeffersonian leaders. But if the people choose Hamiltonian lawmakers, the courts should not rob them of that choice.

HAMILTON, BURR, AND DEFAMATION

Physical versus Verbal Duels

Benjamin Barton

One of the brilliant aspects of *Hamilton: An American Musical* is how well it captures both the depths of the animosity between Burr and Hamilton ("Hamilton, / an arrogant, / immigrant, orphan, / bastard, whoreson")[1] and the sheer ferocity of Hamilton's personal and political attacks of Burr over decades ("But when all is said and all is done, / Jefferson has beliefs, Burr has none").[2] The Hamilton–Burr duel is among the most famous and strangest moments in American history. But what was the duel's actual precipitating incident? The musical (wisely) skips over Burr's actual complaint against Hamilton, partially because it was strange that Burr would suffer years of vituperation at the hands of Hamilton, only to object to a seemingly minor comment. After years of Hamilton abusing Burr, surely it must have been something significant that led to the deadly duel. Weirdly, no.

No one knows what exactly Hamilton said to cause Burr to set the duel in motion. That's because the source of the final conflict was the publication of a letter by Dr. James Cooper in the *Albany Register* on April 24,

1804.[3] In the letter, Cooper claimed that he had heard that Hamilton said Burr was a "dangerous man and one who ought not to be trusted with the reins of the government." (Lin-Manuel Miranda wrote it as, "I look back on where I failed, / and in every place I checked, / the only common thread has been your disrespect. / Now you call me 'amoral,' / a 'dangerous disgrace.' ")[4] The letter also added that Hamilton had expressed a "still more despicable opinion" of Burr, but he gave no further details about what this opinion might be.

Burr did not find out about this letter until June 18, seven weeks after he heartbreakingly lost his election to become the governor of New York, and two months after the letter's publication date.[5] Stung by defeat and fed up with Hamilton, Burr was apparently set off by the letter's hint of a "more despicable" opinion; it led to Burr demanding clarification and apology from Hamilton. Needless to say, Hamilton made little effort to clear the issue up, so we still have no idea what exactly this "more despicable opinion" contained, or even whether Cooper was just exaggerating, and it did not exist in the first place. We do know that, at one point before the duel, Hamilton admitted to Burr that he did not recall much about the conversation and that it only dealt with "political topics and did not attribute to Col. Burr any instance of dishonorable conduct, nor relate to his private character."[6] So even Hamilton cast doubt on whether the alleged conversation was worth dueling over. Nevertheless, at this point the negotiations over the duel were in full swing, so Hamilton was too late to mollify Burr.

Regardless, the "despicable opinion" seems a thin reed in comparison to Hamilton's long career of libeling Burr. Here is just one excerpt from Hamilton's written comments arguing for Jefferson and against Burr in the contested presidential election of 1800: "As to Burr there is nothing in his favor. His private character is not defended by his most partial friends. He is bankrupt beyond redemption except by the plunder of his country. His public principles have no other spring or aim than his own aggrandizement. If he can he will certainly disturb our institutions to secure himself permanent power and with it wealth. He is truly the Catiline of America."[7]

Alexander, tell us how you really feel! It is worth reminding modern readers just what an insult it was to refer to Burr as "the Catiline of America." In eighteenth-century America (as well as England), Cicero's

"Catiline Orations" were required reading in school and were frequently memorized.[8] In the orations Cicero details the character flaws of the villainous and traitorous Senator Catiline, who nearly destroyed the Roman Republic through scheming and licentiousness.[9] To compare Burr to Catiline was thus the harshest possible blow.

Given the ruthlessness of this insult, why didn't Burr sue Hamilton for defamation instead of setting the wheels in motion for a duel? Hamilton and Burr were both intimately familiar with the workings of defamation law, being among the best lawyers in the country in 1804 ("I practiced the law, I practic'ly perfected it. / I've seen injustice in the world and I've corrected it.");[10] both Hamilton and Burr were involved in high-profile defamation actions in the years before their duel.[11] The song "Non-Stop" well captures just how famous Burr and Alexander were, describing their roles as codefense counsel in the "trial of the century," the murder trial of Levi Weeks. ("Are you aware that we're making hist'ry?")[12]

To understand why Hamilton and Burr decided to duel, not sue, you must understand the curvy path that the law represents. American defamation law is a brutal sinkhole. I am not alone in this conclusion. Defamation law has been described as "complicated and at times incomprehensible,"[13] "a mess, [its] trail signs are pointing in many different directions,"[14] "a genuine disaster,"[15] and "a dismal swamp, filled with quaking quagmires" and "mysterious matters [and] strange and incomprehensible jargon."[16]

The hows and whys of the overcomplexity of defamation law would take up pages. As an overview, however, I'll note that the common law tort itself is very old, and thus every element of defamation has sub-elements with (admittedly fun) Latin names—how about "the colloquium" or the "innuendo"?—and unusual procedural steps. There are also very wide variations among the fifty states in how they handle the common law.

But the common law is just the ornate first floor of this palace of confusion because in 1964 the U.S. Supreme Court applied the First Amendment to defamation in the landmark case of *New York Times v. Sullivan*.[17] *Sullivan* launched a decades-long series of cases trying to explain the exact parameters of how the First Amendment limited the reach of state defamation law. This constitutional law is now layered on top of each state's common law of defamation.

In my first-year torts class, by the time I finish teaching the constitutional law of defamation, many students are convinced that the entire project is not worth the candle. At this point I try to reel the students back in by explaining that common law torts, even goofy seeming torts like defamation, exist for a purpose. The judges (and clerics and Roman juriconsults) who originally launched us on this journey did not do so out of sheer malice (torts pun intended). Defamation law arose and survived for centuries because it addresses a serious and persisting societal problem that judges have chosen to keep recompensing for hundreds of years.

Here is where the story of Hamilton and Burr's duel becomes salient. If the students have trouble coming up with what purpose defamation law still serves, I remind them that there are extralegal ways of settling these sorts of reputational/honor disputes. But those ways are often worse than a complicated defamation suit. My two favorite examples are Alexander Hamilton's death and the blood feud between Biggie Smalls and Tupac Shakur.[18] Both of these disputes started as examples of "verbal dueling," where hot and boastful talk eventually led to a physical confrontation as a verbal duel transitioned into the deadly, physical kind of duel.

If these duels/feuds had resulted in defamation lawsuits rather than violent confrontations, we could have enjoyed years of spectacular music, or more years of whatever it was that an overweening and ambitious Alexander Hamilton might have gotten up to later in the nineteenth century. Maybe he would have ended up getting shot by someone else? Or maybe he would have become an even more outspoken advocate of the abolition of slavery.

I then make two additional points. The first is that while any close study of defamation law suggests that it is often used by oversensitive plaintiffs (and actually typically does them little good), that does not mean the law is useless. To the contrary, the world is filled with oversensitive people, so—as we see in the exchange of letters between A. Ham. and A. Burr in Act II[19]—ignoring them is hardly a strategy for success! Instead, the law has to take some account of human nature and repeated types of disputes and attempt to resolve them fairly.

Second, might this purpose for defamation law help explain why the law itself is such a complicated mess? Perhaps the procedural and legal complexity is a feature, not a bug. If one of our goals is to convince people to abandon violent responses, maybe the longer the process the better, as time is often the greatest ameliorator of bad blood. A defamation case gives the participants a structure to air their grievances and move on. It can also helpfully distract anger from the original dispute and onto the law of defamation itself.

But Hamilton and Burr, like my students, believed that—at least on this particular occasion as to this particular matter—a duel appeared more attractive than a defamation lawsuit for several reasons. First, defamation suits rarely lower the profile of the alleged defamation or the defamer. Although Hamilton and Burr both used the existing law (Hamilton the criminal law of sedition and Burr libel) to attempt to silence their critics, they both suffered mightily in the press for their efforts. (Unfortunately for Burr, it turns out that killing your defamer in a duel had even worse effects: "Now I'm the villain in your history.")[20]

Second, a civil suit is only as successful as the depth of the pockets of the defamer. Based on the sheer number of lawsuits filed against a notorious rabble-rouser named James Cheetham—as many as thirty-eight—and the George Clinton– and Thomas Jefferson–supported *American Citizen* newspaper, it is clear that the pro-Clinton, pro-Jefferson faction was willing to pay whatever it took to keep the defamatory spigot open. Under this rationale it appears that they decided that these suits were a cost of doing business and worth it overall. After all, Burr did lose the governor's race of 1804 to Clinton. Burr had already unsuccessfully tried to silence a defamer via a lawsuit. Perhaps a duel would prove more effective. We certainly heard a lot less from Hamilton about Burr after the duel.

Third, the actual language at dispute between Burr and Hamilton was very ambiguous and reported third hand by the time it was published. It is possible that calling Burr a "dangerous man" might have qualified under the law of defamation in 1804, but it is borderline. The hidden "more despicable opinion" would likely have been too speculative. In fact, Hamilton made exactly this point to Burr in his letter replying to Burr's demand for an explanation or retraction of the reference to a more despicable opinion: "'Tis evident that the phrase 'still more despicable' admits of infinite shades, from very light to very dark"[21] or, as Hamilton the musical character sings, "Even if I said what you think I said, you would need to cite a more specific grievance."[22] Burr, ever the cautious lawyer, may have known that a successful defamation action would require a more definite defamatory statement. This may explain why Burr homed in on such a vague statement: he was looking for a duel rather than a legal action. Indeed, Burr was quick to jump from a letter to a duel; after Hamilton says that he does not want to fight, Burr responds, "Careful how you proceed, good man. Intemperate indeed, good man. Answer for the accusations I lay at your feet or prepare to bleed, good man."[23]

Fourth, Burr may have remembered that Hamilton had just argued for the merits of truth as a defense in defamation actions. This would make it likelier that Hamilton might have sought to prove his statements true, all in open court and before a rapacious local and national press.

Last, and most important, though it was socially acceptable for a gentleman to sue a lesser for defamation (like a newspaper editor) it would have been considered grubby and déclassé for a gentleman to sue his equal, especially for monetary damages. Chernow explains: "In theory, Burr could have sued Hamilton for libel, but it was thought infra dig for a gentleman to do so. Hamilton said loftily that he had largely refrained from libel suits because he preferred 'repaying hatred with contempt.'"[24]

For years I have glibly used the Hamilton–Burr duel as support for defamation law, regardless of how tangled and confused that law has become. A deeper dive into the story raises a new and more interesting lesson: the interconnection between societal norms, social opprobrium, and law. As Glenn Harlan Reynolds notes in his chapter on dueling in this volume, the Hamilton–Burr duel was technically illegal and criminal. And yet a norm existed that even duels that ended in death did not result in criminal convictions (and the Hamilton–Burr duel was no exception; although Burr was indicted in two states for the murder of Hamilton, he was not tried).

Similarly, the common law of defamation was generally more favorable to plaintiffs in early America than the law is today, so presumably Burr would be even more incentivized to sue than a current plaintiff. But the societal norm against gentlemen suing other gentlemen trumped the legal and financial advantages of a lawsuit. The fact that the uproar over the duel led to a precipitous decline in duels in New York, and the destruction of Burr's political fortunes also lends further credence to the power of norms and opprobrium to affect law.

In a musical filled with heartbreaking lines, Burr's lament after the duel, "I should've known / the world was wide enough for both Hamilton and me,"[25] is among the saddest. The musical repeatedly establishes that in a duel there are no winners, only losers, and the Hamilton–Burr duel literally destroyed the careers of two great men of such promise. It also draws our attention to the failure of the legal and social structures of the time to defuse battles over honor, making it clear the critical role that defamation law can play in settling these sorts of disputes peaceably. Hopefully, any future Hamilton–Burr verbal duel will be handled in a courthouse rather than a dueling ground.

ELECTIONS AS DUELS

"You Know What? We Can Change That. You Know Why?" 'Cuz We Have the Support of Two-Thirds of Each House of Congress and Three-Quarters of the States!

Joshua A. Douglas

In the song "The Election of 1800," James Madison exclaims, "It's crazy that the guy who comes in second becomes Vice President."[1] Jefferson—who had just won the presidency but faced the reality that his de facto running mate-turned-rival, Aaron Burr, was becoming the vice president, responds, "Yeah, you know what? We can change that. You know why? . . . 'cuz I'm the President."[2]

The Constitution, however, does not give the president the power to change the constitutional structure for electing the president and vice president. As Jefferson knew, only a constitutional amendment can do that. Yet Jefferson's vision of the presidency contributed to the ratification of the Twelfth Amendment, which altered how we select the president and vice president. So while it is a stretch for him to say that he could change the Constitution "'cuz I'm the President,"[3] he was supportive of the amendment that eventually resulted from the hoopla of the election of 1800. ("Congrats on a race well-run. / I did give you a fight.")[4] That story in many ways echoes today's hyperpartisan disputes on the proper way to run our elections.

As initially drafted, the Constitution said that the president was the candidate who received the most Electoral College votes, and the vice president was the person who came in second. Had that system remained in place, Donald Trump's vice president after the 2016 election would have been none other than his political foe, Hillary Clinton. If you think our current politics are deeply factionalized, how much worse might it be if our leader and his second in command were "Diametric'ly opposed, foes,"[5] perhaps contradicting each other all of the time.

The framers, most notably George Washington, recognized the existence of political parties in the states, but most framers shunned the idea of political factionalism as anathema to the proper functioning of the new federal government. They instead thought that the Electoral College could help to foster consensus-building.

Yet here we are, with Democrats and Republicans engaged in political warfare, ideologically dueling in every election. Our continuing partisan clashes stem in part from the Twelfth Amendment, which was a direct response to the controversial election of 1800. The runner-up in the Electoral College no longer becomes vice president; instead, the electoral votes for each office are counted separately. This process allows candidates to run on a ticket, spawning the familiar contentious elections between the nominees of the two major political parties that we know today.

But let's go back to the time before the Twelfth Amendment, to the election of 1800, which was contentious from the outset. At first, Jefferson and Burr were not direct rivals. They were both Democratic-Republicans: Republican leaders backed Jefferson as their preferred presidential candidate and Burr as their vice presidential hopeful. For their part, the Federalists preferred incumbent John Adams for president and Senator Charles Pinckney for vice president. The election was close, and there was even a dispute over the validity of Georgia's Electoral College submission, which Jefferson, as vice president and thus president of the Senate, resolved in favor of counting those votes, adding to his and Burr's tallies.[6]

Ultimately, the Republican candidates had more support in the states, but the Constitution posed a problem: each elector in the Electoral College was given two votes but had no way to designate a preference between candidates for president and vice president. Thus, the electors from states that preferred the Republican candidates cast votes for both Jefferson and Burr, but they could not stipulate that they wanted Jefferson as president and Burr as vice president. The Republicans thought about trying to "game" the system by having some of their electors vote for Jefferson and also Federalist Charles Pinckney instead of Burr to ensure that Jefferson won the most votes and became president. But Jefferson was concerned that such a strategy might result in Burr losing too many votes, such that Pinckney might come in second and become vice president instead. The party leaders told the electors to choose both Jefferson and Burr, leading to a tie in the Electoral College: each candidate received seventy-three votes.

The tie threw the election to the House of Representatives. The winner in Congress would become the president and the runner-up would become the vice president. The Federalists held a numerical majority in the House at that time, but under the Constitution, each state's delegation had one vote—an equal vote per state—to break an Electoral College tie. Representatives from each state would vote among themselves to determine how their state would vote in this "contingent election," with each state having one vote. As some states had a split delegation that deadlocked and could not cast a vote either way, neither party enjoyed a majority of state delegations. The House was thus deadlocked. If the House could not select a president, then secretary of state (and future chief justice) John Marshall, a Federalist, would serve as acting president, thereby depriving one of the Republican candidates of the presidency. Rumors of potential violence, especially if the Federalists blocked Jefferson or Burr from becoming president, swirled in Pennsylvania and Georgia (among other states), with the governors of both states preparing to mobilize their militias. Some Federalists also suggested that the party support Burr over Jefferson or otherwise act as a spoiler. For his own part, Burr initially indicated he would defer to Jefferson as the elder statesman, but Burr ultimately refused to back down—revealing his own ambition for the presidency.

Over six days that included thirty-five votes, the House remained deadlocked. As fans of the musical know, Hamilton weighed in on the dispute, saying Burr was "without Scruple" and was an amoral and "unprincipled . . . voluptuary"[7]—or, in the language of the musical, "And if you were to ask me who I'd promote . . . Jefferson has my vote. . . . I have never agreed with Jefferson once. . . . We have fought on like seventy-five diff'rent fronts. . . . But when all is said and all is done, / Jefferson has beliefs. Burr has none."[8]

The Federalists finally acquiesced, with a few key representatives abstaining on the thirty-sixth ballot, and Jefferson became the president by a vote of ten states to four, with two states (Delaware and South Carolina) abstaining. ("You won in a landslide!")[9] Jefferson was proud that he won the presidency without a single Federalist vote in the House, foreshadowing his views on the political role of the president.

Thomas Jefferson gave his inaugural address on March 4, 1801, to a packed crowd in the Senate chamber. His vision for a political presidency was clear. He listed fourteen "essential principles" of the government that, as political scientist Jeremy Bailey noted, exemplified Jefferson's view of the presidency "as the exponent and protector of the majority will."[10] He spoke not to Congress but to the people themselves, his "friends [and] [f]ellow [c]itizens."[11] Law professor-turned-U.S. senator Joshua D. Hawley explained that Jefferson saw the presidency as "an instrument of popular, majoritarian self-rule"[12] and his role as president as a "popular delegate."[13] As the people's representative, Hawley notes, "Jefferson reimagined the Executive as a political actor."[14]

Yet many of the framers—including Washington and Hamilton—did not share Jefferson's zeal for imagining the presidency as primarily a majoritarian, political office. As Hamilton wrote in *The Federalist Papers* No. 68 regarding the election of the president ("I wrote about The Constitution and defended it well"),[15] "It was also peculiarly desirable to afford as little opportunity as possible to tumult and disorder."[16] Hamilton continued, "And as the electors, chosen in each State, are to assemble and vote in the State in which they are chosen, this detached and divided situation will expose them much less to heats and ferments, which might be communicated from them to the people, than if they were all to be convened at one time, in one place."[17] That is, the election of the president was not dependent on the popular whims of the voters in one state but instead was placed within an independent body representing all states that could ensure the person chosen had "pre-eminent . . . ability and virtue."[18] As Hamilton explained, "talents for low intrigue, and the little arts of popularity, may alone suffice to elevate a man to the first honors in a single State; but it will require other talents, and a different kind of merit, to establish him in the esteem and confidence of the whole Union, or of so considerable a portion of it as would be necessary to make him a successful candidate for the distinguished office of President of the United States."[19]

To be sure, Hamilton was also a political actor; in May 1800, in an effort to harm Jefferson's chances of winning the presidency, Hamilton urged Governor John Jay of New York to convince the state's legislature to change the state's method of appointing presidential electors to a district-based plan instead of giving all of the state's electors to one candidate (Jay refused).[20]

Yet Jefferson's view of the presidency, as expressed in his inaugural address, depended explicitly on the "heats and ferments"[21] of the majority supporting his political viewpoints. As Hawley explains, "The Jeffersonian President was no patriot king; rather, an instrument of majority rule. Indeed, for Jefferson, the election of the President, not Congress, became the primary means by which the people expressed their will in the constitutional system."[22] The original structure of the Electoral College, however, eschewed a pure popularity contest: members of that body could not even designate which candidate should be president and which should be vice president. Popular majorities thus could not directly support a specific candidate for the presidency. The original structure of the Electoral College had the potential to frustrate majority rule, as seen in the contentious dispute between Jefferson and Burr as the House of Representatives remained deadlocked while it tried to resolve the tie between the two candidates.

Soon after Jefferson's electoral victory in 1801, Republican members of Congress began to advocate for a constitutional amendment to change the mechanism for electing the president and vice president. Their plan stemmed directly from Jefferson's vision of the presidency as popularly elected and representative of majority will. They also sought to aggrandize their power over the executive branch.

When *Hamilton*'s Thomas Jefferson says, with much bluster, "We can change [how the vice president is selected]. You know why? . . .'cuz I'm the President," he is speaking more with bravado then with legal accuracy. While a dramatic illustration of the disputed election, the line does not reflect the reality of the Constitution's limits on presidential power. But the lyric does reveal Jefferson's zeal for using the presidency to effectuate majoritarian control and his ultimate support of the Twelfth Amendment.

In real life, Jefferson knew that, as president, he did not possess the unilateral power to amend the Constitution (the process "forbids my interference altogether," he wrote to his Treasury secretary in 1801).[23]

A constitutional amendment requires the approval of two-thirds of each house of Congress and three-quarters of the states, or a constitutional convention called by two-thirds of the state legislatures. (To be fair to Miranda, in a hip-hop musical, the line "You know what? We can change that. You know why? . . .'cuz we have the support of two-thirds of each house of Congress and three-quarters of the states!" just doesn't have the same ring to it.) Although this fact may surprise theatergoers or those who can recite the song "The Election of 1800" from memory, Jefferson was not integrally involved in the passage of the Twelfth Amendment.

After the contentious dispute of 1800, Republicans in Congress began to call for a constitutional amendment to avoid similar turmoil—election duels, if you will—in the future. (Although the Twelfth Amendment may have addressed the problem inherent in the election of 1800, election duels, of course, endure to this day.) There were numerous proposals in 1802, both in Congress and in several state legislatures, but the real action on the amendment did not begin until the fall of 1803, during the Eighth Congress. Republicans enjoyed a 96–38 advantage in the House of Representatives and used that supermajority to enact a rule that would help them more easily retain control of the entire executive branch in the future. As historian Tadahisa Kuroda notes in his book *The Origins of the Twelfth Amendment*, Republicans "played on memories of 1801 when Federalists had tried to foist on the people a person few wanted for President."[24] That is, Burr almost became president even though neither prominent Republicans nor Federalists actually supported him for that position.

Jefferson generally supported the Republicans' action. During the ratification debates in the states, Jefferson noted that the amendment was consistent with his belief in the presidency as a political office to effectuate the views of the majority. Although not directly involved in the introduction and ratification of the Twelfth Amendment, Jefferson supported it both because it vindicated his vision of the political, majoritarian presidency and because it would help his Republican Party. As Kuroda writes, the Amendment went to the states for ratification shortly before the 1804 election with "the obvious intent to guarantee the election of the Republican ticket . . . Party choices were to prevail, not the two best candidates for President as the framers of the Constitution had envisioned."[25] In this way, the Twelfth Amendment contributed to the increased polarization and partisanship of presidential elections—a legacy that endures to this day.

The story of the Twelfth Amendment and its ratification is not all that different from today's disputes on election law and policy: it's politics all-the-way-down. Headlines these days present a doom-and-gloom message when it comes to voting rights and electoral policy. Our national discourse is infused with the notion that the right to vote is under attack. Legislative majorities engage in egregious partisan gerrymanders when drawing district lines in an effort to entrench themselves in power. Influential elites open the floodgates of money in politics to amplify their messages and affect elections. Some politicians support voter suppression measures like strict voter ID laws, proof of citizenship requirements, or voter purges, ostensibly to root out voter fraud, but more accurately to shape the electorate to their favor. The Supreme Court's decision in *Bush v. Gore*, which essentially resolved the 2000 presidential election, demonstrated to both sides the power of using the judiciary to achieve electoral ends. Now the courts are mired in election litigation all the time and election law has become a routine part of campaign strategy.

Although we should do everything we can to prevent partisan abuses of the election process, the history of the Twelfth Amendment shows that today's fights are nothing new. The story of the Twelfth Amendment centers around the Republicans' success in aggrandizing their control over the executive branch. The political minority, the Federalists, were essentially powerless to stop it. The Republicans won the next several presidential elections until the contentious election of 1824, when the party splintered into several factions and the House, in a contingency election, selected John Quincy Adams of the new National Republican Party as president. That's not to say that the Twelfth Amendment was a bad idea or has been harmful in practice. It's just to recognize that political motivations have always been present in how we run our elections.

Jefferson, Burr, Hamilton, and others in the early 1800s were not that much different from today's politicians. ("Can we get back to politics?")[26] Our leaders have often sought to change the rules of the electoral game to their advantage. The controversy over the Twelfth Amendment suggests that we cannot necessarily consider the Founding Fathers as models of purity when it comes to election rules. We have a tendency to look to the

Founders as exemplars of how we should act to sustain our more perfect union. Yet they were just as political as we are today.

That reality does not justify changing election rules unfairly to entrench the current party in power. But it does ground our current disputes in the very Founding of our democracy. Today's partisan abuses, like political gerrymandering or voter suppression measures, often serve to entrench the majority in power and frustrate majority will. Using politics to affect elections may be as old as time, but that does not mean we must accept it as a fact without meaningful solutions. Instead, we must double down on our efforts to bring more independence to today's election administration.[27] Political self-interest, from Jefferson to today, demonstrates the need for an independent judiciary, independent redistricting commissions, nonpartisan election officials, and continued vigilance on those who craft the very rules under which they and their allies run for office. ("Ev'ry action has an equal, opposite reaction")[28]

Modern-Day Protests

As American as Apple Pie

Kimberly Jade Norwood

> I know not what course others may take, but as for me give me
> liberty or give me death.
> —Patrick Henry (1775)

At the tender age of fourteen, just before Alexander Hamilton left his
birthplace in St. Croix for the "mainland," he wrote in a letter to a
friend: "I wish there was a war."[1] A war! Why on earth would a teenager wish for a war? The answer is simple: As he says in *Hamilton: An
American Musical,* Hamilton's fourteen-year-old self instinctively knew in
1769 that "it was the only way to rise up!"[2]

That remains true 250 years later: Protests matter!

The importance, relevance, and power of protests loom large in *Hamilton.* As Frederick Douglass uttered in 1857, as a precursor to America's
Civil War, "power concedes nothing without a demand."[3] Hamilton seemed
to understand this in 1769, and later when he joined a bloody but successful revolution on the mainland to fight for independence against British
rule. His protests contributed to the Founding of this nation. That fundamental right to protest—a right guaranteed under the First Amendment—
is now under attack. Sadly, many Americans have forgotten what protests
have meant to America and the achievement of American ideals.

Protest is the first child America birthed. One of the beauties of the musical is that it both reminds us and makes us fall in love again with the fight for freedom. It reminds us that this country was built on the soil of bloody protests. From the pushback at taxation without representation, to marches in the streets, to the dumping of tea, to a full-blown Revolutionary War, our great country was born out of revolt. This great land of ours was founded by men who, to borrow a phrase, refused to comply, who not only resisted lawful orders but rebelled against the government that issued them. Colonists chased the king's officers through the streets, beat them, tarred and feathered them, and wheeled them through town for all to mock and shame. As distant as it may seem now, that's our national heritage.[4]

The colonies declared independence on July 2, 1776. Over 600,000 soldiers died in a Civil War fought to end slavery.[5] Blood and pain paved the road to the passage of the Nineteenth Amendment giving white women the right to vote.[6] The Civil Rights Act of 1964 and the Voting Rights Act of 1965 were signed on the backs of baton-beaten protesters.[7] What the nation saw in Ferguson, Missouri, in the weeks after Michael Brown's death brought to mind some of the imagery of violence against 1960 protesters. Americans have been protesting for centuries. Protests are as American as apple pie.[8]

Shortly after the 2016 election, Vice President–elect Mike Pence attended a performance of *Hamilton* in New York. The cast knew in advance of his planned presence. The actor scheduled to play Aaron Burr, Brandon Victor Dixon, and the play's creator, Lin-Manuel Miranda, prepared a message to deliver to him. As Mike Pence began his exit, Dixon delivered the following message:

> You know, we have a guest in the audience this evening. And Vice President–elect Pence, I see you walking out, but I hope you will hear us just a few more moments. There's nothing to boo here, ladies and gentlemen. There's nothing to boo here. We're all here sharing a story of love. We have a message for you, sir. We hope that you will hear us out.
>
> Vice President–elect Pence, we welcome you, and we truly thank you for joining us here at *Hamilton: An American Musical.* We really do. We, sir, we are the diverse America who are alarmed and anxious that your new administration will not protect us, our planet, our children, our parents, or

defend us and uphold our inalienable rights, sir. But we truly hope this show has inspired you to uphold our American values and work on behalf of all of us. All of us.

Again, we truly thank you truly for seeing this show, this wonderful American story told by a diverse group of men and women of different colors, creeds, and orientations.[9]

Then President-elect Donald Trump tweeted the next day: "The Theater must always be a safe and special place . . . The cast of Hamilton was very rude last night to a very good man, Mike Pence. Apologize!"[10] This presidential disparagement of a peaceful protest voiced against the backdrop of a play about efforts to govern the birth of a country created from the ashes of protests was priceless. Death threats against the *Hamilton* actors after the tweet followed.[11]

Part of Trump's attack focused on the venue. Does the venue matter? Consider a National Football League playing field. Is this a proper venue for a peaceful protest? At the beginning of the 2016 football season, San Francisco 49ers quarterback Colin Kaepernick started a silent protest against police brutality by refusing to stand during the national anthem.[12] A former NFL player and Green Beret, Nate Boyer, noticed and reached out to Kaepernick. Boyer suggested kneeling as a more respectful way of lodging dissent.[13] Kaepernick agreed.

Kaepernick's stance drew a great deal of attention. Other NFL players, players on college and high school teams, and some cheerleaders also began to kneel.[14] President Trump publicly took the position that not standing for the flag was disrespectful and unpatriotic, and he demanded that players who did not stand be fired.[15] He even went so far as to call those who kneeled "*sons of bitches.*"[16]

Some who kneel have been fired or cut from teams, and some have had their teams threatened with fines.[17] Kaepernick himself has not played on an NFL team since 2016.[18] Ironically, he was punished for exercising the very right military personnel fight to protect.[19]

Those looking to turn a blind eye to the right to peaceful protest by trying to prevent players from taking a knee during the national anthem have not stopped there. Fox News talk show host Laura Ingraham told NBA star Lebron James to stop voicing political opinions and instead just "shut up and dribble."[20] This was after James complained that Trump did not "understand the people" and that some of Trump's comments are "laughable and scary."[21]

Ms. Ingraham's comment ignores the historical role of dissenting athletes in America.[22] Tommie Smith and John Carlos were ousted from the Olympics after they stood on the medal podium at the 1968 Olympics with their heads bowed and fists raised during the playing of the national anthem in protest against civil and human rights violations.[23] Heavyweight champion Muhammad Ali was fined thousands of dollars and banned from boxing for three years for his refusal to fight in the Vietnam War.[24] Protests have always mattered to black athletes.[25]

Some arguing against these protests claim that the First Amendment applies only to action by governmental entities pertaining to public venues, public forums, and government spaces and not on private football fields. This is a smoke screen. For one thing, there has been a near-identical crackdown on public school student athletes. Students who dare to kneel in silent protest in public schools have been threatened with suspensions; and some threatened with physical violence, including lynching.[26] Peaceful refusals to pledge allegiance to the flag in public school classrooms have been met with suspensions and even arrests[27]—this despite settled Supreme Court precedent protecting a student's right not to stand for the Pledge.[28]

What's more, the focus on the existence of First Amendment protection completely misses the mark. Whether a football field is private or publicly owned, why are these peaceful protests viewed as unpatriotic? And why does anyone think that the best way to handle a peaceful protest that some view as unpatriotic is to shut it down? There is even talk of severely limiting protests near the White House and National Mall. President Trump has proposed limiting protest along the north sidewalk of the White House, making it easier to shut down a protest once it has begun, and even charging a fee to protest.[29] Some say had such rules been in effect during the March on Washington era, the march would not have happened.[30] Is this America?

We see similar backlash for protests on public streets.[31] Protests by the civil rights movement, Black Lives Matter, provide some insight. After George Zimmerman was found not guilty for the murder of Trayvon Martin, Alicia Garza posted a message on Facebook, "essentially a love note to Black people," ending her post with the statement "Black people. I love you. I love us. Our lives matter."[32] Shortly thereafter, a close friend of hers started using the Twitter hashtag #BlackLivesMatter, and the concept was born. Ms. Garza's stated goal was not to devalue any lives; rather, it was designed to call attention to police violence, to call for body cams and special prosecutors in police shooting cases, and to address larger issues of socioeconomic racial disparities.[33]

The backlash was swift. A 2016 a petition calling for the movement to be labeled a "terrorist organisation" attracted 140,000 signatures in two weeks, despite the complete lack of any terrorism.[34]

> "What do we want? Justice! When do we want it? Now!"
> —Chant of demonstrators protesting the U.S. Border Patrol announcement to remove existing fencing and build a new wall in downtown El Paso, Texas[35]

Recent protests in the United States have included a variety of issues including school shootings,[36] the Dakota pipeline;[37] LGBTQA rights;[38] women's reproductive rights;[39] immigration reform;[40] and the killings of black and brown people at the hands of police.[41] Astoundingly, these protesters are told that their protests are un-American and unpatriotic. Protesters are told to shut up; or to "get out of *our* country";[42] some are threatened with physical violence; some are killed.[43] All in the land of the free and home of the brave.

The resistance to protests reveals a few things: 1) dissent is being stifled in this country based on who the speaker is, what the speaker is saying, and where the speech occurs; and 2) there is a serious misunderstanding of the rights bestowed by the First Amendment. The First Amendment protects religion and yet Islamophobia is rampant.[44] The First Amendment protects freedom of the press and yet President Trump refers to the "free press" as "the enemy of the people."[45] Legislatures are prohibiting people from filming police interactions, even though federal courts of appeals have upheld the right to do so under the First Amendment.[46] Is this America?

Every single civil and human rights gain in America is a child of a protest movement. Dissent, rage, arrests, blood, and death have consistently been the asphalt on the road to freedom. Is it that violence is sometimes associated with protests enough to clamp down on all protests? Of course not. The violence card is another scare tactic used to justify the assault on this right. Scores of protests have been peaceful and yet we hear the same response: Shut up and dribble!

As the famous comedian turned civil rights activist Dick Gregory eloquently stated: "there's one interesting thing about being an agitator . . . the next time you put your underwear in the washing machine, take the agitator out, and all you're going to end up with is some dirty, wet drawers."[47] Agitation gets results. Protests matter. And they are as American as apple pie.

I have seen *Hamilton*, the musical, three times. And, truth be told, I would go see it again. Without question, I find it to be an incredible piece of art. The music is amazing: hip-hop and rap at their finest! But is that what draws me so strongly?

For many, one of the biggest draws of the musical is that it easily allows them to leave the performance feeling great about how the United States gained its independence from British rule. Some come to admire, even love, Hamilton the man, a poor immigrant who pulled himself up by his bootstraps to become one of the most powerful people in the country. Though I, too, have appreciated the history-brought-to-life aspect of the musical, my appreciation is tempered by the knowledge that the version of events presented in the musical is only a partial picture of our country's history—one from which some of the most painful portions have been omitted.[48]

Alexander Hamilton, the supposed "hero" of the musical, was a slave owner. Indeed, most of the prominent players in the musical were white, male, and owners of enslaved peoples. Hamilton may have been instrumental in establishing America's independence from British rule, but he also helped put a system in place to govern the masses and control property ownership, with rules that benefitted the wealthy. And yet here I have been, happily applauding this man. As a black woman living in twenty-first century America, celebration of such a man feels awkward.

These are the thoughts that swirled in my mind when I was approached about writing a chapter for this book. As much as I wanted to say yes, I had reservations. Given all that I knew about Alexander Hamilton and what he stood for, I wondered if I could find a space to celebrate the man. So I searched for some uncomplicated positive takeaway, a strong theme worth celebrating unabashedly as a black woman in America today. And I found it: *Hamilton* values the power of protests. So do I.

Part 7

"Who Tells Your Story?"

"Every Action's an Act of Creation"

Hamilton *and Copyright Law*

Rebecca Tushnet

Hamilton: An American Musical is one transformative work in an ongoing chain of many such works. Looking at the musical as a product of multiple influences and an influence on future works can help us see how copyright, for good or ill, influences this cultural progression.

In copyright law, a transformative work is a new creative work that takes significant expressive elements from a specific prior work and adds a new purpose, meaning, or message to that prior work. This category is important because transformative works are likely to be fair uses, which means that they don't require the permission of the owner of the copyright in the prior work.[1]

First, we must ask, "What kind of work is *Hamilton*?" The answer depends on who's asking. *Hamilton* reuses and repurposes language from various Founding-era documents and from Broadway and rap songs,[2] as well as rhythms and music from other works; it is inspired by Ron Chernow's biography of Alexander Hamilton.[3] It should not surprise us that Lin-Manuel Miranda's incredible creativity emanated from profound reliance on preexisting materials. Given how human creativity works, drawing inspiration from the world around and using existing languages, techniques, and other building blocks, that kind of reliance is inevitable, whether or not it is obvious.

Hamilton can be identified as Real Person Fiction (RPF), which takes existing historical or current public figures and uses them as characters in new stories, with more or less variation from the characters' factual, public personae. (RPF as a label arose to describe noncommercial works of fiction produced by fans, but the label otherwise fits quite well.) *Abraham Lincoln, Vampire Hunter* is RPF in the same way *Hamilton* is, though its fictionalization is carried out in a different way.

As Christina Mulligan notes in her contribution to this volume, Aja Romano has also argued that *Hamilton* should be understood as a kind of fan fiction.[4] Romano's key insight is grounded in the same kind of new meaning-making that copyright's transformativeness doctrine honors. As she points out, *Hamilton* doesn't pretend to "retell" history. Instead, it remakes and transforms history, asserting ownership of that history for people who have long been excluded from the dominant narrative. That same kind of reversal—from audience to creator, from abject to in control—provides the pleasure and power of all kinds of fan fiction. By using rap, disco, and R&B, by dressing Jefferson like the artist Prince and using a microphone during the rap battles, and by racebending the characters with nonwhite actors, the musical creates a space in which "distinct historical moments . . . magically overlap,"[5] allowing Miranda and the audience to talk back to the historical canon.

Romano argues that critiques of the musical's historical accuracy are beside the point. Eminem and *Sweeney Todd* were just as important as influences as the historical Alexander Hamilton: Miranda was creating a new thing that took what he liked from each of them. His passion for both history and music allowed him to be critical and appropriative; for many in the audience, the criticism and the appropriation reinforce one another, even if they are contradictory to others. It's okay to love problematic things, like American history, and it's also necessary to engage with them in all their imperfections. Audre Lorde said that the master's tools would not tear down the master's house,[6] but stories work differently. As Romano explains, "The fundamental objective of fanfic, especially when it is written by women, queer and genderqueer people, and people of color, is to insert yourself, aggressively and brazenly, into stories that are not about and were never intended to be about or represent you."[7]

Fascinatingly, Richard Primus's chapter in this volume[8] makes almost exactly the same argument about *Hamilton*'s transformativeness in service of a different inquiry: the ability of *Hamilton* to affect constitutional interpretation.[9] As he points out, national identity is a myth rather than an accurate history, and so the appropriate question about *Hamilton*'s myth-making is whether it "builds justice in the present by reallocating the ownership of the republic."[10] *Hamilton*'s reappropriation helps write an origin story that allows "nonwhite Americans [to] directly access . . . the cultural authority that comes from identifying with the nation's already-canonical Founders,"[11] and more generally enables progressives to identify with a myth of the Founders that acknowledges the original sin of slavery but also provides continuity with the past.

None of this discussion directly addresses the considerations that copyright's transformativeness inquiry demands when we ask whether *Hamilton*'s use of other specific works was fair use. There were many such uses. Several references didn't even make the transition from the Public Theater to Broadway, at least initially due to clearance issues.[12] The *Playbill* program notes references to numerous "classics," both works by rap artists and from traditional stage musicals, all of which appear by permission of the copyright owners except for the public domain Gilbert & Sullivan.[13] (Others have identified classical sources as references and inspiration, from the Baroque harpsichord in "You'll Be Back" to a direct quote from Richard Wagner's opera *Lohengrin* in "Helpless," better known now as the classic wedding march, but those too are in the public domain, with no need for fair use to protect them.)[14]

Was Miranda engaging in necessary precautions when he licensed these uses, or was seeking permission optional? The question is highly relevant for creators who could not pay significant licensing fees or who, unlike Miranda, don't have a previous successful Broadway play to show they're worth negotiating with. As lawyer Larry Iser argues, a fair use analysis would conclude that "Miranda created the poster child for 'transformative' works"[15] by changing the meaning and purpose of the songs he quoted so drastically. Fragmentary uses of rappers' braggadocio helped create the character of Jefferson—the kind of use of preexisting elements as "raw materials" for additional creativity that the transformativeness test generally favors.[16] In the musical, the references add new meaning to what's been borrowed, changing it in ways that couldn't reasonably have been foreseen by the original. For example, "Ten Duel Commandments" uses "Ten Crack Commandments" to create a very different "how-to guide for illegal activities in the 1790s" from the original "how-to guide for illegal activity in the [19]90s."[17] Miranda's version uses different music as well as a new dialogic form: he replaces the single God-like dictation of the crack "commandments" with a back-and-forth depiction of a specific duel to illustrate how the general rules worked—and failed to work—in practice.[18]

Pro-licensing partisans might argue that these changes are not transformative because they still have the basic entertainment (and even self-aggrandizing) purpose as the original Biggie Smalls raps, but "entertainment" is too broad a category to count as having the same purpose or meaning. Courts have regularly found transformation in purpose and meaning when one creative work mines another for material to repurpose, even when both are works of fiction. The biggest barrier to a fair use finding, other than the fact that *Hamilton* was a hit and a court might want to reward identifiable influences, is the question of whether a meaning-transformative use has to somehow target or comment on the original in order to be "fair." Though "Ten Duel Commandments" sheds some new light on the original, mostly it's using the original as a guide through an unfamiliar historic world. Viewed through that lens, interpretive use is clearly a transformative purpose; the original is no longer an end in itself, but rather a waystation that helps us learn and experience new things.

What's more, the use of several of the credited sources was limited; as Zahr Said discusses in her contribution to this volume, even in the absence of a fair use defense, they were so brief that copyright law would not even have deemed them infringing if they'd been unauthorized. For example, Aaron Burr sings, "I'm with you, but the situation is fraught. / You've got to be carefully taught,"[19] echoing part of a well-known line from *South Pacific*. The brevity of the quote indicates that not enough has been taken to infringe; it also has been completely recontextualized. The post–World War II lyric's "you've got to be carefully taught to hate"[20] signals a very different sentiment than Burr's, both in terms of the singer's approval of the teaching and in terms of the group described (children versus angry young men); this different meaning is an indicator of transformativeness. Less transformative is the quote from "Say No to This," which ends with the words "Nobody Needs to Know," a common sentiment about infidelity that is also the title of another song about infidelity from the musical *The Last Five Years*.[21] Nonetheless, this is the kind of short phrase, banal in context, that copyright does not protect.[22]

Considering fair use also raises the question: could the references that were cut have nonetheless been acceptable as noninfringing, no-permission-required uses under copyright law? Because of the principals' decisions to cut what they didn't license, we'll never know for sure—and to the extent that this decision was because of fear of litigation and contributes to a "permission is always required" culture, we are the worse for it. If artists seek permission out of fear of the expense and risk of being sued, even if they have strong defenses against infringement claims, then the practical scope of current copyright owners' rights will increase, to the detriment of future artists and general cultural freedom.[23] If future would-be licensors invoke *Hamilton* to prove that uses of short phrases of this sort should be licensed, then the brilliance of this work will have to be balanced against the harm it did to future creators. We should recognize that the decision to seek permission was not about what the law mandated, but about avoiding uncertainty and providing credit that Miranda affirmatively wanted to give to the creators who inspired him.[24]

But it is not just the creators of previously published works who may argue that they hold copyrights to the musical. Cast members helped form the show as it was developed, first in rehearsals and then off-Broadway. Javier Muñoz wrote that the second act "was created during the rehearsal process of the off-[Broadway] production," while an understudy stated that rehearsals included "huge blocks of time" during which the choreographer had the cast with "no structure, not setting the show, just mining our brains." "We CREATED this show"[25] was another common refrain—one that might read as overstatement, but if it would have been a different show without them, the "we" is justifiable.

As a result, the original cast had a moral claim to some share in ownership of the results, but their legal claims are different than the claims of the artists Miranda quoted. Under current copyright doctrine, only "masterminds" who have the ability to veto or demand changes can be "authors" entitled to copyright. This rule is related to copyright doctrine's puzzling and unnecessary insistence that all people deemed coauthors have equal shares. Because of the seeming windfall that equal shares would bring to many cocreators, copyright law usually declines to award the status of "author" to anyone who is unable to get her cocreators to agree with her that she was an author before she sues. Thus, the rappers and lyricists credited in *Playbill* had a far stronger legal argument for ownership by contributing small, discrete amounts, rather than pervasive but intermingled participation in the overall musical.

Fortunately for the cast members, the owners of *Hamilton* agreed to give them a small share of subsequent net profits from U.S. productions.[26] Moreover, the deal inspired other Broadway actors to ask for more from their work in other shows, suggesting another way in which the musical may have been transformative.[27]

Just as the cast contributed to the musical's creation, fans of the musical have generated endless commentary about the musical and imitated or added to its story. As a result of *Hamilton*'s writerly openness, as well as Miranda's deliberate courting of modern fan culture, fans have responded in kind, creating thousands of retellings and reworkings of the story—a surprising number of them reimagining the characters as modern young adults, in college or working in coffee shops or otherwise trying to survive another time that seems full of threat and possibility.

Hamilton is a remix, and it is also almost infinitely remixable. It is a text of enough openness that it can be claimed by conservatives celebrating its message that poverty and low class are no barrier to a sufficiently motivated (male) individual in America[28] as well as by progressives like Primus celebrating its inclusiveness and reclamatory gestures toward the "canon" of American politics. Open, "writerly"[29] texts of this sort allow multiple plausible readings and responses, some of them in direct contradiction to one another. The more writerly a text is on its face, the more obviously it participates in a chain of interpretation and reinterpretation, although there is a persuasive argument to be made that no work can actually prevent the reader from responding by treating the text as open to revision.

These revisions and responses might take one of several forms. First, there is the classic fanwork: it (re)tells a part of the story, but with a different meaning, exploring the musical's internal world. The same words mean something different when said over Washington's grave (see figure 26.1)

Figure 26.1. "Call Me Son" (cartoon by Arieryn, http://arieryn.tumblr.com/post/135124909918/blame-darkseid-for-this).

Most copyright lawyers, I think, would have little trouble calling this cartoon a fair use. It adds a new meaning to the original; it's noncommercial; it takes only a small amount of the original; and it's hard to imagine that this cartoon harms the licensing market for Hamilton or for a musical's ordinary derivative works (novelizations, cast albums, etc.) in any way. (Although *Hamilton* is a work of fiction, and in theory gets more protection than highly factual works, the presence of transformativeness usually negates that extra protection.)

Figure 26.2 gets a little more complicated. I would still call this image a transformative work: the attribution of *Hamilton* Washington's gravitas and reputation to the fictional, female General Leia Organa Solo changes the meaning of the original, just as making Washington a black man changed the meaning of the historic George Washington's gravitas and reputation. Numerous works online meld *Star Wars* with *Hamilton*, often invoking Leia's role in leading a rebellion. The combination also brings transformative meaning to *Star Wars*, taking it from a story with no obvious direct political analogs to a specific allegory of Resistance in the age of Trump, especially as represented by a female leader haunted but not crushed by her losses.

Figure 26.2. "Here Comes the General" sticker (https://www.redbubble.com/people/xbernathy/works/21065072-here-comes-the-general).

Unlike the cartoon, the image in figure 26.2 is being sold as a sticker, so that commerciality would weigh against fair use, though many fair uses are in fact commercialized in similar ways. Transformativeness often outweighs commerciality, especially when there's no developed market for the copyright owner to control. Like the cartoon, the sticker takes very little from *Hamilton*, just a recognizable catchphrase—less than the cartoon takes, given the absence of any *Hamilton* visuals. (The strongest argument in favor of the sticker is that fair use isn't even required: a four-word quote is too small to infringe.) Returning to the fair use analysis if necessary, one could argue that there's a market for *Hamilton*-related merchandise, but there might not be a market for *Hamilton/Star Wars* crossovers, especially given the notorious reluctance of the latter's owner Disney to engage in anything overtly "political" and Miranda's polar opposite reputation for passionate progressive commitments.

Finally, in this protest sign (figure 26.3), we have an externally facing fanwork. Rather than transforming rap to read history as "Ten Duel Commandments" does, this protest sign from the 2018 March for Our Lives turns *Hamilton* outward to perform a reading of the present

Figure 26.3. Poster from March for Our Lives in New York City, March 2018 (Wikimedia Commons, https://commons.wikimedia.org/w/index.php?title=File:March_For_Our_Lives_20180324-0058_(40993596861).jpg&oldid=293594814).

American situation. We are at another turning point in history, the sign argues; "you" the viewer/participant can be as significant an actor as Washington or Hamilton, should you choose to be so. In fair use cases not involving direct criticism of the original, courts have often wondered whether the secondary works "needed" the original work to make their point. This protest sign makes clear why externally facing works should also be recognized as transformative for fair use purposes. The new meaning functions differently than the original by treating the original as an interpretive tool, not as a standalone work. And this new use conveys an important political message, exactly the kind of speech that the First Amendment should protect. The Supreme Court has identified fair use as one of the key mechanisms that prevents copyright from conflicting with the First Amendment; recognizing externally transformative works as fair uses implements that speech-protective promise.

Hamilton is a mash-up of types of authorship: borrowing, licensing, quoting, cocreating. No artistic work is free of outside influences, but some do not wear their influences as proudly as *Hamilton* does. In its conscious, complicated participation in a chain of meaning-making stretching from the flawed past to the unknown but influenceable future, *Hamilton* offers a showcase of the best that transformative works have to offer.

HOLLERING TO BE HEARD

Copyright and the Aesthetics of Voice

Zahr K. Said

In *Hamilton: An American Musical*'s exuberant and unlikely soundscape, Lin-Manuel Miranda gives voice to his heroes—Tupac Shakur, Notorious B.I.G., Grandmaster Flash, Beyoncé, Gilbert and Sullivan and, of course, Alexander Hamilton. It is through integration and interpolation of their voices that Miranda creates the intense and brilliant stuff of *Hamilton*. What makes *Hamilton* truly "ingenuitive"[1] (in the play's lexicon) is its combination of styles, sources, and historical moments, its fluid shifts between different cultural registers.

Exploring *Hamilton*'s fragmentary borrowings and allusions from the perspective of U.S. copyright law suggests that copyright doctrine does not account for all forms of borrowing equally well. In particular, copyright case law seems inattentive to what we might call the aesthetics of voice: the effects produced by appropriating parts of existing works and repurposing them in ways that enable speaking in new and perhaps socioculturally diverse ways. Two potential problems embedded in copyright jurisprudence should give us pause, in light of *Hamilton*'s success. The first of these concerns fragmentary uses and uncertainty over the amount and kind of borrowing necessary to trigger infringement. The second concerns the nature of the unauthorized use when the second work reflects something more like homage than critique. Both problems touch on how authors speak through these earlier works, how much they use to do so, and why they are speaking in the first place. Ultimately, *Hamilton* illustrates that copyright's infringement and fair use doctrines would benefit from a greater understanding of the aesthetics of voice.

Copyright law is the legal domain responsible for regulating property interests in the expressive products of the mind, including literature, theater, and music, the primary sources on which Miranda draws. Copyright law protects "original works of authorship fixed in a tangible medium of expression."[2] Its originality standard is deliberately low, requiring little more than a "modicum" of creativity, a "creative spark." *Hamilton* is original in both the lay and legal senses. Yet *Hamilton* draws insistent and deliberate attention to its quotations and rewriting, to the works it cites and the styles and voices to which it alludes as it weaves strands of language and music together. In so doing, *Hamilton* highlights the indebtedness of art to everything prior to it and undermines the idea that any single text is wholly original. Copyright's low originality standard, in theory, accounts for that indebtedness, by not requiring works to show they are original relative to existing works, and by anticipating that art will resemble and recycle earlier works in certain ways. That anticipation is reflected in various doctrines, such as the idea/expression dichotomy, the exclusion from protection for stock characters, and the de minimis doctrine.

Given that the standard for originality is so low, the system, by design, assumes that many works will receive copyright protection, and most will not be worth fighting over. Audiences, the theory goes, are better off with more works, even on similar or overlapping topics, and the similarity among works may not reflect wrongful copying but rather audience preferences.

Copyright litigation over similar but nonidentical works exists when a creator identifies work by a second creator and asserts that (1) the similarities are not coincidental, such that copying can be inferred (whether or not it is proven) and (2) these similarities pertain to a sufficient number or kind of the expressive elements in both works that the relationship between the works satisfies the legal standard of "substantial similarity."

When there is little borrowed from the first work, or the borrowing is trivial, the second work may be shielded by the de minimis doctrine. This operates as it does in other fields of law, to exclude technical violations that amount to mere trivialities. Knowing when the de minimis doctrine applies presents a challenge, given the deliberately vague way that copyright sets its entitlements, granting protection easily ex ante and then using litigation as a forcing function that defines and delimits the rights in a particular work.

In some cases, courts seem to conflate the substantial similarity and de minimis doctrines, lowering the question of infringement to "more than de minimis" as opposed to treating the de minimis doctrine as a true exception to infringement that would operate in a manner that remained distinct from the substantial similarity assessment.[3] Such courts seem to say that the de minimis doctrine operates only when an average audience would not recognize the use of an underlying work, and that a work fails the substantial similarity test only when a use is so trivial as to be de minimis.[4] This problematic conflation of substantial similarity and de minimis raises the standard for noninfringement. Worse, it runs counter to artistic practices in which creators use allusions and fragmentary borrowings precisely to trigger audience recognition. The nature of these allusions ought not to put a thumb on the infringement scale when the use is trivially small or fleeting; a rule to the contrary would discourage artists from making references to common works or sources for fear of infringement or out of reluctance to grapple with the hassles and costs of seeking permissions.

Hamilton's allusion to Shakespeare's *Macbeth* provides an example of how an artist might use an allusion in ways that copyright might fail to shield from liability but should. In "Take a Break," Miranda borrows famous lines from *Macbeth* (" 'Tomorrow and tomorrow and tomorrow / creeps in this petty pace from day to day' "),[5] compares his characters to *Macbeth*'s central characters ("Madison is Banquo, Jefferson's Macduff / And Birnam Wood is Congress on its way to Dunsinane."),[6] and refers to a long-standing theatrical superstition that holds it unlucky to say the name of "the Scottish play." The text emphasizes the connection, as though to ensure the audience won't miss it ("I trust you'll understand the reference to / another Scottish tragedy without my having to name the play").[7]

The song moves through several registers before returning to *Macbeth*. Eliza draws Hamilton over to listen to Philip's piano and poetry in a moment of parental tenderness, and then Eliza and Angelica both beseech Hamilton to accompany them on vacation. Eliza's plea is soft and pastoral ("There's a lake I know . . ."),[8] while Angelica's is anything but, as she quotes Lady Macbeth's famous incitement of her husband to murder: "Screw your courage to the sticking-place."[9]

The references to *Macbeth* in "Take a Break" are brief, embedded in a rich linguistic and musical array of other original choices. The references, however glancing, are clearly purposeful in the sense that Miranda links and emphasizes them. Yet they are trivial to the play. Moreover, if Shakespeare's work were still under copyright, these references to *Macbeth* would likely be considered de minimis both qualitatively and quantitatively. Even if these references were infringing, they would be fair uses under copyright law.

These *Macbeth* allusions highlight the problems of the de minimis doctrine's application. They are fleeting but recognizable, and they are chosen and deployed purposefully, not accidentally or incidentally in the background. Copyright controversies significant enough to lead to early stage litigation reveal that artists do sue others over mere snippets, or background glimpses of works under copyright. Usually these involve repeated uses of snippets or refrains but sometimes truly glancing borrowings give rise to litigation. Cases in which artistic works appear in the background of a movie or television set, for instance, have split both ways on infringement; cases of unauthorized musical sampling of very brief snippets have likewise gone both ways.[10] Fair use may save such cases, but should a defendant have to litigate fair use when the de minimis doctrine would, if operating more robustly, properly screen allusions like this?

The failure of de minimis to screen disputes over small and or fleeting uses is especially unfortunate when parties sue over short verbal phrases. Two recent cases concerning, respectively, Taylor Swift's song "Shake it Off" and the song "Walk It Like I Talk It," by Migos featuring Drake, reflect that artists lack certainty about the scope of protection in short phrases used in new works, and demonstrate that this uncertainty can cost artists significant resources even when the amounts borrowed are no more than snippets of text with little originality contributed by the plaintiff.[11] Copyright excludes from protection any short phrases or titles. Hence if creators want to protect those, they may do so only by litigating use of the larger registrable work from which the phrase has allegedly been borrowed. A flurry of legal activity—and significant expenditure of attorneys' fees—typically follows. Often, such cases settle after an initial conflagration even though, on the merits, these disputes appear quite weak and should not require even the costs and time of settlement; they ought to amount to letters that defendants can, as a legal matter, safely ignore.

For creators whose works engage in fragmentary borrowings, litigation over snippets is problematic and likely to chill expression. Permissions may be unavailable or expensive, and it may be prohibitive, especially for underresourced creators, to justify small or fleeting uses, even though wellheeled appropriation artists can afford either the licenses or the lawsuits. These consequences are far from ideal from the perspective of copyright policy, given that it supports fair uses that are discernibly transformative under the fair use analysis.

In theory, the de minimis doctrine could shield from infringement a narrow class of works that rely on fragmentary and fleeting allusions. In practice, the de minimis limitation does little to clarify the noninfringement of sampling, remixing, quotation, and fleeting or background uses. The de minimis doctrine maps poorly onto artistic practice. For instance, courts in many cases have interpreted the scope and strength of rights to control snippets of works in ways that seem medium-specific, and that may defy logic if viewed from an artist's perspective, given the function of the snippet as an allusion, and often an homage. The medium shouldn't matter in an homage, just as it doesn't matter in a parody. A creator may be using an underlying work in a less explicitly homage-oriented way, as well, using snippets to create a textured sound or collage of voices. In both the homage and the textural modes, the creator intends that the audience recognize at least some of the underlying work(s). Audience recognition is usually the very point of an allusion, and this is probably true of homage, too: if a creator wants to celebrate the work of a prior artist, this effort fails if the reference sails above the audience's head. Yet even if the snippets are minimal—perhaps because they are not repeated, and form very small parts of a larger backdrop—their very recognizability, their aesthetic raison d'être, may mean that some courts will fail to find them de minimis since the standard for infringement in many courts is interpreted as audience recognition of the underlying work in the second work. A finding of infringement could still lead to a court's conclusion that a snippet's use was fair.

Fair use may be the jewel in the crown of United States copyright. As Rebecca Tushnet explains in her chapter in this volume, fair use typically protects uses whose purpose is to engage in recognizable acts of appropriation, collage, or borrowing (depending on facts specific to the given work and context). But it does so in ways that arguably privilege particular kinds of borrowing: specifically, works that display an aesthetic of critique. Somewhat counterintuitively, copyright case law may inadvertently privilege extended allusions or more extensive borrowings given that fair use requires that a purpose be discernible (or plausible), and borrowing too little can make that difficult in some cases.[12] When judges find a work transformative, the use is usually deemed fair, and the rest of the analysis tends to fall in line.

As Tushnet argues, the purpose of Miranda's uses ought to qualify as transformative, thus making a finding of fair use likelier. While the meaning of "transformative" has grown somewhat clearer over time, it can often be interpreted in ways that privilege certain uses (critical works and parodies) over others (celebratory or non-critical works such as homages, fleeting uses, or textural uses of snippets). When a later work is critical of earlier works, and its critical purpose can be discerned, fair use is an easier conclusion, but when the engagement is affective—not critical—the fair use case is sometimes harder to discern. A more inclusive and updated understanding of creativity requires moving beyond critique to affect and other forms of engaging with preexisting works.

A key missing point in copyright jurisprudence is the turn to affect as a way of engaging interpretively and creatively with expressive works. For at least a decade, literary and cultural studies have questioned older modes of analysis, which privileged critique and downplayed affective engagement. In the humanities, a long-standing default to reading "against the grain" of a work—known as a "hermeneutics of suspicion"—yielded more recently to a query: why should critique be the default approach? Affect has surfaced as a mode of reception wrongly and curiously displaced by the fetish for critique.[13]

In *Hamilton*, Miranda used various forms of cultural heritage—from Gilbert and Sullivan to Grandmaster Flash—to diversify his audience and speak across traditional genre barriers. He writes that he "built this score by dream casting my favorite artists. I always imagined George Washington as a mix between Common and John Legend . . .; Hercules Mulligan was Busta Rhymes; and Hamilton was modeled after my favorite polysyllabic rhyming heroes, Rakim, Big Pun, and Eminem."[14] But in this celebratory tenor, Miranda displays almost no critical impulse. What Miranda is really doing with his fragmentary borrowings is not so much transforming them as creating a new aesthetic texture through homage to the authors, texts, and traditions that have guided and inspired him.

Recall *Hamilton*'s allusion to *Macbeth*. When Macbeth worries their murderous plan might fail, Lady Macbeth minimizes his fear and goads him with the image of slaughtering an animal: "We fail! / But screw your courage to the sticking-place, / And we'll not fail."[15] This reference to the sticking-place—which is the place on an animal's neck to insert the knife during slaughter—signifies the mixture of violence and resolve for which Lady Macbeth's plan calls. As Angelica sings it, the phrase encourages Hamilton not to political or physical violence, but to a different kind of courage, either to committing time to family or—perhaps, given her feelings for him—to joining her in some sort of intimate connection. (The line follows her asking him about one of his letters, in which he has referred to her as "my dearest, Angelica.")

With this allusion, perhaps Miranda momentarily engenders sympathy for Hamilton by casting Angelica as pushy, or as a woman trying to manipulate him to act one way or another; this is a reading that the reference to Lady Macbeth permits. Or perhaps this allusion to an archetypally too-powerful woman triggers meanings that help the audience make better sense of the action in *Hamilton*. However, it would be hard to say that the reverse is true, namely, that the allusion reflects transformative light onto *Macbeth*; it's simply too fleeting and underdeveloped to do so. Hence at the level of the line, *Hamilton*'s reference to the sticking-place does not seem to transform *Macbeth* in any ordinary understanding of the word "transform," even if it deploys it in a novel way. Nor is *Hamilton*'s larger purpose, as courts would likely interpret it, transformative of Shakespeare's. Both works are expressive; their purpose is to entertain through the performing arts, and to do that, one draws meaning through allusion to the other.

Hamilton makes an interpretive use of *Macbeth*, setting itself up in a textual lineage with *Macbeth*. Tushnet's theory of interpretive use is promising, and ought to be taken seriously, even if it is judicially untested as of yet.[16] In a word, Miranda's use is a form of homage. Especially in

Miranda's use of Shakespeare's phrase as a nod to a whole theatrical tradition, it becomes clearer that creators may use allusions for evocative and textural reasons and as interpretive uses that lie beyond a narrow understanding of transformation.

This broader sense of texture arises also from the layering of Miranda's allusions. Miranda intended the sticking-place reference as "a nod to both Shakespeare and Howard Ashman," the Disney lyricist who wrote, among many hits, "The Mob Song," from Disney's animated musical, *Beauty and the Beast* (itself a retelling of an older work). The boorish antagonist, Gaston, gathers surrounding villagers, preying on their fears and superstitions, and urges them to help him destroy his competitor. The refrain alludes to *Macbeth*: "Kill the Beast! Light your torch, mount your horse / Screw your courage to the sticking-place / We're counting on Gaston to lead the way."[17] *Hamilton* does not transform *Beauty and the Beast*, nor does its purpose differ from it, in the commonly understood legal sense. The point of its reference, again, is homage. It may conjure emotion, an exhortation to violence, but it seems textural and affective more than anything. And under a cramped reading of the first factor of fair use analysis into nature and purpose of the defendant's use, it's possible to imagine a court's failure to see this purpose as qualifying, which seems a regrettable and unintended consequence with potential real-world implications for creators.

Hamilton provides us with an example of a highly successful work that did not court copyright trouble, but arguably could have met with it under only slightly different facts. Regardless of the likelihood of a fair use finding, some parties litigate because they believe they will win on the contest of their resources rather than the merits. In the context of the performing arts, in which many industry participants are underresourced, this ought to be concerning for copyright policymakers. Miranda's work offers a helpful extended example of affective borrowing that relies on many fragments, but it may represent the unusual case in which the artist had the diverse resources and reputational cachet to seek and receive permissions. Other artists might face the same conditions of uncertainty and be unable to proceed with their artistic projects as desired even though copyright's principles would protect their work on the merits.

Hamilton suggests the need for continued development of copyright's infringement and fair use doctrines, to continue to encourage the multivoiced expressive creation in evidence throughout the play. If the de minimis doctrine were more robust, courts could deploy it more regularly to screen out trivial uses and thus to avoid comprehensive litigation on the question of fair use. Furthermore, fair use requires clear-eyed assessment of the artist's purpose, which in turn requires that courts understand that fragmentary borrowings are less likely than extensive borrowings to make a critical, or even a transformative, purpose clear. And homage or affective and textural uses ought to be considered just as "transformative" as parody and criticism.

Hamilton's multilayered textuality challenges copyright law's approach to both fragmentary borrowings and unauthorized homage. The musical thus exposes gaps in copyright's scheme that undercut the premise that copyright intends to treat all original works alike, not favoring one over another based on aesthetic merit or artistic intention. It also suggests the risks of leaving copyright's de minimis doctrine underdeveloped: under-resourced artists are considerably less likely to use works once they learn they must seek a license. If these practices are ones that can provide a means of augmenting underrepresented voices, or simply diversifying artistic domains by means of collage and cross-cutting samples, copyright policy ought to do more to reflect a commitment to the aesthetics of voice and ensure that creators who rely on fragmentary borrowings do not find themselves hollering to be heard, or worse, silenced before they start to speak.

TAKING LAW SCHOOL
MUSICALS SERIOUSLY

A Little Love Letter to Legal Musicals
and the Lawyers Who Love Them

Robin J. Effron

Can music teach us about the law? Even before *Hamilton: An American Musical*, many of us intuited that the answer might well be yes. But to those who have not considered the rhythm and beat of the law, *Hamilton* might seem, at first glance, to be an anomaly or a curiosity. Those people might question whether a somewhat forgotten historical figure and the stories of our Founding could be the genesis of the most successful Broadway musical of our generation.

To those of us who have existed at the juncture of musical theater and the law (and, yes, that is a cognizable category of people), *Hamilton* was nothing short of a dream come true. Suddenly masses of people were thirsting for more knowledge and critical thought about law and history. About federalism! And separation of powers! And the relationship between governmental structure and economic structure! Within weeks of the musical's opening, many otherwise serious-looking law-types were lining up to pay hundreds, nay, thousands of dollars to see this musical, not because it was a place to be seen, but because of a genuine passion for the show.[1]

But, *Hamilton* is not an anomaly at all. It is simply an extraordinarily popular example of the fascinating relationship of law and music, particularly law and theatrical music. Music lifts supposedly dull and often arcane issues of law out from the dusty, heavy leather-bound volumes behind which lawyers and historians often hide (or, at least, used to—it's a bit of an earned stereotype nowadays, when almost all legal research takes place online) and launches them into a world of popular accessibility. The language of law has its own dialect, rhythm, and drama. The less successful musical depictions of law and history are those that merely use music to amplify and decorate law's own language. *Hamilton*'s success comes from Lin-Manuel Miranda's intuition that a different set of melodic, rhythmic, and linguistic tools can be used to transform an old story and fussy concepts into fresh ideas that are not reserved for specially educated insiders. And for the insider, it is instructive to awaken to the new ideas that emerge from a novel musical interpretation of the old chestnuts.

Theater and music were central to my law school education. I arrived at NYU Law School in the fall of 2001 determined not to fall into the clichéd law school "bubble" of all-consuming first-year studies. No one wants to be the law student who obsessively masters the Rule Against Perpetuities, yet is unable to maintain normal human connections with other people or the outside world (another stereotype, but one that does reflect real law student life, even today). I promised myself that I would keep at least one foot in the real world, no matter how intense my three years of study might be. My concrete step in that direction was to continue performing with my chorus, the New York Choral Society. Those weekly rehearsals and periodic performances of the great works were nothing short of a sanity saver at stressful moments during all three years of my legal education.

Late in the fall of my first year, I found out that I didn't even have to leave campus to keep my musical feet wet; I could audition for the Law Revue, the law student musical that law students wrote each fall and performed each spring. The Law Revue was as formative an experience in law school as my classes, or even the vaunted *NYU Law Review* itself, for which I was an editor.

The law school musical serves an obvious purpose: it is the steam valve for the pressure cooker that is law school. It's the place where students lampoon their professors and administrators. At NYU, the Law Revue was the forum to spoof the general power structure that we all bristled against, yet desperately wanted to be a part of—perhaps not unlike the feelings that the Founding Fathers themselves had for King George and the powers that be across the pond. For me, it was more than a place to do my best impression of my civil procedure professor. (Spoiler alert: I grew up to become a civil procedure professor.) I started to realize that I had things to say about the law. And they weren't things that I could express in an exam, or a brief, or a law review article. No, these were things that I wanted to express through the medium of melody and rhythm. These were the things that I could imagine given voice by an actor emoting with outsized gestures, wearing a costume, and strutting in front of a rickety set.

I realized how much more I could communicate in song and verse. Instead of writing a dull essay bemoaning the use of Latin signals for footnotes and citations (supra, infra, cf., and so on), I could turn them into a parody of "Supercalifragilisticexpialidocious" from *Mary Poppins*. My Law Revue comrades arrived at our weekly meetings with a similar outpouring of rhyme and parody and satire. We'd work until the wee hours of the morning to fashion our raw material into smart and snappy songs and skits that we cobbled together into a coherent show. We transformed first-year classes into an episode of *Survivor* where students had to toe the line between "very competent" yet not "too good," lest they get voted off the proverbial classroom island. Nine Supreme Court justices bumped and grinded to a raunchy "It's Getting Hot in Here (So Take Off All Your Robes)." And the too-cool-for-J.D.-School LL.M. students sang "LL.M's Smoke Out in the Courtyard" to the tune of "Me and Julio Down by the Schoolyard." Meanwhile, a core cast of characters would wind their way through a predictable yet satisfying story arc of high law school hope, terrifying law school peril, and ultimately a social and academic redemption with a happy ending.

Our law school musical was limited to the derivative work of parody and satire. Much as we would have loved it to be the actual legal work for which we were judged, it was just an extracurricular activity. And yet we gladly joined the fight.[2] There were always whispers of greater glory, if we lived to see it. Didn't you hear, we would ask each other, that one of the cowriters of *Avenue Q* is a lawyer? His name is Jeff Marx and he went to law school! We're not doomed! We, too, could take our dutifully learned lessons of equal protection and race discrimination in constitutional law and dash off a cheerful ditty like "Everyone's a Little Bit Racist."

Years later, when I was back in those musty law books full time as a professor, came *Hamilton*. Much has been made of *Hamilton*'s innovative style. Hip-hop and rap were not the musical vernacular of the time of the Founding; they have only recently achieved a tentative foothold as a mainstream musical theater style, especially in legal circles, because lawyers might be creative, but they are also cautious and staid. Miranda gets a good deal of expressive mileage simply by using a contemporary style to animate and refresh a historical time and legal concepts. Like the magic of the parodies that we wrote for Law Revue—dull topics could become fun and accessible when attached to the catchy and familiar—at its core, *Hamilton* is captivating and entertaining. *Hamilton* is about far more than just making old ideas new again. Hip-hop is a musical conduit for expressing important things about law and legal history that go beyond just setting an old story to new music.

Hamilton does much more than make law and history relevant by attaching the stories and concepts to perky earworms. The music itself is a part of the legal and historical thesis. Most of us who have ever tried to "set the law to music" have aspired to do what Miranda—who did not go to law school!—has achieved. He moved beyond the superficial task of using the words to make the law rhyme or the music to make history toe-tapping hummable fun, to use the nature of the music to connect and dramatize the legal and historical points. For me, *Hamilton*'s music and structure communicate something important about law and history that words alone (even rhyming words) do not fully convey.

As many critics have already observed, rap and hip-hop enable an especially sharp focus on words and lyrics.[3] Hip-hop emphasizes the centrality of the words and language themselves. The underlying chords, rhythms, and melodies are there to augment rather than overshadow the text. But this emphasis on language is not unique to hip-hop—some of the best musicals (much of Sondheim's work comes to mind) center on sharp and delicate wordplay.

There is something more in hip-hop generally and *Hamilton* in particular that makes this music an especially good fit for conveying legal ideas. Rap and hip-hop are characterized by a repetitive structure. Rhythms, chord sequences, short melodies, and lyrics churn in subtle loops. Repetitive, however, does not mean redundancy. Rap and hip-hop are driven by predictable repetition accompanied by subtle changes in chords, rhythm, or lyrics as the song progresses. The comforting stability of predictable phrasal iterations that simultaneously drives the listener forward with a slight yet sophisticated evolution in words and structure—this, of course, might also be a description of the common law. Or, dare I say, constitutional meaning.

The law, both codified and common, is replete with well-worn phrases that have come to have their own rhythm and even phrasal melody infused into their meaning. The study of law is the ability to internalize these rhythms and recognize the subtle differences as they diffuse out over a code or across generations of common law opinions. The rhythm and repetition give lawyers a shared language in which the shorthand is both the words themselves and the common rhythmic thrum is always running underneath them.

This is why *Hamilton* resonated with such a broad audience. Listeners who have grown up with hip-hop find it a natural bridge to connecting with an old narrative and the personal struggles and stories of key figures of the Founding. Audience members really do feel like they are right there in "The Room Where It Happen[ed]."[4] And for law geeks who have not spent much time listening to Jay Z and Kanye West, the structure and appeal of hip-hop as a vehicle for expressing the repetitive yet evolving nature of law and government is immediately apparent.

Most important, *Hamilton* allows us to relive the oral expression that is a central part of any generation's formative experience and hear it as our own instead of as antiquated. So much of law school is devoted to teaching our students how to "think like a lawyer" and write like one too. It's no wonder that my students have reacted with such enthusiasm to *Hamilton*'s joyful and intricate mode of expression. Finding my own happiness in a legal history musical has forced me to remember how much of law school I spent both absorbing and resisting the mandate to think, read, and write in prescribed ways. It was the repetition and evolution of law in the books and law on the stage that kept me afloat and propelled me toward my career in which I find utter joy and satisfaction. I write primarily in civil procedure—a field that many might see as picky, technical, and arcane. But I find it structured, beautiful, and comforting, much like the "Cabinet Battles" in *Hamilton*, which almost trick the audience into absorbing detailed political information that they might otherwise glaze over.

Although my formal performing days are behind me, I'll keep coming up with elementary puns and jokes to reinforce key concepts in my law school classes. I'll bring in my guitar on *Shady Grove*[5] day to give them the bluegrass version of *Erie*. Maybe, someday, there will be another musical with the perfect style and the perfect form and the perfect legal subject—civil procedure, perhaps? We'll all flock to see it—coming soon to a venue (civil procedure pun intended) near you.

"THE WORLD TURNED UPSIDE DOWN"

Hamilton *and Deconstruction*

Bret D. Asbury

Jack Balkin's "Deconstructive Practice and Legal Theory" introduces legal audiences to French philosopher Jacques Derrida's approach to textual interpretation, commonly known as deconstruction. Balkin asserts that Derrida's approach—focused on "teasing out the antimonies in our language and thought"—"raises important philosophical issues for legal thinkers."[1] Deconstruction encourages scholars, judges, lawyers, and critics to identify and question presuppositions underlying legal texts in order to "shed light on theories of ideological thinking: how people form and use ideologies, consciously and unconsciously, in legal discourse." But as Balkin later notes, "we can also use deconstruction as a tool for ideological and historical analysis."[2]

The strength of the deconstructive project lies in defamiliarization. "By challenging what is 'given,' deconstruction affirms the infinite possibilities of human existence. By contesting 'necessity,' deconstruction dissolves the ideological encrustations of our thought." "Deconstruction is thus revelatory,"[3] and reading *Hamilton* through its lens helps to explain its remarkable success. Taken together, the play's text, music, casting, and staging offer a master class in teasing out antimonies—contradictions between two incompatible beliefs or conclusions—and in so doing set forth counternarratives that complicate audience understandings of America's Founding and reframe modern cultural and artistic hierarchies.

Balkin identifies two deconstructive practices applicable to legal interpretation, each of which *Hamilton* employs in interpreting history: the inversion of hierarchies and the liberation of text from the author. As to the first, deconstruction seeks to identify "hierarchical oppositions" in a given text, then invert them. The temporary inversion is meant not to establish a new privileging, but rather "to investigate what happens when the given, 'common sense' arrangement is reversed." This investigation serves as "a means of intellectual discovery, which operates by wrenching us from our accustomed modes of thought."[4]

On the page and stage, *Hamilton* unabashedly rejects conventional wisdom by inverting hierarchies, forcing its audience to look at the events it depicts with fresh eyes. Alexander Hamilton is paradigmatic of this approach. Though the play can be read as an exercise in historical revisionism meant to elevate the status of its title character, it opens with Aaron Burr's describing Hamilton as the "bastard, orphan, son of whore and a Scotsman."[5] Two lines later Burr adds that Hamilton was born poor and in the Caribbean, of all places.[6] Further details soon emerge. Hamilton's father left when he was ten; he and his mother then soon together grew gravely ill—"half-dead sittin' in their own sick, the scent thick"—but only he survived; the relative with whom he moved in after his mother's death died by suicide.[7] All this is revealed within two minutes of the play's first notes. *Hamilton*'s opening makes clear the improbability of its protagonist's journey, setting forth as its American hero an indigent, illegitimate, foreigner who has suffered deep childhood trauma. Though the Horatio Alger framing of heroism has been a constant in American letters since at least the late 1800s, Lin-Manuel Miranda's choice to degrade rather than elevate the play's protagonist as the play opens foreshadows his interest in the inversion of hierarchies throughout the play.

The decision to focus a play about the revolutionary period on Hamilton is also deconstructive. Pre-*Hamilton*, it was customary to place Hamilton within, but near the bottom of, a cohort of Founding Fathers that included George Washington, John Adams, Thomas Jefferson, and James

Madison—our first four presidents—as well as the incomparable Benjamin Franklin and John Jay, our first chief justice. Despite his having been largely forgotten prior to when the play opened in 2015, *Hamilton* makes the case that its protagonist should be placed at or near the top of this hierarchy. (Adams, Franklin, and Jay do not even appear in the play as characters, only in mentions, and Adams is treated with disdain. ["Tell my wife John Adams doesn't have a real job anyway."[8] and "That poor man, they're gonna eat him alive!"])[9]

Other inversions of hierarchies abound. Most obvious is the play's casting of nonwhite actors to play Hamilton, Burr, Washington, the Marquis de Lafayette, the Schuyler sisters, and other white characters. As other authors in this volume have theorized, casting actors of color forces audiences to reimagine the revolutionary period as multicultural, as it was. Furthermore, it opens the door to pondering the role nonwhites whose names do not appear in *Hamilton*—such as Crispus Attucks and Benjamin Banneker—played in the march to independence and the early years of the republic. True to form, this deconstructive casting inverts the white/nonwhite hierarchy only temporarily; Miranda is not making the claim that Hamilton was Latino or Washington was black. But the inversion achieved through casting successfully wrenches us "from our custom modes of thought," opening the door to new readings of the era.

Hamilton's presentation of gender is also of note. Not only do women of color depict all three Schuyler Sisters—allowing the audience to consider the challenges of intersectionality in this era—but two of them, Eliza and Angelica, play crucial roles in retelling the story of America's birth. Traditional narratives of the Revolution focus almost exclusively on clever, brave, and powerful white men. But in *Hamilton*, it is only Angelica, originally cast as a black woman—not Washington, Jefferson, Madison, Burr, or Lafayette—who matches Hamilton's wit and energy, and it is she who orchestrates the history-altering marriage between Eliza and Alexander.

Eliza, for her part, evolves from being a more traditionally portrayed female shrinking violet of a character who, unlike Angelica, is too shy to approach Hamilton at the Winter's Ball in "Helpless," to a young woman who implores her husband in "That Would Be Enough," "let me be a part of the narrative in the story they will write someday."[10] She ultimately succeeds beyond her modest expectations, as it is Eliza who tells Alexander's story, putting herself "back in the narrative"[11] after withdrawing in

"Burn" due to his infidelity. Following a brief introduction by Washington, Jefferson, and Madison, Eliza seizes control of the play's final song, "Who Lives, Who Dies, Who Tells Your Story," to address Burr's questions: "When you're gone, who remembers your name? / Who keeps your flame? . . . Who tells your story?"[12]

In shaping her husband's legacy over the fifty years by which she outlives him, Eliza interviews every soldier with whom he served in the Revolutionary War, reads and rereads thousands of pages of his writings, collaborates with Angelica to tell his story, speaks out against slavery (as he presumably would have more zealously had he lived longer), and establishes an orphanage in honor of her orphaned husband. That *Hamilton* closes in Eliza's voice is both notable and deconstructive. As Michael Schuman has noted in the *New Yorker*, "in placing Eliza front and center, Miranda is reinforcing his over-all project, which is in part to displace the founding story as the province of white men. . . . And by implicitly equating Eliza's acts of narration with his own, he's acknowledging the women who built the country alongside the men."[13] This choice is quintessentially deconstructive, and by privileging women over men even modestly, Miranda further promotes the intellectual discovery that is the hallmark of deconstructive practice.

Finally, Miranda's heavy reliance on hip-hop—rather than more traditional genres of Broadway storytelling—is perhaps his most deconstructive choice. Though there are exceptions, staged theater is generally considered a "higher" art form associated with cultural and intellectual elites, while hip-hop is considered a "lower" art form associated with the poor and subaltern (primarily blacks). To be sure, *Hamilton* contains several traditional songs containing no hip-hop elements. But hip-hop is core to *Hamilton* in a manner unlike any other Broadway musical, the closest parallel being *In the Heights*, Miranda's prior work. From the two "Cabinet Battles" (pitting Hamilton versus Jefferson in rap battles reminiscent of Eminem's 2002 film *Eight Mile*)[14] to the "Ten Duel Commandments" and its peer "Ten Things You Need to Know" at the beginning of "The World Was Wide Enough" (both modeled after The Notorious B.I.G.'s "Ten Crack Commandments"),[15] the influence of hip-hop music and culture is express and undeniable.

These are only the most obvious examples. More subtle ones include the use of record scratching in the introduction of "Your Obedient Servant" (which itself can be read as a protracted and more genteel rap battle), Hamilton's spelling out his name in "My Shot" in the same cadence that The Notorious B.I.G. does in his "Going Back to Cali,"[16] and the repetition of the elongated "laaaadies" in "A Winter's Ball," which is reminiscent of the chorus of the Beastie Boys' "Hey Ladies."[17] Though each of these examples could be missed by audience members not well versed in hip-hop, their presence speaks to the extent to which *Hamilton* is steeped in hip-hop and seeks to bridge (and at times invert) "high" and "low" forms of artistic expression.

Perhaps most interesting are the musical juxtapositions between hip-hop and traditional Broadway sounds Miranda creates. "Satisfied" provides a prime example. What begins as a quiet, tender love song celebrating Alexander and Eliza's marriage flashes back around the one-minute mark to show Hamilton's first encounter with Angelica. Two minutes in, Angelica unleashes an electric, staccato rap verse in which she explains her attraction to Hamilton. ("So so so– / so this is what it feels like to match wits / with someone at your level!")[18] Then, turning to see her sister's face, appropriately "helpless,"[19] Angelica returns to singing, further explaining the predicament that she believes requires her to marry someone else and steer Hamilton toward Eliza. Resigned to her fate, Angelica raps no more in "Satisfied," calmly describing her melancholy at the necessary choice she has made ("But when I fantasize at night / it's Alexander's eyes"),[20] while simultaneously toasting her sister and new brother-in-law ("To the groom! . . . To the bride!").[21] The song is a breathtaking mixture of genres "low" and "high," mirroring the emotional roller coaster Angelica experiences.

At its best the inversion of hierarchies causes audiences to rethink familiar tropes and promote intellectual discovery. Miranda invites us to reimagine the nation's Founding through a series of different lenses, inverting multiple hierarchies (rich/poor, native born/immigrant, legitimately/illegitimately born, white/nonwhite, man/woman, high/low culture, and other Founders/Hamilton). Though any one of these inversions might not result in intellectual discovery for everyone, acting together they ensure that few leave *Hamilton* regarding the period and characters depicted in the same way as when they entered.

Hamilton also features the second deconstructive technique Balkin highlights, the liberation of text from author. Balkin explains, "much of deconstructive criticism involves the discovery of unintended connections between words."[22] The liberation of text from the author is premised on the notion that any text is subject to many readings, and that in some sense all readings are misreadings (in the sense that they negate other readings of the text and can themselves be negated in the future). As Balkin explains, quoting Jonathan Culler, "the claim that all readings are misreadings can . . . be justified by the most familiar aspects of critical and interpretive practice. Given the complexities of texts, the reversibility of tropes, the extendability of context, and the necessity for a reading to select and organize, every reading can be shown to be partial. Interpreters are able to discover features and implications of a text that previous interpreters neglected or distorted."[23]

By decontextualizing both hip-hop lyrics and the words of the Founding Fathers, Miranda forces audiences to consider the words separate and apart from their initial creation and meaning, thereby liberating texts from their authors. Upon liberation, authorial intent and contemporaneous meaning are no longer relevant—texts can be read (or misread) standing alone, which opens up new pathways of interpretation.

Miranda employs this technique through the use of a single rap lyric, twice quoting Mobb Deep's "Shook Ones Part II."[24] Prodigy, one of two Mobb Deep rappers, declares in the song, "I'm only nineteen but my mind is older"[25] by way of introduction to the fact that despite his youth, his hardscrabble upbringing has foisted on him a lifetime's worth of experiences. Miranda seizes on this line in both "My Shot," spoken by Hamilton ("Only nineteen but my mind is older"),[26] and "Blow Us All Away," spoken by his son Philip ("I'm only nineteen but my mind is older").[27] So it is that we have Philip alluding to his father's words from Act I, while simultaneously both young men are alluding to Prodigy. But the two Hamiltons employ the line to different effect—Alexander is referencing not just his difficult childhood, but also his prodigious talents ("I got a lot of brains but no polish. . . . My power of speech: unimpeachable"),[28] while Philip, who grew up in comfort, seems to be referring only to his intellect ("The scholars say I got the same virtuosity and brains as my pops!").[29] In this way Miranda liberates Prodigy's line from Prodigy, fostering the discovery of new features and implications within the text and revealing an otherwise unseen connection between the twentieth-century rapper and the two Hamiltons.

Other examples are more contemporaneous. When the Schuyler sisters sing, "We hold these truths to be self-evident. That all men are created equal,"[30] they are quoting directly from the Declaration of Independence. But as revealed in Angelica's next line—"And when I meet Thomas Jefferson, . . . I'm 'a compel him to include women in the sequel!"[31]—the sisters are seeking to liberate the phrase from Jefferson and provide it with a more aspirational and inclusive meaning, one that courts and the nation would eventually embrace. As Balkin explains, "there is generally great critical importance in discovering that a text says more than the author meant it to say."[32] Here the sisters reveal that they have made such a discovery within Jefferson's famous words.

Miranda gives Washington a similar treatment in "One Last Time." In this instance we have Christopher Jackson, a black actor playing Washington, bidding farewell to the office of the presidency by quoting the historical Washington. Under these circumstances, the line "Though . . . I am unconscious of intentional error, I am nevertheless too sensible of my defects not to think it probable that I may have committed many errors"[33] takes on a new meaning. Jackson likely would have been an enslaved person in Washington's time, and certainly owning scores of slaves for most of his adult life and throughout his presidency should be counted among the "many errors" of Washington's administration. But this deconstruction is not that simple, for as Jackson continues to utter Washington's eloquent and humble parting words, he liberates them from the slaveholder he portrays, allowing the audience to hear them anew. The words can now stand for themselves and, unburdened by their author's imperfections, they are even more beautiful. This liberation proves exceedingly moving on stage—"we celebrate the manner in which the authors' words have worked themselves pure in spite of the authors' intentions."[34]

Liberating text from the author brings about this possibility. The words of Washington's farewell address have not changed, but coming out of Jackson's mouth they land differently than when read online or in a book. Similarly, Jefferson's words take on a different meaning when sung by Angelica, and it is her interpretation, not his, that ultimately wins out (as Kim Roosevelt describes in-depth in his chapter in this volume, both Lincoln's Gettysburg Address and King's I Have a Dream Speech set forth readings similar to Angelica's). And connecting both Alexander and Philip to Prodigy through the use of the latter's lyric both reimagines the phrase and reminds us of the centrality to the overall narrative of Hamilton's "comin' up from the bottom,"[35] as so many rappers do. Once one accepts that all readings are misreadings in at least some sense, the range of interpretive possibilities expands drastically, and though some interpretations are better than others, all have the potential to uncover features unseen or unremarked upon by previous interpreters. *Hamilton*'s deconstructive techniques—the inversion of hierarchies and liberation of text from the author—defamiliarize traditional narratives and open the door to fresh interpretations. The effect is that *Hamilton* leaves audiences changed—anyone reading this volume most likely came across some form of revelation upon experiencing *Hamilton* for the first time, and for many of us these revelations continue to this day. Just as Balkin shows that the deconstructive project can prove fruitful with respect to legal analysis, so does Miranda illustrate it can be richly applied to historical analysis. The intellectual discovery resulting from taking in *Hamilton* inevitably will vary person to person, but, as Balkin stresses, it is the journey deconstruction takes us on—rather than the destination—that is most important. *Hamilton*'s enduring success is a testament to just how rare it is for art to take us on this journey and just how enjoyable it can be.

Part 8

"What Is a Legacy?"

Lessons from Hamilton *beyond
the Libretto*

"Cabinet Battle #1"

The Structure of Federalism

Erwin Chemerinsky

One of the most powerful scenes in *Hamilton: An American Musical* is the debate between Alexander Hamilton and Thomas Jefferson over the constitutionality of creating a national bank. I confess to rarely using technology of any kind in the classroom, but I do play for my students "Cabinet Battle #1,"[1] the debate between Alexander Hamilton and Thomas Jefferson over whether to create a Bank of the United States.

In the musical, George Washington declares: "The issue on the table: Secretary Hamilton's plan to assume state debt and establish a national bank. Secretary Jefferson, you have the floor." Jefferson opposes the bank and argues for a limited national government:

> But Hamilton forgets
> his plan would have the government assume state's debts
> Now, place your bets as to who that benefits:
> the very seat of government where Hamilton sits
>
> . . .

This financial plan is an outrageous demand,
and it's too many damn pages for any man to understand.[2]

Hamilton responds and defends the need for broad national powers, but
also raises the issue of slavery:

Thomas. That was a real nice declaration.
Welcome to the present, we're running a real nation.

. . .

If we assume the debts, the union gets
A new line of credit, a financial diuretic.
How do you not get it? If we're aggressive and competitive
The union gets a boost. You'd rather give it a sedative?[3]

The cabinet battle ends with Washington telling Hamilton that he needs
to get the votes and make it happen. Washington admonishes Hamilton:
"Winning was easy, young man. Governing's harder. . . . You have to find
a compromise."[4] The difficulty? As fans of the musical know, Hamilton
wasn't great at compromise—"Hey, turn around, bend over, I'll show you
where my shoe fits."[5] And Thomas Jefferson sought to take advantage
of Hamilton's combative nature to win arguments—or "battles"—by appearing reasonable and grounded, if somewhat snarky.

In real life as in the musical, Washington sided with Hamilton ("It
must be nice, it must be nice to have / Washington on your side.")[6] over
Jefferson's objections, and Congress did approve the plan for a Bank of
the United States. But, as Mehrsa Baradaran describes in her chapter in
this volume, it contributed to the rift between Jefferson's camp and Hamilton's.[7] The bank existed for twenty-one years until its charter expired
in 1811, several years after Hamilton's death. However, after the War of
1812, the country experienced serious economic problems, and the Bank
of the United States was recreated in 1816. Although he had opposed
such a bank a quarter of a century earlier when he was a congressman
from Virginia, as president, James Madison endorsed its recreation. ("He
took our country from bankruptcy to prosperity. I hate to admit it, but he
doesn't get enough credit for all the credit he gave us.")[8] The United States
government owned only 20 percent of the new bank.

The Bank of the United States did not solve the country's economic
problems and many blamed the bank's monetary policies for aggravating
a depression. State governments were particularly angry at the bank, just

as Jefferson (speaking on behalf of Virginia) had been at its concept in "Cabinet Battle #1," especially because the bank called in loans owed by the states. Thus, many states adopted laws designed to limit the operation of the bank. Some states adopted laws prohibiting its operation within their borders. Others, such as Maryland, taxed it. The Maryland law required that any bank not chartered by the state pay either an annual tax of $15,000 or 2 percent on all of its notes.

The bank refused to pay the Maryland tax, and John James sued for himself and the State of Maryland in the County Court of Baltimore to recover the money owed under the tax. The defendant, McCulloch, was the cashier of that branch of the Bank of the United States. The trial court rendered judgment in favor of the plaintiff, and the Maryland Court of Appeals affirmed.

The constitutionality of this tax came to the Supreme Court in *McCulloch v. Maryland*.[9] It became the most important Supreme Court decision in American history defining the scope of Congress's power and the relationship between the federal government and the states. It laid out a framework for federalism that has been followed ever since. Although the specific issue posed in *McCulloch* is whether the State of Maryland could collect a tax from the Bank of the United States,[10] Chief Justice John Marshall used the case as an occasion to broadly construe Congress's powers and narrowly limit the authority of state governments to impede the federal government. In doing so, he echoed the arguments made by Hamilton in the *Federalist Papers*, briefly presented by him in "Cabinet Battle #1."

Although in the musical Hamilton is the primary spokesperson for a strong central government, arguing against Madison and his pals, who wanted to give the states much more power ("You're gonna need congressional approval / and you don't have the votes!"),[11] in actuality, other branches of the federal government and the states played a large part in establishing the limits of federal power. In the words of *Law & Order*, this is their story. Or at least the story of one point in time, one case, one Supreme Court.

In examining the issue of federal versus state power, Marshall's opinion in *McCulloch v. Maryland* considered whether Congress had the authority to create the Bank of the United States. Undoubtedly, Marshall recognized this case as an ideal opportunity to articulate a broad vision of federal power, much as he used *Marbury v. Madison*—the stuff of every eleventh-grade government class—to establish the power of judicial review.

Marshall's argument was rhetorically powerful; it concluded that "the government of the Union . . . is, emphatically, and truly, a government of the people."[12] Marshall began his opinion by declaring: "It has been truly said, that this can scarcely be considered as an open question, entirely unprejudiced by the former proceedings of the nation respecting it. The principle now contested was introduced at a very early period of our history, has been recognized by many successive legislatures, and has been acted upon by the judicial department, in cases of peculiar delicacy, as a law of undoubted obligation."[13]

In other words, Marshall invoked the history of the first Bank of the United States as authority for the constitutionality of the second bank. Marshall expressly noted that the first Congress enacted the bank after great debate and that it was approved by an executive "with as much persevering talent as any measure has ever experienced, and being supported by arguments which convinced minds as pure and as intelligent as this country can boast."[14] Although he did not mention Madison by name, Marshall remarked that even those who opposed the first bank (and Hamilton, its creator) endorsed creating the second bank. Marshall concluded that "it would require no ordinary share of intrepidity, to assert that a measure adopted under these circumstances, was a bold and plain usurpation, to which the constitution gave no countenance."[15] Simply put, Marshall relied on Hamilton's triumph in "Cabinet Battle #1" as a reason why the bank was constitutional.

In considering the constitutionality of the Bank of the United States, Marshall's opinion emphatically rejected "compact federalism," a view that sees the states as sovereign because they created the United States by ceding some of their power and by ratifying the Constitution. This idea implies that if the states are sovereign, then they would have the authority to veto a federal action, such as the creation of the Bank of the United States.[16] Marshall contended that it was the people who ratified the Constitution, and the people were therefore sovereign, not the states.[17] The Court thus rejected the view that the Constitution should be regarded as a compact of the states and that the states retain ultimate sovereignty under the Constitution.

In discussing the constitutionality of the creation of the bank, the Court's third major point was to address the scope of congressional powers under Article I. Chief Justice Marshall admitted that the Constitution does not enumerate—or spell out—a power to create a Bank of the United States, but said that this omission was not dispositive as to Congress's power to establish such an institution. Marshall explained that "a constitution, to contain an accurate detail of all the subdivisions of which its great powers will admit, and of all the means by which they may be carried into execution, would partake of the prolixity of a legal code, and could scarcely be embraced by the human mind."[18] Marshall then uttered some of the most famous words in United States law: "In considering this question, then, we must never forget that it is a *constitution* we are expounding."[19]

Marshall's conclusion was that Congress is not limited to those acts specified in the Constitution. Although the Constitution does not mention a power to create a Bank of the United States, Congress can create one as a means to carrying out many of its other powers. This was a dramatic expansion in the scope of congressional authority in exactly the direction that Hamilton contemplated. If Congress were limited to the powers specifically enumerated in Article I, the range of laws would be finite. But if Congress can choose any means not prohibited by the Constitution to carry out its powers, it has an almost infinite range of options that can be enacted into law. Indeed, in opposing Hamilton in the initial creation of the Bank of the United States, Jefferson saw how broad Congress's power would be if it could choose any means to implement its authority: "Congress [is] authorized to defend the nation. Ships are necessary for defence; copper is necessary for ships; mines, necessary for copper; a company necessary to work the mines; and who can doubt this reasoning who has ever played at 'This Is the House that Jack Built.'"[20]

If Congress's powers had been narrowly restricted to those enumerated in the Constitution, it is doubtful that the Constitution could have survived, at least without extensive amendments. The problems of the twentieth and twenty-first centuries, and the range of laws needed to deal with them, can be dealt with under an eighteenth-century Constitution only because of the broad construction of congressional powers found in *McCulloch*.

The fourth and final point that Marshall made in explaining the constitutionality of the creation of the Bank of the United States concerned the meaning of the "necessary and proper" clause.[21] Chief Justice Marshall said that this provision makes it clear that Congress may choose any means not prohibited by the Constitution to carry out its express authority. In some of the most important words of the opinion, Marshall wrote: "Let the end be legitimate, let it be within the scope of the constitution, and all means which are appropriate, which are plainly adapted to that end, which are not prohibited, but consist with the letter and spirit of the constitution, are constitutional."[22]

Chief Justice Marshall rejected a restrictive interpretation of the necessary and proper clause. The necessary and proper clause is placed in Article I, Section 8, which expands Congress's powers, and not in Article I, § 9, which limits them. Its "terms purport to enlarge, not to diminish the powers vested in the government,"[23] he noted. *Necessary* here means useful or desirable, not indispensable or essential. In part, Marshall again explained that this is because of the nature of a Constitution. Marshall observed that the "provision is made in a constitution, intended to endure for ages to come, and consequently, to be adapted to the various crises of human affairs."[24]

The Court, however, rejected any contention that this interpretation gives Congress limitless authority. Marshall stated that "should congress, in the execution of its powers, adopt measures which are prohibited by the constitution; or should congress, under the pretext of executing its powers, pass laws for the accomplishment of objects not intrusted to the government; it would become the painful duty of this tribunal . . . to say, that such an act was not the law of the land."[25] Marshall thus reaffirmed *Marbury v. Madison* and the power of the judiciary to review the constitutionality of federal laws.

McCulloch v. Maryland established several crucial aspects of constitutional law and the relationship between the federal government and the states. All were in accord with Hamilton's vision.

First, by rejecting "compact federalism," *McCulloch* emphatically declares that the federal government is supreme over the states and that the states have no authority to negate federal actions. This was very much in line with Hamilton's vision of the relationship between the national and state governments. In *The Federalist* No. 32, Hamilton spoke of "the division of sovereign power": each level of government needs it to function with "full vigor" on its own. Hamilton saw "strong States and a strong Federal Government." Unlike his foes Madison and Jefferson, he did not see a federal government subordinate to state governments.

Second, the Court expansively defined the scope of Congress's powers. The Court saw Congress as having the authority to do anything reasonably needed to carry out its authority, even apart from the necessary and proper clause, exactly the position that Hamilton took in *The Federalist* No. 33. Hamilton contended that this clause is implicit in the Constitution—if Congress is granted a power, it must necessarily be able to draft laws that enable it to execute that power. Arguments against this power, he argues, are based on misrepresentations and exaggerations.[26]

Hamilton expressly addressed why the necessary and proper clause was needed if Congress already had the power to adopt laws to carry out its authority. Hamilton said that the clause is included "to guard against all cavilling refinements in those who might hereafter feel the disposition to curtail and evade the legitimate authorities of the Union." In other words, to guard against those who would seek to evade the authority of the Union by an overly literal interpretation of the Constitution. In his essay he stated—much like John Marshall did in *McCulloch*—that "to make all laws which shall be necessary and proper for carrying into execution the powers by that Constitution vested in the government of the United States . . . and the treaties made by their authority shall be the supreme law of the land, anything in the constitution or laws of any State to the contrary notwithstanding."[27]

And so you can see why, although I have declined to use technology teaching techniques, I've figured out how to show the students a critical scene from *Hamilton*. "Cabinet Battle #1" was about one of the most basic questions concerning American government: the power of Congress, especially relative to the states. Hamilton won during the Washington administration and a Bank of the United States was created. But it was a couple of decades later, in a case ironically about the constitutionality of a different Bank of the United States, that the Supreme Court adopted Hamilton's vision. It has been the basis for crucial aspects of constitutional law ever since.

Talk about a legacy.[28]

HAMILTON'S BANK AND JEFFERSON'S NIGHTMARE

Mehrsa Baradaran

Before the U.S. Constitution was signed, debate raged over how to create a thriving banking system that would meet the needs of the developing economy and populace. There were many disagreements about what sort of system would best serve the country. Alexander Hamilton pushed for a national, centralized, and government-coordinated banking system. He argued that only this system of banking would produce a world-class economy and a unified, prosperous nation. While a twenty-four-year-old soldier, he saw the bank as much more than a way to fund the war. He wrote, "tis by introducing order into our finances by restoring public credit not by gaining battles that we are finally to gain our object." His time in the army ("We have resorted to eating our horses. / Local merchants deny us equipment, assistance.")[1] had convinced him that "military operations could not be made more effective without more money and more money could not be procured without new means."[2]

Hamilton understood that banks created money—they were not just intermediaries, but creators of wealth. Banks, he explained in a letter to

Washington, enabled the "augmentation of the active or productive capital of a country."[3] Gold and silver, he said, "acquire life" and become "active and productive" only through the operation of a bank. "Banks in good credit can circulate a far greater sum than the actual quantum of their capital in Gold & Silver."[4] Describing bank lending and the money multiplying magic of banking, Hamilton explained that bank "credit keeps circulating, performing in every stage the office of money."[5] In other words, it was through banking that American wealth would be created.

Hamilton emphasized that successful banking required a strong partnership with the federal government. He told Congress in 1790 that a bank is "not a mere matter of private property, but a political machine of the greatest importance to the state."[6] A healthy government needed a centralized and powerful banking system to survive, and strong banks needed government support. As *Hamilton: An American Musical* makes clear, a large federal bank was Thomas Jefferson's worst nightmare. ("But Hamilton forgets / his plan would have the government assume states' debts. / Now, place your bets as to who that benefits / the very seat of government where Hamilton sits.")[7] Jefferson feared that powerful, centralized banking would threaten democracy and suffocate credit for the nonelite small farmers that would be the lifeblood of this nation. The character argues in the musical, "Our poorest citizens, our farmers, live ration to ration / as Wall Street robs 'em blind in search of chips to cash in."[8] He proposed that these inequalities should be remedied by forcing banks to serve only local markets. Jefferson won in the short term, but Hamilton was more prescient about what the country would need and the central role the federal government would take on in the banking sector.

The small-and-local versus big-and-national banking models represented ideological differences that were at the heart of the negotiations that formed our country. ("Thanks to Hamilton, our cab'net's fractured into factions / Try not to crack under the stress, we're breaking down like fractions.")[9] The debate did not die down after the initial clash between the Founders, but only strengthened over time. Yet for most of American history, the sides outlined in the initial debate held steady even as the nation transformed. In the Jeffersonian tradition, populists, Southerners, and farmers demanded small-and-local banking as a bulwark against an alliance of federal power and Wall Street money. Even as a second national bank was established (as Erwin Chemerinsky describes in his chapter in this volume about *McCulloch v. Maryland*), drafting banking policy meant protecting the people from too much bank power, which would inevitably lead to inequalities in access. Thus, Jefferson's vision of localized banking was embraced for over a century, even though it became clear that the United States would not persist as an agrarian society but was destined to grow into a complex economic machine.

For much of U.S. history, the answer to banking for the poor—whether the rural farmer or working-class city dweller—has been through local and community control of credit. Over the past several decades, most of the government and industry initiatives aimed at financial inclusion have focused on community efforts to bank the poor—Jefferson's localism still runs deep in banking politics. However, the problem of access is fundamentally different today than it was historically. Disparities in access are not regional but based almost exclusively on income. There is a straightforward economic reason banks, local or otherwise, do not lend to the poor: there are more profits to be made elsewhere.

Any effort to bank the poor must recognize that centralized, national, and large banking is the world we live in. Hamilton was right that government-controlled central banking was essential to coordinating a modern economy. But Jefferson was also right that banking power permitted to accumulate in the hands of a few does so at the expense of the many. The dilemma of living in a Hamiltonian banking world without addressing the Jeffersonian nightmare of inequality has led to the current crisis of the unbanked.

But there is a Hamiltonian solution to Jeffersonian fears: a public option in banking—a central bank for the poor. The core function of the central bank or Federal Reserve is to infuse liquidity into troubled banks so that they could withstand a temporary credit crunch and get back on their feet. A public option would provide the same short-term credit help. Indeed, in the modern banking landscape, only a lender that is large and liquid is able to lower the costs of lending to the poor.

One way the federal government might become involved is through the existing U.S. Postal Service structure. Using the post office to achieve financial inclusion has historical roots. From its founding, the U.S. Post Service was the practical means that gave effect to our Founders' democratic ideals. Postal banking was also the largest and most successful experiment with financial inclusion in U.S. history and remains the primary tool for financial inclusion across the world. A public option in banking balances the scales of government support for the banking industry and has the potential to drive out the usurious fringe lending sector, which profits from the American people when they are down on their luck.

This idea was based on the ones shared by many Founders. The Post Office Act of 1792, supported by George Washington, James Madison, and Alexander Hamilton (an alliance that we do not see in the musical), has been called "one of the most important single pieces of legislation to have been enacted by Congress in the early republic."[10] The act made several crucial decisions that would shape our first-rate democracy and economy. First, it was decided that the post office would be financially supported by the federal government and not required to produce a surplus like its counterparts in Europe. It was to be self-sustaining, but not profitable, and when needed, supplemented by the Treasury. At the time, this made the post office the largest government agency by far. Second, the post office would serve every community without regard to profit. In other words, profitable routes (along the Eastern Seaboard) would subsidize the East to West routes.

The post office did not offer savings accounts right away, but beginning in 1870 almost every postmaster general advocated postal banking until it was finally passed in 1910 and dubbed "the Poor Man's Bank."[11] Early advocates of post office savings banks were not just trying to expand savings banks across the country; they were interested in providing a state-supported institution. In 1882, Congressman Edward Lacey said, "private enterprise alone does not, and cannot, in this respect, meet the necessities of the industrious poor in any country, and least of all in the United States."[12] The point was that "the working poor . . . would be more inclined to deposit earnings in the Post Office, a *public* institution, than in the local savings bank run by sanctimonious clergymen and philanthropists."[13] The post office, with its rich history and public mission, was the obvious choice for providing this service. With branches in communities where no bank and certainly no savings bank would go, the post office had the potential to do with savings what it had done with information—democratize the country.

Postal banking was seen by many as a boon to rural farmers and the poor. Marion Butler, a Populist Party senator from North Carolina, offered the most passionate endorsement for postal banking during congressional debates around the end of the nineteenth century. Although the post office was the largest federal government agency at the time and many Southern bankers opposed its expansion, Butler channeled the spirit of Jefferson as he advocated for postal banks. "With all who stand on the money question where Jefferson, Jackson, and Lincoln stood," Butler claimed, "it is a strong argument in favor of postal savings banks."[14]

Why? Because as the nation industrialized and urbanized, banks were forbidden to join other industries in forming nationwide conglomerates in pursuit of high profits in money centers.[15] Because it was so important that rural regions have sufficient access to credit, these laws were zealously protected even though they resulted in chronic panics, runs, and crises. For better or for worse, equality of access trumped bank profitability and stability. For two centuries, the democratic political process decided it would rather have less efficient banks that were available to all than more powerful and profitable banks that were only available to some. Andrew Jackson vigorously fought a "bank war"[16] to defeat the renewal of the Second National Bank's charter (even though the Supreme Court had held in *McCulloch v. Maryland* that the federal government did have the power to establish it, the government was not required to do so). Jackson saw his success as a victory of the common man against the powerful banking industry. The absence of a central bank may have caused the unfettered Wall Street excess and the widespread banking panics that led to the Great Depression.

Forcing local banking and opposing the central bank were not economic ideals, but policy principles that had to counter market forces that naturally favored growth and concentration. Jefferson and Jackson may have been wrong in their solutions, but they were prophetic in their fears. They worried that money tended to flow where there was more money and when banks became too large and powerful, they would only lend where profits were highest, creating inequalities. But they miscalculated that keeping banks geographically dispersed could preclude centralized banking power. The modern world has made that solution insufficient. There is no doubt Jefferson would have been just as uncomfortable with our current bifurcated nationwide banking systems (one for the rich and one for the poor) as he was with a big city banking monopoly leaving out poor rural farms. The point was that the rich and poor should operate in credit markets governed by the same rules; that banks must not have the power to anoint winners and losers.

The fight for equality in banking that started before the ink was dry on the Constitution—the fight that, although it endured for most of our nation's history, has only a cameo in the musical—ended sometime in the last few decades as deregulation did away with most meaningful attempts to restrict bank power. What eventually happened was predictable: banks became powerful and stopped serving a large sector of the population. Instead of bank wars or even bank skirmishes, politicians pushed laws favoring bank profitability and efficiency over public needs. Any suggestion that banks should be forced to lend to less profitable borrowers was seen as a government intrusion into the private market. And because the people's representatives have gone from fighting the centripetal force of bank power to helping it along, the accumulated power of banks has become harder to dislodge.

Although Hamilton is the hero of sorts in the musical that bears his name, it is important to understand that his nemesis Jefferson's fears—rejected by Washington, but wholeheartedly embraced by other Founders—had merit. As banks became larger and more concentrated as Hamilton predicted they would in an industrial economy, Jefferson's nightmare has come to pass. Banks rely on federal government support and are Wall Street institutions. Access to credit and capital for the rest of the country has diminished. As bank mergers accelerated, many banks serving low-income communities disappeared. Once community banks left the scene, fringe lenders filled the void. These lenders extract unconscionable interest rates from the most vulnerable populations and deepen inequalities in wealth.

Economies of scale and the backing of the government can be used to bring down the costs of lending to the poor. The federal government is in a unique position to lend to the poor and cover its costs without having to answer to shareholder pressure to maximize profits.

Postal banks led to increased saving by the broader public for half a century, and their rebirth can do the same. By offering low-barrier savings accounts, the post office can again offer a refuge for the countless small savers in the United States who have been shut out of the banking system because their too-small savings accounts are no match for high bank fees. Increased access to low-cost savings accounts can benefit a population living without any financial cushion. Postal savings accounts could provide much-needed financial buffers that could even diminish the need for short-term credit. Having even a few hundred dollars stored away can make a significant difference to a moderate-income family who may face a financial emergency such as an unexpected medical crisis or an extensive roof repair. Postal savings can even reinvigorate a culture of savings that has been long lost in the United States, but retained in Japan and Germany precisely because of their strong network of postal banks.

The high cost of credit exacerbates the already-strained lives of the poor and makes it that much more difficult for them to escape poverty. Low-cost credit alone cannot eliminate poverty; nor is credit an adequate substitute for better employment or higher wages. Still, access to reasonably priced credit can help a large portion of the population improve their financial lives. Reasonable credit not only serves as a bridge over financial trouble, but for millions of Americans, credit is the only means to build assets, start a business, or get an education.

Although postal banking has the potential to save an institution that predated the Constitution and made our first-rate democracy possible, the crucial argument in favor of postal banking is that it has the potential to bank the unbanked. The most important potential benefit would be access to savings accounts. Consider the social and economic benefits of a system that enables the unbanked in the United States to leave the expensive and time-wasting cash economy and pay their bills online, send money to family, make debit card purchases, and save money without worrying about draconian overdraft fees. And it is not just the unbanked that stand to benefit; an even larger portion of the population has a bank account but has been forced to rely on high-cost fringe loans. Postal banking can provide the creditworthy among the low and middle-income small loans without life-crushing fees and interest.

Even though Hamilton, in the words of Lin-Manuel Miranda's Madison, took our country "from bankruptcy to prosperity,"[17] even though "his financial system is a work of genius,"[18] his national banking system must be adapted to avoid Jefferson's nightmare. Hamilton "doesn't get enough credit for all the credit he gave us"[19] and his vision for the future is the world we currently inhabit. But so too with Jefferson, who feared the power and conglomeration of the banking industry. Both visions can be honored, and the entire country can be included in the banking system.

Alexander Hamilton's Legacy

The American Board of Directors

M. Todd Henderson

Ev'ry American experiment sets a precedent.
— "What'd I Miss," *Hamilton*

One of the central dramatic tensions in *Hamilton: The Musical* is a conflict between Hamilton and the duo of Jefferson and Madison on the nature of federal power in the new Republic. As Erwin Chemerinsky and Mehrsa Baradaran discuss in their chapters in this volume, the debate set out in the lyrics is about debts and banks, but the resolution (not seen in the musical) had a profound impact on American corporate law as well. The precedent Hamilton set by outfoxing Jefferson and Madison can be seen in every boardroom of every American corporation to this day.

Alexander Hamilton did not invent the idea of a board of directors—the antecedents of the modern board can be found in human cooperation from the Middle Ages, if not before—but his use of a board of directors for The Society for Establishing Useful Manufactures (SUM) and the Bank of the United States undoubtedly provided a foundation for American capitalism. Boards created by Hamilton were prominent when New York liberalized corporate law in the early nineteenth century, and this model is still used today. Interestingly, the functions that Hamilton envisioned for the boards that he created fell out of fashion as economic, legal, and political conditions changed over the next two hundred years. Today we have come almost full circle back to the original Hamiltonian board.

Establishing the governance model was neither easy nor straightforward. In the musical, we first witness the conflict over corporate governance—the charter of the First Bank of the United States—when Thomas Jefferson's character returns home from France. He's confronted by his fellow Virginian and co-author of the Constitution, James Madison.

Jefferson:	But who's waitin' for me when I step in the place?
	My friend James Madison, red in the face
	He grabs my arm and I respond,
	"What's goin' on?"
Madison:	Thomas, we are engaged in a battle for our nation's very soul
	Can you get us out of the mess we're in? . . .
	Hamilton's new financial plan is nothing less than government control . . .
	We have to win . . .
Jefferson:	Headfirst into a political abyss![1]

The "political abyss"? The abyss, in Jefferson's view, represented Hamilton's plan to have the federal government assume the debts of the Revolution and to establish a national bank but, in broader terms, the allocation of authority between states and the federal government under the new Constitution—a central conflict in the musical and in American politics today.

The origin of the conflict was in three reports Hamilton wrote and delivered to the first Congress:[2] a report on public credit (1790), a report on a national bank (1790), and a report on manufacturing (1791). All advocating a fulsome role for the new federal government, these reports put Hamilton at sharp odds with two of the other leading statesmen of the day, Secretary of State Thomas Jefferson and James Madison, serving then as a representative from Virginia. Hamilton wanted Congress to play an active role in developing the financial and industrial capacity of the fledgling nation. By contrast, Jefferson romanticized the agrarian farmer (not the factory worker) and Madison advocated the federal government hewing strictly to the enumerated powers found in Article II of the Constitution.

In the next song, "Cabinet Battle #1," Hamilton debates the role of the federal government with Jefferson and Madison, all under the watchful eye of President George Washington. The latter tees up the question: "The issue on the table: Secretary Hamilton's plan to assume state debt and establish a national bank,"[3] before turning the floor over to Jefferson, who cries, "This financial plan is an outrageous demand!"[4]

Hamilton turns to Washington for help, but Washington reminds Hamilton:

Washington: You need the votes.
Hamilton: No, we need bold strokes. We need this plan.
Washington: No, you need to convince more folks . . . Figure it out, Alexander.[5]

Hamilton figured it out. He created semipublic entities for his purposes, outside of the government to appease Jefferson and Madison, but enough inside the ambit of government control to accomplish his goal of fortifying national power.

To appreciate how Hamilton accomplished this finesse, we must first consider the approach he took regarding the third of his bold plans presented to the first Congress—Hamilton's proposal for a federally managed investment in industrial capacity centered around the falls near Patterson, New Jersey. Hamilton wrote of the importance of his project to build a new manufacturing hub for the nascent United States:

> The establishment of Manufactures in the United States when maturely considered will be found to be of the highest importance to their prosperity. It is an almost self evident proposition that that community which can most completely supply its own wants is in a state of the highest political perfection. And both theory and experience conspire to prove that a nation (unless from a very peculiar coincidence of circumstances) cannot possess much *active* wealth but as the result of extensive manufactures.[6]

In Hamilton's view, "the union gets a boost,"[7] and he looked down on the agrarian South, not the least of which because he knew "who's really doing the planting."[8] The vision was bold, but a threat to the South, which he noted was holding the nation "hostage."[9] But as Washington, Jefferson, and Madison told him—he didn't have the votes.[10]

Instead of trying to convince Madison—"a nonstarter"[11]—Hamilton petitioned the New Jersey legislature for a charter for a corporation to promote industrial development of the Passaic River near the town of Patterson, about fifteen miles west of Manhattan. Its goal was to "produce paper, sail linens, women's shoes, brass and ironware, carpets, and print cloth,"[12] among other items. To raise the private funds—about $600,000 ($10 million in today's dollars)—Hamilton partnered with financier William Duer and four other business leaders of the day. They solicited funds from investors, rather than funding the construction and operation through the public fisc.

The decision to make SUM a "private" entity was a less radical step than it would appear today. Corporations were not then what they are now. A private corporation in those days existed solely with the blessing of the legislature, not in the sense of creating background rules that permitted limited liability or the like, but in the sense of authorizing a specific corporation to be formed for a particular purpose. In addition, corporations were typically authorized only for projects with a social mission, not run-of-the-mill businesses. For instance, the majority of the thirty corporations chartered up to 1790 in America were for infrastructure or other projects that fit easily within the ambit of government services;[13] the use of private business was often merely a means of finding the most efficient mechanism to raise funds and to undertake the activity. Early corporations were government by other means. This is why they required the imprimatur of the government, in the form of a legislature-issued charter and were limited in scope to the purposes set out in their charter. And SUM's charter—vesting in it government functions such as being able to take land for its use by process of condemnation—made the quasi-governmental nature of its existence clear.

Although SUM was a private corporation, Hamilton designed its governance to reflect its origin in his mind as a public operation. He appointed a "governor" and "deputy governor" to manage SUM's day-to-day operations. To provide checks and balances over their power, Hamilton employed a structure that would fundamentally shape the governance of every corporation from then to now—he constituted a board of thirteen "directors" chosen by the shareholders to oversee the governor and deputy governor. SUM was to be governed as a representative democracy with layers of power designed to limit the potential for abuse by any one person or small interest group of persons, just as it would have been had it been created and funded directly by Congress.

The governance structure did not work as intended. Duer squandered the money raised for SUM on other speculative ventures, and by 1792 was in debtor's prison, where he would spend the rest of his life.[14] Hamilton took over SUM. But even he couldn't turn around SUM's fortunes and, by 1796, the factories lay idle and Patterson was "a ghost town."[15] But the lasting legacy of SUM was not its factories or their output, but its corporate governance structure—the board of directors, which became the norm for American corporations. SUM's charter became a template for corporate governance, and by 1811, when New York passed the first antecedent to modern corporate legislation, the idea of a board of directors was baked into corporate law. That statute provided that "the . . . concerns of such company shall be managed and conducted by [directors], who . . . shall be elected . . . as shall be directed by the bylaws of the said company."[16] This requirement is ubiquitous today. Nearly every American corporation, from a ten-person real estate business to General Motors, uses the Hamiltonian board of directors.

SUM's governance structure borrowed heavily from the one used by Hamilton earlier that year when he helped establish the first Bank of the United States. Like SUM, the bank was originally envisioned as a public entity designed to serve a public purpose—to create financial infrastructure for the nation.[17] The bank idea ran into the same political opposition as SUM: Jefferson and Madison argued that it exceeded the federal government's powers under the Constitution. To overcome these objections, Hamilton structured the bank as a quasi-governmental entity. The bank was to be federally chartered for twenty years, and only 20 percent of the capital would be provided by taxpayers, with the remaining $8 million raised from individuals in the United States and abroad. This was sufficient to garner enough votes in Congress and President Washington's signature. Befitting its public purpose, the bank was to be governed by a board of twenty-five directors, elected annually by the shareholders, the biggest of which was the U.S. government.[18] As with SUM, political governance befitted the public purpose of the enterprise.

Like most American innovations of the Founding era, the model of "corporate" governance drew heavily on English antecedents. The 1694 charter of the Bank of England vested management authority in twenty-four directors, and this would likely have been a ready and powerful example for early American officials.[19] As in America with the Bank of the United States, the Bank of England was originally chartered to bring stability to England's financial situation following a costly war with France. The Bank of England was also private company cloaked with public purpose. Parliament created the Bank of England (with the Tonnage Act of 1694), just as Congress created the Bank of the United States (with the Bank Act of 1791).[20] It is not surprising that both banks borrowed their governance model from politics—the directors were chosen by the shareholders to represent the interests of each bank's stakeholders, just as representatives to the House of Commons or Congress represented citizens.

In stark and revealing contrast, most businesses at this time did not use boards or any other type of collective governance approach. Given the nature of economic production, most businesses were akin to modern sole proprietorships or partnerships. These were most often family-run affairs, under the control of a single individual. Economic activity was not collectively managed, but governed and directed by individuals. This was true even for some big businesses of the era. For instance, the banking empires of Renaissance Italy—the Peruzzi (1275–1343) and Medici (1397–1494) companies—were "partnerships operated under the domination of a family leader or trusted manager,"[21] and were run by the head of the family. Businesses great and small were purely private affairs, and they were governed as such.

The connection between the board of directors and politics is evident from these examples, but it can be made even clearer by looking back to antecedents to the Bank of England. Franklin Gevurtz locates the origins of modern corporate boards in medieval Europe, on both the Continent and in England.[22] The reason for using a group to oversee an individual leader's authority arose from the explicitly political origins of corporations. Early corporations were not private entities seeking private ends, but rather government entities in disguise, for whatever reason. The political nature of early boards can be more clearly seen several hundred years earlier in the proto-corporations of Europe.

In England, two early companies that pioneered the modern board of directors approach were the Company of Merchants of the Staple (granted a royal charter in 1319) and the Company of Merchant Adventurers (granted a royal charter in 1505). These "companies" were established to consolidate the various exporters of wool and cloth (respectively) from England to the Continental Europe. The idea was to achieve economies of scale and to increase regulatory control over English tradesmen operating on the Continent. (Traders were based initially in Antwerp, far beyond the reach of the English monarch.) The function of these companies was governmental—the policing of merchants through a sort of proto self-regulatory apparatus. For instance, the twenty-four directors of the Company of Merchant Adventurers did not direct the strategy of the various English tradesmen operating in the export business, but rather promulgated rules and sat in judgment of their alleged misbehavior.[23] If one English merchant defrauded a wool buyer in Belgium, this would potentially harm all English wool merchants, since they might get a reputation for shady dealings as a group. If the English merchants were less able to be regulated by the local authorities and beyond the reach of their sovereign, this presented a problem for the noncheating traders. If you think you might be cheated and you can't sort the good traders from the bad ones before the fact, then you will lower the amount you are willing to pay for a certain quantity and quality of wool. A "corporation" of all traders internalizes these potential negative effects and raises overall quality.

Hamilton brought this quasi-public governance approach to the most prominent early American corporation. The idea took hold. But over time the Hamiltonian innovation evolved to meet the needs of the era. After New York liberalized corporate formation in 1811, businesses no longer needed legislative authority for limited liability and the other benefits of incorporation, so the form spread like wildfire. Businesses that did not need political oversight were using the corporate form. But they kept the board that Hamilton used for SUM. Instead of providing checks and balances and offering political accountability, for the tens of thousands of corporations formed before the Civil War, the board provided sources of funding, connections, credibility with regulators, and wisdom about management, production, and markets.

After the Civil War, the emergence of large industrial conglomerates—such as Standard Oil—provided a way for boards to evolve again. At the time, states prohibited companies from owning interests in companies in other states—a significant barrier to efficient economic production at a national scale, and entrepreneurs, like John Rockefeller, found a solution in the board. Putting individuals on multiple boards—for example,

Rockefeller's brother served on boards of oil firms in Ohio and New York—enabled investors to control companies across state lines.

Modern corporate law obviates the need for this function, but boards evolved again. From the 1950s through to the late 1980s, boards were staffed with long-serving executives of the firm, and served as strategic advisers as American companies grew at unprecedented rates at home and expanded across the globe. After a series of governance failures and several important court cases and federal statutes, the board transitioned again. The Sarbanes-Oxley Act required new independence for audit committees, and empowered boards to hire advisers independent of the CEO. The Dodd-Frank Wall Street Reform and Consumer Protection Act of 2010 mandated a similar independence obligation for compensation committees. Both laws emphasized the board as a monitor of the corporation, and not just as a means of reducing agency costs within the firm, but also as a means of ensuring compliance with external law and regulation. The board is in a sense the agent of not just the shareholders, but also of society writ large. In this sense, the modern board, which is largely independent of management and acts as an oversight mechanism to ensure compliance with legal requirements, is a return to the Hamiltonian ideal.

In the end, Hamilton got the votes. And he created a legacy, even if it was one he did not live to see.[24]

"I Never Thought I'd Live Past Twenty"

Hamilton *through the Lens of Anticipated Early Death*

Sarah Fishel

The threat of death looms over Lin-Manuel Miranda's *Hamilton: An American Musical*. From the first song, the audience is introduced to the death of three people close to Alexander Hamilton, and then reminded of Hamilton's death. Throughout the musical, characters like George Washington ("Dying is easy, young man. Living is harder")[1] and Eliza Hamilton ("Stay alive . . .")[2] discuss death, but Hamilton thinks differently about death than the other characters do. After experiencing the loss of his mother, the suicide of his cousin, the violence of the slave trade, poverty, and even natural disasters, Hamilton's outlook on life becomes fatalistic. Hamilton expects to die young, saying, "I never thought I'd live past twenty. / Where I come from some get half as many."[3] Given the circumstances surrounding Hamilton's childhood, this viewpoint is understandable. Hamilton has been exposed from an early age to profound death and violence in a way that shapes his later behaviors. Early in his life, he resigns himself to the belief that he will die young.

Hamilton brings to the forefront a new narrative surrounding the American Revolution that has excited audiences and legal scholars alike. At its heart, *Hamilton* is about a determined young man who, by his own account, never should have lived to adulthood. Although Miranda's Hamilton lives past his twenties and is able to focus on his legacy, today's youth who anticipate an early death are more likely to find themselves involved in the justice system than in an award-winning Broadway musical. The law has started to change in response to the idea that youth think differently and make decisions differently than adults. Going one step further and using frameworks that acknowledge these thinking patterns to understand why youth engage in risky behaviors is vital to creating a justice system that is better able to respond to their needs.

Feeling as though death is imminent can have a powerful impact on a person's decision making; it can alter personal values and impact the risks they are willing to take. A popular way that people respond to considering their life expectancy is by creating a bucket list of adventures, activities, and experiences that they would like to "check off" before "kicking the bucket." Each person's bucket list can look different, but all reflect the same kind of thinking. After all, if you believe that your life is near its end, why "wait for it"?[4]

This type of fatalistic thinking can become a problem when death is not actually imminent, when those who anticipate an early death begin to take more dangerous risks, or when the risks are illegal. Hamilton's brashness in the face of anticipating an early death was often rewarded ("Hamilton doesn't hesitate. / He exhibits no restraint. / He takes and he takes and he takes / and he keeps winning anyway"),[5] but for many young people today, their risky behaviors stemming from similar beliefs can lead to potentially life-altering legal consequences.

Research on anticipated early death suggests that the potentially problematic framework can develop as a result of exposure to violence, abuse, or a dangerous or unpredictable environment early in life.[6] Hamilton experienced his share of adversity at a young age; he was exposed to the social consequences of being a "bastard, orphan, son of a whore . . . impoverished, in squalor,"[7] witnessing his mother's death, his cousin's suicide, and the devastation of a natural disaster all before leaving the Caribbean and everything he knew to travel to New York as a teenager. Given this shocking exposure to death and dying early in life, Eliza Hamilton even tells her husband, "Look at where you are. / Look at where you started. / The fact that you're alive is a miracle."[8]

High levels of unpredictability early in a person's life can lead him to conclude that all of life will be unpredictable; this, in turn, affects his decision making. If someone does not believe he will live to see the consequences of his actions, or, alternatively, believes that the potentially fatal consequences of his actions are inevitable, he is more likely to take risks than someone who expects to live a long life.[9] In modern-day America, anticipating an early death may lead people to discount the future and any long-term consequences resulting from risky behaviors that produce short-term rewards.[10] This way of thinking is associated with later risk-taking behaviors such as delinquency, violent offending, and involvement in gang activities.[11] Where others may step away from risky or dangerous situations before they escalate, or mentally weigh the choices and consequences thereof, youth who anticipate an early death are more likely to step into that situation with a cavalier attitude toward the consequences, as, like Hamilton, "[They] could never back down, / [they] never learned to take [their] time."[12]

In *Hamilton*, the Revolutionary War amplifies the threat of death for Hamilton and many of Miranda's other characters, but Hamilton again distinguishes himself by his willingness to challenge death and push boundaries that other characters are not willing to push. For example, at the beginning of the war, while other soldiers are abandoning their posts around the Battery, Hamilton runs toward the fight ("Hamilton won't abandon ship, / Yo, let's steal their cannons").[13] Hamilton's risk paid off, and he caught the eye of George Washington, which unquestionably changed the trajectory of his career.

Alexander Hamilton was able to channel his desire to prove his "nerve" and willingness to take dangerous risks in the Revolutionary War, where his fearlessness was rewarded. But what would have happened to Hamilton if there was no war? Or if the war was not waged by a fledgling country, but was instead between two neighborhoods in a city? What would happen to a young, poor Hamilton if he lived his life today as if he would die before the age of twenty? Instead of joining a militia, a young Hamilton may have found himself in the juvenile justice system.

The theme of war is familiar to the study of anticipated early death. In interviews with researchers in Atlanta, Georgia, adolescent offenders (youth who have committed crimes) described life in their neighborhoods as living in a "war zone," where death was both omnipresent and seemingly senseless.[14] As a result, many of those youth believed that they would die young, and developed a "here and now" orientation and attraction to risky, and often criminal, behaviors. Similarly, in inner-city Philadelphia, youth have spoken about having "nerve," which "expresses a lack of fear of death," and demonstrating that they have conquered their fear of death by engaging in risky and violent confrontations.[15] These confrontations exist outside of the context of war as Hamilton knew it. Researchers interviewed one nineteen-year-old from Atlanta who drew the parallel between his life and war: "I grew up with shootin' and fightin' all over . . . It's like a war out there. People die every day . . . Bullets be lying on the street in the morning."[16] The same risky, and sometimes violent, actions of youth today usually have legal consequences that Hamilton never faced.

Historically, the law has acknowledged that youth think differently than adults, and so the majority of youth who come in contact with the justice system are processed through the juvenile justice system.[17] This system was built on the understanding that young people think differently, and so act and react differently, from adults.[18] Hamilton, at eighteen years old, would have been on the cusp between the juvenile and adult systems if he were tried for stealing the cannons at the Battery in 1775.[19] Though the pendulum of juvenile justice policy has swung back and forth between prioritizing rehabilitation or retribution for youth, the juvenile system has remained structurally distinct from the adult justice system for this reason.[20]

Case law has also recognized that juveniles, even those who do not believe that death is just around the corner, take unnecessary risks and fail to think through the consequences of their actions. In *Roper v. Simmons*, the Supreme Court abolished the death penalty for juvenile offenders, reasoning in part that "the character of a juvenile is not as well formed as that of an adult."[21] Similarly, in *Graham v. Florida*, the Court restricted juvenile life in prison without parole to homicide cases and acknowledged that "juveniles are more capable of change than adults" due to their developmental stage, and should be allowed the opportunity to demonstrate that change.[22] In *Miller v. Alabama*, the Court extended its holding in *Graham* to prohibit mandatory sentencing of juveniles to life without parole for any crime, considering it important to allow individual consideration of "age and age-related characteristics" in sentencing.[23]

Though these landmark cases focus on the most serious juvenile offenders, in each case the Court cited the elasticity of adolescence and the potential for change as reasons to treat juveniles who have committed the most violent of crimes differently than their adult counterparts. Adolescents, in addition to demonstrating a propensity for forming potentially problematic worldviews that impact their behavior at a young age, also demonstrate a propensity for change.

Miranda showcases this change in Hamilton by following his story from his childhood in the Caribbean, through the Revolutionary War, and into adulthood. Contrary to his expectations, Hamilton does not die at twenty years old, and his outlook on his lifespan adjusts to that reality.[24] The anticipation of an early death may have impacted Hamilton's willingness to engage in risky activities during his youth, but once his future began to solidify and he could see beyond his twentieth birthday, his decision-making processes had to change.

Many events can help to facilitate a shift in the mindset of an individual who, like Hamilton, anticipates an early death. The event could be as mundane as living past the age at which the person expected to die, or as dramatic as marriage or parenthood—events that tend to signal a major life transition.[25] For Hamilton, his attitude noticeably shifts when the end of the war is in sight. In "Yorktown," he again references the presence of death, but something has changed for him. Hamilton begins the familiar phrase, "I imagine death so much it feels just like a memory," but then, instead of reflecting on his perceived imminent death, his worldview changes: "Then I remember my Eliza's expecting me / Not only that, my Eliza's expecting / We gotta go, gotta get the job done / Gotta start a new nation, gotta meet my son!"[26]

Instead of charging into the field and confronting death head on, his battle plans make a sharp turn. He orders his men to take the bullets out of their guns and instead sneak up on the enemy, for the first time specifically choosing to follow a careful and cautious plan, one that is most likely to let him "live another day."[27] The parallel between this reference and his first words outlining a more cavalier and fatalistic attitude toward death demonstrate how Hamilton's "world[view] turned upside down."[28] Though Hamilton transitioned naturally out of the mind-set of anticipating an early death, interventions that target the "here and now" mind-set may encourage youth who anticipate an early death to reconsider this belief system before they may naturally mature out of this way of thinking.[29]

Under the theoretical framework of anticipated early death, youth who commit crimes because they believe that they will die or be killed prematurely do not live without fear or completely disregard the consequences of their actions.[30] Instead, the framework suggests that these considerations do not stop them *because* they have already resigned themselves to living a short life.[31] A shorter life means that they have already accepted that their death is imminent and that they will likely not live to experience the consequences of their actions. For some, they would rather "Die on the battlefield in glory."[32] It makes sense, then, that the best interventions to address this thinking style may be to disrupt the "here and now" mindset.[33] By challenging the belief systems of these youth and encouraging those who do not believe they have a future to plan as if they would live a full life, targeted interventions may disrupt this problematic belief system, improve self-control and rational decision-making, and reduce the likelihood that they will make risky decisions, such as engaging in dangerous or criminal activities.[34]

The shift in Hamilton's belief system did not mitigate his intensity. He still poured himself into his work, fiercely defended his legal clients, and wrote "day and night like [he was] running out of time."[35] The essence of Hamilton's character did not change, but the risks he took had a new focus. Rather than fixating on the present moment, Hamilton began to obsess over planning for the future and solidifying his legacy. In the end, the death he anticipated in asking, "when's it gonna get me?"[36] was not in Hamilton's youth, but after half a century of scholastic contribution to the country he helped create.

NOTES

Preface

1. Throughout the musical, Alexander Hamilton declares his interest in leading his own command.

2. Miranda, "What Comes Next?," *Hamilton*.

3. This riffs on "And so the American experiment begins" from Miranda, "Yorktown (The World Turned Upside Down)," *Hamilton*.

4. Miranda, "Non-Stop," *Hamilton*.

5. As of February 2018, *Hamilton* was one of the five-highest selling cast albums in history, even though it had been available for only two-and-a-half years. See Logan Culwell-Block, "Hamilton Cast Recording Enters Top 5 Highest-Selling Cast Albums in Nielsen Music History," *Playbill*, February 16, 2018, http://www.playbill.com/article/hamilton-cast-recording-enters-top-5-highest-selling-cast-albums-in-nielsen-music-history.

6. See http://www.playbill.com/article/the-10-most-streamed-cast-albums-of-2019-and-of-the-decade and https://www.billboard.com/charts/year-end/cast-albums.

7. As of December 2017, according to Carolyn Juris, "This Week's Bestsellers: December 4, 2017," *Publishers Weekly*, December 1, 2017, https://www.publishersweekly.com/pw/by-topic/industry-news/bookselling/article/75524-this-week-s-bestsellers-december-4-2017.html. It was number 14 on the Adult Non-Fiction Best-Seller list in 2016. John Maher, "The Bestselling Books of 2016," *Publishers Weekly*, January 20, 2017, https://www.publishersweekly.com/pw/by-topic/industry-news/bookselling/article/72566-the-bestselling-books-of-2016.html. According to the publisher, as of May 23, 2018, Grand Central Publishing has

printed 778,313 copies of the book over seven printings. Jimmy Franco, senior director of publicity, Grand Central Publishing, email message to author, May 23, 2018.

8. Miranda, "Right-Hand Man," *Hamilton*.

9. Miranda, "The Schuyler Sisters," *Hamilton*.

10. Miranda, "Non-Stop," *Hamilton*.

11. Miranda, "Satisfied," *Hamilton*.

1. Lin-Manuel Miranda and the Future of Originalism

A longer version of this chapter was originally published as Richard Primus, "Will Lin-Manuel Miranda Transform the Supreme Court?," *The Atlantic*, June 4, 2016, https://www. theatlantic.com/politics/archive/2016/06/lin-manuel-miranda-and-the-future-of-original ism/485651/. Reprinted with permission.

1. Lin-Manuel Miranda, "Guns and Ships" *Hamilton: An American Musical* (Atlantic Records 2015).

2. *Printz v. United States*, 521 U.S. 898, 915 at n 8, 117 S. Ct. 2365, 2375, 138 L. Ed. 2d 914 (1997).

3. Miranda, "My Shot," *Hamilton*.

4. Miranda, "Alexander Hamilton," *Hamilton*.

5. Ibid.

6. Ibid.

7. Ibid.

8. Miranda, "Who Tells Your Story?" *Hamilton*.

9. Ibid.

10. Miranda, "Washington on Your Side," *Hamilton*.

11. Miranda, "Alexander Hamilton," *Hamilton*.

2. Some Alexander Hamilton, but Not so Much *Hamilton*, in the New Supreme Court

I thank Max D. Bartell, Rachel N. Harris, and Danielle M. Stefanucci for excellent research assistance.

1. U.S. Constitution, Art. 3, Sec. 1.

2. See, e.g., *Marbury v. Madison*, 5 U.S. 137 (1803).

3. Lin-Manuel Miranda, "Non-Stop," *Hamilton: An American Musical* (Atlantic Records 2015).

4. Ibid.

5. See Buckner F. Melton, Jr., "The Supreme Court and *The Federalist*: A Citation List and Analysis, 1789–1996," *Kentucky Law Journal* 85 (1996–97): 243; Buckner F. Melton, Jr. and Jennifer J. Miller, "The Supreme Court and *The Federalist*: A Supplement, 1996–2001," *Kentucky Law Journal* 90 (2001–2): 415; Buckner F. Melton, Jr. and Carol Willcox Melton, "The Supreme Court and *The Federalist*: A Supplement, 2001–2006," *Kentucky Law Journal* 95 (2006–7): 749.

6. A few examples from a prominent cases: Brief for Respondents at 2, *Trump v. Hawaii*, 585 U.S. ___, 138 S. Ct. 2392 (2018) (No. 16-1540) (quoting *Federalist No. 47* [by Madison], explaining the principle that legislative, executive, and judicial powers should not be held by a single person or branch of government); Brief for Petitioners at 51–52, *Obergefell v. Hodges*, 576 U.S. ___, 135 S. Ct. 2584 (2015) (No. 13–354) (quoting from *Federalist No. 78* [Hamilton]: the "independence of the Judges is equally requisite to guard the Constitution and the rights of individuals from . . . serious oppressions of the minor party in the community"); Brief of Amicus Curiae Judicial Watch, Inc. in Support of Respondents at 3–4, *Sebelius*

v. Hobby Lobby Stores, Inc., 573 U.S. 682 (2014) (No. 13-354) (citing to *Federalist Nos. 58* [by Madison] and *78* [Hamilton], supporting the separation of powers between the three branches of government).

7. See, e.g., Transcript of Oral Argument at 54 [by Paul D. Clement, on behalf of the Petitioner], *Franchise Tax Bd. v. Hyatt*, 578 U.S. ___, 136 S. Ct. 1277 (2016) (No. 14-1175) (describing *Federalist No. 81* [by Hamilton] as one of the original explanations of States' sovereign immunity from lawsuits by individuals); Transcript of Oral Argument at 20–22 [by U.S. Solicitor General Donald B. Verrilli, Jr., on behalf of the Petitioner], *NLRB v. Noel Canning*, 573 U.S. 513 (2014) (No. 12–1281) (referring to *Federalist Nos. 76* [by Hamilton] and 51 [by Madison] as support for the ideas that the Senate's advice and consent function should be "rarely exercised" and "would operate, if at all, invisibly or silently," and that the Executive needed to be "fortified" against Congress's potential to "amass authority and drain authority from the Executive").

8. See Charles C. Hileman et al., "Supreme Court Law Clerks' Recollections of October Term 1951, Including the Steel Seizure Cases," *St. John's Law Review* 82 (2008): 1239.

9. *Youngstown Sheet & Tube Co. v. Sawyer*, 343 U.S. 579 (1952).

10. Ibid., 634 (Jackson, J., concurring in the judgment & opinion of the Court).

11. Ibid.

12. Ibid., 634–35.

13. See Brief for Plaintiff Companies, Petitioners in No. 744 and Respondents in No. 745, *Youngstown Sheet & Tube Co. v. Sawyer*, 343 U.S. 579 (1952) (Nos. 744 & 745), at 37.

14. 343 U.S. at 635n1 ("A Hamilton may be matched against a Madison. 7 The Works of Alexander Hamilton, 76–117; 1 Madison, Letters and Other Writings, 611–54").

15. Richard Primus, "Will Lin-Manuel Miranda Transform the Supreme Court?," *The Atlantic* (June 4, 2016), https://www.theatlantic.com/politics/archive/2016/06/lin-manuel-miranda-and-the-future-of-originalism/485651.

16. *Printz v. United States*, 521 U.S. 989, 915 n.9 (1997).

17. "Obama Job Approval (Monthly)," Gallup, https://news.gallup.com/poll/151025/obama-job-approval-monthly.aspx.

18. Nick Romano, "Hamilton: Hillary Clinton Fundraiser Performance Announced for July 12," *Entertainment*, June 25, 2016 (quoting a Clinton campaign email to supporters), https://ew.com/article/2016/06/25/hamilton-performance-hillary-clinton-fundraiser/.

19. "Transcript: Hillary Clinton's Speech at the Democratic Convention," *New York Times*, July 28, 2016, https://www.nytimes.com/2016/07/29/us/politics/hillary-clinton-dnc-transcript.html, quoting Miranda, "The Story of Tonight," and "The World Was Wide Enough," and perhaps referencing "What Did I Miss?"

20. Alisa Chang, "Justice Stephen Breyer on What the Court Does Behind Closed Doors and Hamilton," National Public Radio, December 13, 2015, https://www.npr.org/2015/12/13/459365840/justice-stephen-breyer-on-what-the-court-does-behind-closed-doors-and-hamilton.

21. See Christopher Jackson (@ChrisisSingin), Twitter, November 26, 2015, 11:27 a.m., https://twitter.com/ChrisisSingin/status/669915356174131200.

22. Ariane de Vogue, "Justice Kennedy Reflects on This Year's Tough Cases, Scalia and 'Hamilton,'" CNN, July 13, 2016, https://www.cnn.com/2016/07/13/politics/justice-anthony-kennedy/index.html.

23. Mark Walsh, "High Court Justice Spotlights Civics Education at 9th Circuit Conference," *Education Week*, July 18, 2017, http://blogs.edweek.org/edweek/school_law/2017/07/high_court_justice_spotlights_.html; "Gorsuch Can't Escape Travel Ban at San Francisco Meeting," CBS News, July 18, 2017, https://www.cbsnews.com/news/gorsuch-cant-escape-travel-ban-at-san-francisco-meeting/.

24. See John Paul Stevens, reviewing Noah Feldman, "The Three Lives of James Madison: Genius, Partisan, President," *Michigan Law Review* 117 (2019): 1019, 1022. ("I am told this episode [Thomas Jefferson's June 1790 dinner in Philadelphia with Hamilton and Madison, producing their agreement that the United States would assume states' Revolutionary War debts and that the U.S. capital would move from Philadelphia to a new city to be built on the Potomac River] provides the basis for one of the more well-known numbers ["The Room Where It Happens"] in the Broadway musical, Hamilton.")

25. See *Franchise Tax Bd. v. Hyatt*, 587 U.S. ___, 139 S. Ct. 1485 (2019).

26. Ibid., 587 U.S. at ___, 139 S. Ct at 1495 (quoting *Nevada v. Hall*, 440 U. S. 410, 437 (1979) (Rehnquist, J., dissenting)).

27. *See Nielsen v. Preap*, 586 U.S., 139 S. Ct 954, 979 (2019) (Breyer, J., joined by Ginsburg, Sotomayor, & Kagan, JJ., dissenting). Justice Alito, writing the plurality opinion that reached the statutory interpretation issue, ignored Justice Breyer's *Hamilton* example.

3. Tragedy in the Supreme Court

Epigraph: Lin-Manuel Miranda, "Take a Break," *Hamilton: An American Musical* (Atlantic Records 2015).

1. Miranda, "Take a Break."

2. Miranda, "Yorktown (The World Turned Upside Down)," *Hamilton*.

3. Miranda, "Take a Break," *Hamilton*.

4. Although Miranda was talking about an actual war—the American Revolution—when he wrote "I'll see you on the other side of the war" in "The Story of Tonight," an adaption of this line seems apropos in this context.

5. Ron Chernow describes how Maria Reynolds was likely involved in a blackmail plot with her husband, but the musical portrays her as more of a victim. See Ron Chernow, *Alexander Hamilton* (New York: Penguin Group, 2004), 366–67.

6. Miranda, "Take a Break," *Hamilton* (quoting William Shakespeare, *Macbeth*, 1.7.59–62).

7. This is not to say that the left is free of misogyny, but at least in recent years, the left has been far more likely to cast out the accused than the accuser.

8. Miranda, "Washington on Your Side," *Hamilton*.

9. Miranda, "Take a Break," *Hamilton*, referring to a prophecy in *Macbeth*.

10. Miranda, "The Reynolds Pamphlet," *Hamilton*.

11. Miranda, "History Has Its Eyes on You," *Hamilton*.

12. Miranda, "History Has Its Eyes on You," *Hamilton*.

13. Clarence Thomas, confirmation hearing testimony before the U.S. Senate, 102nd Cong., 1st sess., October 11, 1991.

14. Letter on July 8, 2019, "Campaign for Supreme Court Term Limits," signed by more than sixty legal scholars, including three authors in this volume. "Campaign for Supreme Court Term Limits," https://fixthecourt.com/wp-content/uploads/2019/07/July-8-law-profs-letter.pdf.

15. Joe Biden, Confirmation Hearings for John G. Roberts, Jr., September 14, 2005, https://www.judiciary.senate.gov/imo/media/doc/GPO-CHRG-ROBERTS.pdf.

16. The Supreme Court makes significant decisions about executive power, as well as about voting rights and procedures which contribute to the outcome of elections. And in 2000, the Supreme Court all but decided the outcome of the election.

17. Miranda, "We Know," *Hamilton*.

18. Shakespeare, *Macbeth*, 1.7.27.

19. Kenji Yoshino, *A Thousand Times More Fair: What Shakespeare's Plays Teach Us about Justice* (New York: Ecco, 2011).

20. Miranda, "Aaron Burr, Sir," *Hamilton*.

21. Miranda, "History Has Its Eyes on You," *Hamilton.*

22. Miranda, "Yorktown (The World Turned Upside Down)," *Hamilton.*

23. Banquo, *Macbeth*, 1.3.87.

24. Miranda, "Burn," *Hamilton.*

25. "Campaign for Supreme Court Term Limits," https://fixthecourt.com/wp-content/uploads/2019/07/July-8-law-profs-letter.pdf.

26. *Hamlet*, 1.4.42 (this line is what you say if you accidentally say "Macbeth" in a theater).

4. Alexander Hamilton's "One Shot" before the U.S. Supreme Court

I thank Soren Schmidt for his many contributions to this essay, and Lindsay Baxter for her assistance in researching this chapter.

1. Lin-Manuel Miranda, "Alexander Hamilton," *Hamilton: An American Musical* (Atlantic Records 2015).

2. Ron Chernow, *Alexander Hamilton* (New York: Penguin Group, 2004), 190.

3. *Annals of Congress*, 3rd Cong., 1st sess., 730 (1794); James Madison, "Letter from James Madison to Thomas Jefferson," *Letters and Other Writings of James Madison Fourth President of the United States*, vol. 2 (Philadelphia: J.B. Lippencott & Co., 1865), 14.

4. U.S. Constitution, Art. 1, Sec. 9, Cl. 4.

5. Miranda, "Non-Stop," *Hamilton.*

6. *The Federalist* Nos. 12, 21, 30, 31, 32, 33, 34, 35, 36 (Alexander Hamilton).

7. *Hylton*, 3. U.S. (3 Dall.) 172 (Chase, J.).

8. "Letter from William Bradford to Alexander Hamilton (July 2, 1795)," in *Papers of Alexander Hamilton*, vol. 18, ed. Harold C. Syrett (New York: Columbia University Press, 1973), 393–97.

9. See Chernow, *Alexander Hamilton*, 485–500.

10. "Letter from Alexander Hamilton to George Washington (May 10, 1796)," in *Papers of Alexander Hamilton*, vol. 20, 173–74.

11. Miranda, "Non-Stop," *Hamilton.*

12. Maeva Marcus, ed. *The Documentary History of the Supreme Court of the United States, 1789–1800*, vol. 1 (New York: Columbia University Press, 1985), 262.

13. Miranda, "History Has Its Eyes on You," *Hamilton.*

14. "Letter from John Adams to Abigail Adams, 24 February 1796," Adams Family Papers: An Electronic Archive, Massachusetts Historical Society, https://masshist.org/digitaladams/archive/doc?id=L17960224ja&rec=sheet&archive=&hi=&numRecs=&query=&queryid=&start=&tag=&num=10&bc=/digitaladams/archive/browse/date/all_1796.php.

15. "Letter from James Iredell to Hannah Iredell—February 26, 1796," in *Documentary History of the Supreme Court of the United States, 1789–1800* vol. 7, ed. Maeva Marcus (Columbia University Press: New York, 2003), 490.

16. "Alexander Hamilton's 'Brief'—[Before February 17, 1796]," in *Documentary History of the Supreme Court of the United States*, vol. 7, 456.

17. There is no transcript of Hamilton's oral argument but, fortunately, Justice Iredell took copious notes. "James Iredell's Notes of Arguments in the Supreme Court—February 23–25, 1796," in *Documentary History of the Supreme Court of the United States*, vol. 7, 477.

18. "Alexander Hamilton's 'Opinion'—[before February 17, 1796]," in *Documentary History of the Supreme Court of the United States*, vol. 7, 465.

19. Ibid.

20. Ibid.

21. *Hylton*, 3. U.S. (3 Dall.) 175 (citing Adam Smith, *An Inquiry into the Nature and Causes of the Wealth of Nations*, vol. 1 (London: W. Strahan, 1776), 482–83, 490–91.

22. "James Iredell's Notes of Arguments," 477.

23. "Alexander Hamilton's 'Opinion,'" 466.

24. Ibid., 467.

25. "Letter from James Iredell to Hannah Iredell," 490–91.

26. Ibid., 490.

27. "Letter from John Adams to Abigail Adams (Feb. 27, 1796)," in *Adams Family Correspondence: The Adams Papers*, vol. 11, ed. Margaret A. Hogan (Cambridge, MA: Belknap Press of Harvard University Press, 2013), 186–87.

28. "Letter from James Iredell to Hannah Iredell," 490.

29. "Gazette of the United States—February 26, 1796," in *Documentary History of the Supreme Court of the United States*, vol. 7, 490. The *Gazette* may have been a bit biased in favor of Hamilton, as it was the leading, pro-Federalist paper of the day.

30. "Letter from Jeremiah Smith to William Plumer—February 27, 1796," in *Documentary History of the Supreme Court of the United States*, vol. 7, 492–93.

31. Ibid.

32. See note 1 in "Gazette of the United States, February 25, 1796," in *Documentary History of the Supreme Court of the United States*, vol. 7, 490.

33. "Letter from William Plumer to Jeremiah Smith—March 15, 1796," in *Documentary History of the Supreme Court of the United States*, vol. 7, 503.

34. "Letter from James Madison to James Monroe—February 26, 1796," in *Documentary History of the Supreme Court of the United States*, vol. 7, 491.

35. "Letter from James Madison to Thomas Jefferson—March 6, 1796," in *Documentary History of the Supreme Court of the United States*, vol. 7, 494–95.

36. See note 1 in "Jeremiah Smith to William Plumer, February 27, 1796," in *Documentary History of the Supreme Court of the United States*, vol. 7, 493.

37. Miranda, "My Shot," *Hamilton*.

38. "Philadelphia Gazette—March 8, 1796," in *Documentary History of the Supreme Court of the United States*, vol. 7, 501.

39. *Hylton*, 3. U.S. (3 Dall.) 175 (Chase, J.), 177 (Paterson, J.), 183 (Iredell, J.).

40. *Hylton*, 3. U.S. (3 Dall.) 174 (Chase, J.), 179–80 (Paterson, J.), 181–83 (Iredell, J.).

41. Ibid., 175 (Chase, J.), 180 (Paterson, J.), 182–83 (Iredell, J.).

42. Ibid., 175 (Chase, J.).

43. 157 U.S. 572 (1895).

44. *Nat'l Fed'n of Indep. Bus. v. Sebelius*, 567 U.S. 571 (2012) (citing *Hylton*, 3. U.S. (3 Dall.), 175) (Chase, J.)).

45. "Letter from David Hunter to Alexander Hamilton (July 7, 1796)," in *Papers of Alexander Hamilton*, vol. 20, 249.

46. "To Alexander Hamilton from David Hunter, 7 July 1796," Founders Online, National Archives, https://founders.archives.gov/documents/Hamilton/01-20-02-0160.

47. Miranda, "My Shot," *Hamilton*.

5. "Never Gon' Be President Now"

All errors or omissions are mine alone. I dedicate this chapter to my daughter, Izzy Secunda, who has had a bad case of "Hamilaria" now for a number of years. See "Hamilaria," Urbandictionary.com ("An incurable disease in which one feels the need to sing Hamilton lyrics in public, usually after being prompted by normal everyday speech."), https://www.urbandictionary.com/define.php?term=hamilaria.

1. Joanne B. Freeman, *Affairs of Honor: National Politics in the New Republic* (New Haven: Yale University Press, 2001), 262.

2. Lin-Manuel Miranda, "History Has Its Eyes on You," *Hamilton: An American Musical* (Atlantic Records 2015).

3. Miranda, "The Adams Administration," *Hamilton*.

4. Miranda, "The Reynolds Pamphlet," *Hamilton*.

5. Miranda, "The World Was Wide Enough," *Hamilton*.

6. Miranda, "Alexander Hamilton," *Hamilton*.

7. Miranda, "The World Was Wide Enough," *Hamilton*.

8. *The Federalist* No. 65 (Hamilton).

9. Jeffrey Rosen, "The Framers' Broad View of Constitutional Corruption," National Constitution Center October 11, 2013, https://constitutioncenter.org/blog/the-framers-broad-view-of-constitutional-corruption (quoting Lessig's Amicus Brief in Support of the Appellate *McCutcheon v. FEC* [2013]).

10. Miranda, "The Reynolds Pamphlet," *Hamilton*.

11. Miranda, "Right Hand Man," *Hamilton*.

12. Miranda, "Non-Stop," *Hamilton*.

13. Miranda, "Cabinet Battle #2," *Hamilton*.

14. Miranda, "Non-Stop," *Hamilton*.

15. Miranda, "One Last Time," *Hamilton*.

16. Miranda, "Say No to This," *Hamilton*.

17. Miranda, "My Shot," *Hamilton*.

18. Miranda, "The World Was Wide Enough," *Hamilton*.

19. Miranda, "Washington on Your Side," *Hamilton*.

20. Miranda, "The Election of 1800," *Hamilton*.

21. Miranda, "Washington on Your Side," *Hamilton*.

22. By the end of Jefferson's first term, the Constitution was amended to correct for this oversight by the framers in the Twelfth Amendment to the Constitution.

23. Miranda, "The Election of 1800," *Hamilton*.

24. Letter from Alexander Hamilton to Harrison Gray Otis, December 23, 1800, https://www.gilderlehrman.org/sites/default/files/inline-pdfs/t-00496-028.pdf.

25. *The Federalist* No. 65 (Hamilton).

26. James Bryce, *The American Commonwealth* (London: Macmillan, 1889), 208.

27. Miranda, "Your Obedient Servant," *Hamilton*.

28. Freeman, *Affairs of Honor*, 163.

29. Ibid., 162.

30. Miranda, "Blow Us All Away," *Hamilton*.

31. See Freeman, *Affairs of Honor*, 178. ("Fatalities in political duels were uncommon, for killing one's opponent was more of a liability than an advantage, leaving a duelist open to charges of bloodthirstiness and personal ambition. By law, a politician who slew his opponent was also guilty of murder, though ironically these lawyers and lawgivers were rarely charged.")

32. U.S. Constitution, Art. 2, Sec. 4.

33. These were the facts that gave rise to the Supreme Court's unanimous opinion, written by Chief Justice Marshall, in the landmark case of *Marbury v. Madison*, 5 U.S. 137 (1803), which helped to uphold the power of judicial review—courts' authority to assess the constitutionality of federal legislation and action.

34. On these and other impeachments from that era to the present, see Michael J. Gerhardt, *The Federal Impeachment Process: A Constitutional and Historical Analysis*, 3rd ed. (Chicago: University of Chicago Press, 2019).

35. David O. Stewart, *American Emperor: Aaron Burr's Challenge to Jefferson's America* (New York: Simon & Schuster, 2011), 302–3.

36. See, for example, Nancy Isenberg, *Fallen Founder: The Life of Aaron Burr* (New York: Penguin, 2007); Andrew Burstein and Nancy Isenberg, "What Michelle Bachmann Doesn't Know about History, Salon, January 4, 2011, http://www.salon.com/2011/01/04/burstein_isenberg_bachmann_bur/.

37. U.S. Constitution, Art. 1, Sec. 3.

38. See Michael J. Gerhardt, *Impeachment: What Everyone Needs to Know* (New York: Oxford University Press, 2018).

39. Miranda, "The Reynolds Pamphlet," *Hamilton.*

40. Miranda, "The Room Where It Happens," *Hamilton.*

6. Hamilton: Child Laborer and Truant

Epigraph: Lin-Manuel Miranda, "Alexander Hamilton," *Hamilton: An American Musical* (Atlantic Records 2015).

1. Miranda, "Alexander Hamilton," *Hamilton.*

2. Ibid.

3. Ibid.

4. Ibid.

5. Miranda, "My Shot," *Hamilton.*

6. See Jessica Contrera, "The searing photos that helped end child labor in America," *Washington Post*, September 3, 2018, https://www.washingtonpost.com/news/retropolis/wp/2018/09/02/the-incredible-photos-that-inspired-the-end-of-child-labor-in-america. ("In the early 1900s, [Lewis] Hine traveled across the United States to photograph preteen boys descending into dangerous mines, shoeless 7-year-olds selling newspapers on the street and 4-year-olds toiling on tobacco farms . . . Hine's searing images of those children remade the public perception of child labor and inspired the laws to ban it.")

7. Fair Labor Standards Act of 1938, Public Law 75–718, U.S. Statutes at Large 52 (1938): 1060–69.

8. Jeffrey M. Hirsch, Paul M. Secunda, and Richard A. Bales, *Understanding Employment Law*, 2nd ed. (Newark, NJ: LexisNexis, 2013).

9. See Paul M. Secunda, "Sources of Labour Law in the United States: Contract Supra Omnis," *Marquette Law School Legal Studies Paper No. 18-21* (2018), https://papers.ssrn.com/sol3/papers.cfm?abstract_id=3255712 (over 150 pieces of state workplace protective legislation was struck down by the Supreme Court from about 1905–35).

10. *Lenroot v. Interstate Bakeries Corp.*, 55 F. Supp. 236 (D. Mo. 1944), *aff 'd in part and rev'd in part*, 146 F.2d 325 (8th Cir. 1945). The FLSA child labor restrictions, in combination with compulsory school attendance laws, as discussed below, attempt to keep children in school rather than at work.

11. 29 U.S.C. § 212.

12. 29 C.F.R. §§ 570.1(b), (c), 570.2; *Martin v. Funtime, Inc.*, 963 F.2d 110 (6th Cir. 1992).

13. 29 C.F.R. § 570.2(a)(1)(i). The types of permissible jobs were expanded in a 2010 DOL amendment of this regulation. See 29 C.F.R. §§ 570.33, 570.34.

14. Ibid. §§ 570.31, 570.33 (not permitting work in mining, with most power machinery, helping with motor vehicles, public messenger services, transportation, communications, public utilities, construction, and warehouse storage), 570.34, 570.35 (work time maximums).

15. Ibid. § 570.2(a)(1)(ii). Examples of such jobs include excavation, manufacturing explosives, mining, and operating many types of power-driven equipment. However, the permissible bounds for employment for children in hazardous industries are constantly in flux. See

Rebecca Rainey, "Not Safe for Kids?," *Politico*, September 27, 2018 ("The Labor Department will publish a proposal today that would allow 16- and 17-year old workers to operate, unsupervised, patient lifting devices in nursing homes and hospitals. Today's proposed regulation would reverse an Obama-era policy that permitted teens to operate such machinery only if they had 75 hours' training and were supervised by an adult."), https://www.politico.com/newsletters/morning-shift/2018/09/27/not-safe-for-kids-353952.

16. See Marie E. Failinger, " 'Too Cheap to Work for Anybody but Us': Toward a Theory and Practice of Good Child Labor," *Rutgers Law Journal* 35, no. 3 (2004).

17. See International Labour Organization, "Conventions and Recommendations," https://www.ilo.org/global/standards/introduction-to-international-labour-standards/conventions-and-recommendations/lang—en/index.htm. ("The ILO's Governing Body has identified eight conventions as 'fundamental,' covering subjects that are considered as fundamental principles and rights at work: the elimination of all forms of forced or compulsory labour; the effective abolition of child labour. These principles are also covered in the ILO's Declaration on Fundamental Principles and Rights at Work [1998].")

18. International Labour Organization, "C138 Minimum Age Convention, 1973 (No. 138)," https://www.ilo.org/dyn/normlex/en/f?p=NORMLEXPUB:12100:0::NO::P12100_ILO_CODE:C138.

19. Ibid.

20. See International Labour Organization, "Ratifications for Saint Kitts and Nevis," https://www.ilo.org/dyn/normlex/en/f?p=1000:11200:0::NO:11200:P11200_COUNTRY_ID:103373.

21. See International Labour Organization, "Declarations of the United States Virgin Islands," https://www.ilo.org/dyn/normlex/en/f?p=1000:11200:22435527407783::::P11200_INSTRUMENT_SORT:4.

22. See Ravi Nagi, "How the Fair Labor Standards Act Applies to USVI Employers," *Virgin Islands Law Blog*, February 2, 2015, https://lawblog.vilaw.com/2015/02/articles/labor-employment/how-the-fair-labor-standards-act-applies-to-usvi-employers. ("For business owners in the U.S. Virgin Islands, the laws governing employees' hours and pay are based for the most part upon the standards set forth in the federal Fair Labor Standards Act.")

23. Ron Chernow, *Alexander Hamilton* (New York: Penguin Group, 2004), 31.

24. Miranda, "Alexander Hamilton," *Hamilton*.

25. Miranda, "Satisfied," *Hamilton*.

26. Miranda, "Alexander Hamilton," *Hamilton*.

27. See Chelsea Lauren Chicosky, "Restructuring the Modern Education System in the United States: A Look at the Value of Compulsory Education Laws," *Brigham Young University Education and Law Journal* 1, no. 1 (2015): 71 (table II outlines the compulsory education attendance law of every state). Most states require kids to start some form of schooling by age six and continue through sixteen or eighteen.

28. Ibid., 26. ("As a result of modern educational theory and practice, numerous alternatives to compulsory public education—private schools, school vouchers, and charter schools [collectively referred to as "school choice" options], and homeschooling [with regulations across a wide spectrum]—have developed.")

29. Miranda, "Alexander Hamilton," *Hamilton*.

30. Ibid.

31. See Jan Pudlow, "Blind Judge Works to Assist Children," *Florida Bar News*, October 1, 2012, https://www.floridabar.org/the-florida-bar-news/blind-judge-works-to-assist-children. ("92 percent of the prison population was chronically truant in elementary and middle school.")

7. Hamilton's America—and Ours

1. Lin-Manuel Miranda, "Guns and Ships," *Hamilton: An American Musical* (Atlantic Records 2015).

2. Miranda, "Yorktown (The World Turned Upside Down)," *Hamilton.*

3. Miranda, "The Schuyler Sisters," *Hamilton.*

4. Lyric from "Cabinet Battle #3," which was cut from the show, https://genius.com/Lin-manuel-miranda-cabinet-battle-3-demo-lyrics.

5. Miranda, "Washington on Your Side," *Hamilton.*

6. See, e.g., Edward Delman, "How Lin-Manuel Miranda Shapes History," *The Atlantic*, September 29, 2015 https://www.theatlantic.com/entertainment/archive/2015/09/lin-manuel-miranda-hamilton/408019.

7. This move, too, has been criticized from the left. While Hamilton does show us people of color in leading roles, those people are the actors, not the characters. Hamilton could have done more to include black characters, not just black actors.

8. U.S. Constitution, Art. 2, Sec. 1, Clause 5; emphasis added.

9. Miranda, "Yorktown (The World Turned Upside Down)," *Hamilton.*

10. Liz Mineo, "Correcting 'Hamilton,' " *Harvard Gazette*, October 7, 2016, https://news.harvard.edu/gazette/story/2016/10/correcting-hamilton/.

11. Ishmael Reed, " 'Hamilton: The Musical': Black Actors Dress Up like Slave Traders . . . and It's Not Halloween," *Counterpunch*, August 21, 2015, https://www.counterpunch.org/2015/08/21/hamilton-the-musical-black-actors-dress-up-like-slave-tradersand-its-not-halloween.

12. Nawal Arjini, "Ishmael Reed Tries to Undo the Damage 'Hamilton' Has Wrought," June 3, 2019, https://www.thenation.com/article/ishmael-reed-haunting-of-lin-manuel-miranda-hamilton-play-review/.

13. *Dred Scott v. Sandford*, 60 U.S. 393, 407 (1857).

14. *Brown v. Board of Education* 347 U.S. 483 (1954).

15. U.S. Constitution, amend. 15.

16. As someone said, they were never more English than when they rebelled.

17. *Brown v. Board of Education of Topeka,* 347 U.S. 483 (1954); *Loving v. Virginia,* 388 U.S. 1 (1967); *Miranda v. Arizona,* 384 U.S. 436 (1966); *Gideon v. Wainwright,* 372 U.S. 335 (1963); *Roe v. Wade,* 410 U.S. 113 (1973); *Obergefell v. Hodges,* 576 U.S. ___ (2015).

18. Bingham's life featured plenty of drama: in addition to drafting the amendment, he participated in the trial of the Lincoln assassins and the impeachment of Andrew Johnson before losing his seat in Congress after being implicated in the Crédit Mobilier scandal. He was also ambassador to Japan. See Gerard N. Magliocca, *American Founding Son: John Bingham and the Invention of the Fourteenth Amendment* (New York: New York University Press, 2013).

8. Hamilton and Washington at War and a Vision for Federal Power

1. Lin-Manuel Miranda, "Right Hand Man," *Hamilton: An American Musical* (Atlantic Records 2015).

2. See Risa L. Golubuff and Richard C. Schragger, "The Real World: Why Judicial Philosophies Matter," *Slate*, September 7, 2005, https://slate.com/news-and-politics/2005/09/the-real-world.html.

3. The Heritage Foundation, Twitter, February 6, 2017, 4:41 a.m., https://twitter.com/heritage/status/828584433863254016.

4. Miranda, "That Would Be Enough," *Hamilton.*

5. Miranda, "Guns and Ships," *Hamilton.*

6. Lin-Manuel Miranda and Jeremy McCarter, *Hamilton: The Revolution* (New York: Grand Central Publishing, 2016), 52–53.

7. Miranda, "You'll Be Back," *Hamilton.*

8. Miranda, "Take a Break," *Hamilton.*

9. Miranda, "Non-Stop," *Hamilton.*

10. Articles of Confederation, art. 3 (1781).

11. Articles of Confederation, art. 5.

12. Miranda, "Right Hand Man," *Hamilton.*

13. George Washington, "Letter to Joseph Jones, May 31, 1780," in *The Writings of George Washington*, ed. John C. Fitzpatrick (Washington, DC: U.S. Government Printing Office, 1931), 18:453.

14. George Washington, "Circular to State Governments, October 18, 1780," in *Writings*, ed. John Rhodehamel (New York: Library of America, 1997), 398.

15. Ibid., 283 ("Letter to Henry Laurens").

16. Ibid., 282.

17. Ibid., 292 ("Letter to George Clinton").

18. Miranda, "Stay Alive," *Hamilton.*

19. Washington, "Letter to Alexander Hamilton, March 4, 1783," *Writings*, 488.

20. Miranda, "Stay Alive," *Hamilton.*

21. Washington, "Letter to Alexander Hamilton, March 31, 1783," *Writings*, 505.

22. Washington, "Letter to Alexander Hamilton, March 4, 1783," *Writings*, 490.

23. *The Federalist* No. 15 (Hamilton).

24. Ibid.

25. Miranda, "Yorktown (The World Turned Upside Down)," *Hamilton.*

26. Miranda, "Dear Theodosia," *Hamilton.*

27. U.S. Constitution, Art. 1, Sec. 8.

28. *The Federalist* No. 30 (Hamilton).

29. Ibid.

30. *The Federalist* No. 12 (Hamilton).

31. Akhil Reed Amar, *America's Constitution: A Biography* (New York: Random House, 2005), 107.

32. U.S. Constitution, Art. 1, Sec. 8.

33. Alexander Hamilton, "Letter from Alexander Hamilton to George Washington, Opinion on the Constitutionality of an Act to Establish a Bank, 1791," in *The Papers of George Washington Digital Edition*, ed. Theodore J. Crackel (Charlottesville: University of Virginia Press, 2008).

34. Miranda, "Washington on Your Side," *Hamilton.*

35. Hamilton, "Letter from Alexander Hamilton to George Washington," *The Papers of George Washington Digital Edition.*

36. George Washington, "Letter to David Humphreys, July 20, 1791," in *The Papers of George Washington: Presidential Series* 8, ed. Theodore J. Crackel (Charlottesville: University of Virginia Press, 2008), 359.

37. Miranda, "Cabinet Battle #1," *Hamilton.*

38. See David H. Gans and Douglas T. Kendall, "The Shield of National Protection: The Text & History of Section 5 of the Fourteenth Amendment," *Constitutional Accountability Center* (2009), https://www.theusconstitution.org/wp-content/uploads/2017/12/Shield_of_National_Protection.pdf.

9. Two Oaths

Thank you to CDR Russell Evans, USN (Ret.); Col William McCollough, USMC; Michael Pine, and the Hamilton Operational Planning Team. Views expressed in this piece are my own and do not represent those of Marine Corps University, the Department of Defense, or any other arm of the U.S. government.

Epigraph: Lin-Manuel Miranda, "Non-Stop," *Hamilton: An American Musical* (Atlantic Records 2015).

1. *Act of Congress 29 September 1789* (sec. 3, chap. 25, 1st Congress).

2. 1st Cong., 2d sess., statute 2, chap. 10, April 30, 1790.

3. July 2, 1862, 27th Cong., 2d sess., chap. 128.

4. August 10, 1956, chap. 1041, 70A Stat. 17, § 501; Pub. L. 87-751, § 1.

5. 5 U.S.C. 1331 (1966). The Presidential Oath is specified by Article II section 1 of the Constitution. Federal judges take the same oath as civil servants along with a second oath. 28 U.S.C. 453.

6. Richard M. Swain and Albert C. Peirce, *The Armed Forces Officer* (Washington, DC: National Defense University Press, 2017).

7. Ibid., 5.

8. Ibid., 6.

9. Ibid., 10.

10. See Carol Rice Andrews, "The Lawyer's Oath: Both Ancient and Modern," *Georgetown Journal of Legal Ethics* 22 (2009): 21–23; Leonard S. Goodman, "The Historic Role of the Oath of Admission," *American Journal of Legal History* 11, no. 4 (1967): 404–11.

11. Utah, for example, requires its lawyers to "support, obey, and defend" the Constitution. See Wendell K. Smith, "Why We Take an Oath," *Utah Bar Journal* 8, no. 1 (1995): 12.

12. The words are not mandatory for those who object to them on the grounds of religion or conscience.

13. The definition of these words differed somewhat, but not significantly, at the time of the Founding. I have chosen to analyze modern definitions because these are the meanings that oath-takers reflect on today, and because I share the view that the Constitution is a living document. For discussion of the dictionary definitions as of 1812, see Col Thomas J. Sadlo, "Oath of Office: Can the Military Defend the Constitution Against Domestic Enemies?," Research Report, Air War College, 2010.

14. Merriam-Webster.com, "support," https://www.merriam-webster.com/dictionary/support.

15. See Andrews, "The Lawyer's Oath."

16. See Sanford Levinson, "Constituting Communities through Words That Bind: Reflections on Loyalty Oaths," *Michigan Law Review* 84, no. 7 (1986).

17. DoD Directive 1344.10, *Political Activities by Members of the Armed Forces on Active Duty* (February 19, 2008).

18. Ibid.

19. Contrary to common belief, sharp political divisions exist among servicemembers. See Leo Shane III, "Military Times Poll: What You Really Think about Trump," *Military Times,* October 23, 2017, https://www.militarytimes.com/news/pentagon-congress/2017/10/23/military-times-poll-what-you-really-think-about-trump/ (noting that 44% of troops surveyed have a favorable view of President Donald Trump while roughly 40% have an unfavorable opinion, and that 48% of enlisted personnel approve of Trump while about 30% of officers do); Statista, "Exit Polls of the 2016 Presidential Elections in the United States on November 9, 2016, Percentage of Votes by Military Service," 2018, https://www.statista.com/statistics/631991/voter-turnout-of-the-exit-polls-of-the-2016-elections-by-military-service/

(showing that 61% of military members who voted did so for Trump and 34% voted for Clinton).

20. See "Partisan Political Activity Rules for 'Less Restricted' DoD Civilians," Department of Defense—Office of the General Counsel, http://ogc.osd.mil/defense_ethics/resource_library/hatch_act_q_a_less_restricted.pdf.

21. Besides making clear that one is acting in one's personal capacity and not as a representative of the DoD when engaging in partisan activity, restrictions for "Less Restricted" DoD civilians primarily deal with fundraising. Use of government resources to engage in partisan activity is also prohibited. See ibid.

10. Finding Constitutional Redemption through *Hamilton*

1. Aja Romano, "Hamilton Is Fanfic, and Its Historical Critics Are Totally Missing the Point," *Vox*, April 14, 2016, https://www.vox.com/2016/4/14/11418672/hamilton-is-fanfic-not-historically-inaccurate.

2. Lin-Manuel Miranda, "My Shot," *Hamilton: An American Musical* (Atlantic Records 2015).

3. Miranda, "The Schuyler Sisters," *Hamilton*.

4. Annette Gordon-Reed, "The Intense Debates Surrounding Hamilton Don't Diminish the Musical—They Enrich It," *Vox*, September 13, 2016, https://www.vox.com/the-big-idea/2016/9/13/12894934/hamilton-debates-history-race-politics-literature.

5. Andrew M. Schocket, "Hamilton and the America Revolution on Stage and Screen," in *Historians on Hamilton: How a Blockbuster Musical Is Restaging America's Past*, ed. Renee C. Romano and Claire Bond Potter (New Brunswick, NJ: Rutgers University Press, 2018), 183 (citing Andrew C. Butler et al., "Using Popular Films to Enhance Classroom Learning: The Good, the Bad, and the Interesting," *Psychological Science* 20, no. 9 [2009]: 1161; Sharda Umanath, Andrew C. Butler, and Elizabeth J. Marsh, "Positive and Negative Effects of Monitoring Popular Films for Historical Inaccuracies," *Applied Cognitive Psychology* 26, no. 4 [2012: 556]).

6. Rob Weinert-Kendt, "Rapping a Revolution," *New York Times*, February 5, 2015, https://www.nytimes.com/2015/02/08/theater/lin-manuel-miranda-and-others-from-hamilton-talk-history.html.

7. Clay Skipper, "How to Maintain Your Chill When You're Starring in Hamilton," *Gentleman's Quarterly*, December 7, 2015, https://www.gq.com/story/hamilton-moty (interview with Lin-Manuel Miranda, Jonathan Groff, and Daveed Diggs).

8. Lin-Manuel Miranda and Jeremy McCarter, *Hamilton: The Revolution* (New York: Grand Central Publishing, 2016), 149.

9. Ibid.

10. Weinert-Kendt, "Rapping a Revolution."

11. John McWhorter, "The Exhausting and Useless Accusations of Racism in 'Hamilton,'" *Daily Beast*, April 16, 2016, https://www.thedailybeast.com/the-exhausting-and-useless-accusations-of-racism-hamilton.

12. Patricia Herrera, "Reckoning with America's Racial Past, Present, and Future in Hamilton," in *Historians on Hamilton*, 260.

13. Ibid., 261.

14. Ibid., 260, 270.

15. See Sean Gorman, "Goodlatte Says U.S. Has the Oldest Working National Constitution," *Politifact*, September 22, 2014, https://www.politifact.com/virginia/statements/2014/sep/22/bob-goodlatte/goodlatte-says-us-has-oldest-working-national-cons/. Gorman notes that the United Kingdom and San Marino "have some written documents still in effect that

predate the 1789 enactment of the U.S. Constitution." Still, the United States has the old-est working "single document laying out an overall framework for governing a country." See also Comparative Constitution Project, http://comparativeconstitutionsproject.org/ccp-rank ings/ (listing the year national constitutions were enacted, and dating the United Kingdom's at 1215 because of *Magna Carta*).

16. Evan Thomas, "Founders Chic: Live from Philadelphia," *Newsweek*, July 8, 2001, https://www.newsweek.com/Founders-chic-live-philadelphia-154791.

17. David Waldstreicher and Jeffrey L. Pasley, "Hamilton as Founders Chic: A Neo-Federalist, Antislavery Usable Past?," in *Historians on Hamilton*, 141–43.

18. Ibid., 143.

19. Ibid.

20. Ishmael Reed, " 'Hamilton: the Musical:' Black Actors Dress Up like Slave Traders...and It's Not Halloween," *Counterpunch*, August 21, 2015, https://www.counterpunch.org/ 2015/08/21/hamilton-the-musical-black-actors-dress-up-like-slave-tradersand-its-not-hal loween/.

21. Ta-Nehisi Coates, "Letter to My Son," *Atlantic*, July 4, 2015, https://www.theatlan tic.com/politics/archive/2015/07/tanehisi-coates-between-the-world-and-me/397619/.

22. Jack Balkin, *Constitutional Redemption* (Cambridge, Mass.: Harvard University Press, 2011), 6.

23. Ibid., 5.

24. Ibid., 27.

25. See Winthrop D. Jordan, *White over Black: American Attitudes toward the Negro, 1550–1812* (Williamsburg, VA: Penguin Books, 1968), 429–81 (describing Jefferson's *Notes on the State of Virginia* and assertions of black inferiority); see also Annette Gordon-Reed, *Thomas Jefferson and Sally Hemings: An American Controversy* (Charlottesville: University of Virginia Press, 1997); Thomas Jefferson Memorial Foundation, *Report of the Research Committee on Thomas Jefferson and Sally Hemings* (2000), https://www.monticello.org/site/ plantation-and-slavery/report-research-committee-thomas-jefferson-and-sally-hemings (con-cluding based on DNA evidence that Sally Hemings had one or more children with Thomas Jefferson).

26. Balkin, Constitutional Redemption, 5 (citing Pirke Avot 2:21).

27. Richard Primus, "Will Lin-Manuel Miranda Transform the Supreme Court?," *Atlan-tic*, June 4, 2016, https://www.theatlantic.com/politics/archive/2016/06/lin-manuel-miranda-and-the-future-of-originalism/485651/.

28. Jack Balkin, *Living Originalism* (Cambridge, MA: Belknap Press of Harvard Univer-sity Press, 2011), 85.

29. Balkin, *Constitutional Redemption,* 6.

30. Miranda and McCarter, *Hamilton: The Revolution,* 208.

31. Ibid.

11. Race, Nation, and Patrimony, or, the Stakes of Diversity in *Hamilton*

1. Audre Lorde, "Poetry Is Not a Luxury," in *Sister Outsider: Essays and Speeches* (Berkeley, CA: Crossing Press, 2007), 36–37.

2. Ibid., 36.

3. James Langston Hughes, "Let America Be America Again," in *The Collected Poems of Langston Hughes*, ed. Arnold Rampersad (New York: Alfred A. Knopf, 1994), 191.

4. Ibid.

5. Ibid.

6. Miranda, "Alexander Hamilton," *Hamilton.*
7. Miranda, "A Winter's Ball," *Hamilton.*
8. Miranda, "That Would Be Enough," *Hamilton.*
9. Ibid.
10. Miranda, "Yorktown (The World Turned Upside Down)," *Hamilton.*
11. Miranda, "That Would Be Enough," *Hamilton.*
12. Somerset v Stewart 98 ER 499 (1772).
13. Ibid.
14. Ibid.
15. Miranda, "My Shot," *Hamilton.*
16. 60 U.S. (19 How.) 393 (1857).
17. Lorde, "Poetry Is Not a Luxury," 38.
18. *Dred Scott v. Sandford* 60 U.S. (19 How.) 393 (1857).
19. Ibid.
20. Ibid.
21. Ibid.
22. Ibid.
23. Gerald Ford, "Remarks upon being sworn in as President of the United States, August 9, 1974," Gerald R. Ford Presidential Library & Museum, https://www.fordlibrarymuseum.gov/grf/quotes.asp.
24. *Dred Scott v. Sandford* (1857).
25. Ibid.
26. Lorde, "Poetry Is Not a Luxury," 36.

12. "The World Turned Upside Down"

1. Lin-Manuel Miranda, "Non-Stop," *Hamilton: An American Musical* (Atlantic Records 2015).
2. Miranda, "Cabinet Battle #1," *Hamilton*; Miranda, "Cabinet Battle #2," *Hamilton*; Miranda, "Cabinet Battle 3 (Demo)," *The Hamilton Mixtape* (Atlantic Records 2016).
3. Miranda, "The Room Where It Happens," *Hamilton.*
4. Rebecca Mead, "All about the Hamiltons," *New Yorker*, February 2, 2015, https://www.newyorker.com/magazine/2015/02/09/hamiltons.
5. Ibid. See also Lin-Manuel Miranda and Jeremy McCarter, *Hamilton: The Revolution* (New York: Grand Central Publishing, 2016), 94–95 (describing the intentional musical allusions throughout the songs in Hamilton and the link Miranda saw between Hamilton's life and death and the life and death of Christopher Wallace).
6. Rembert Browne, "Genius: A Conversation with 'Hamilton' Maestro Lin-Manuel Miranda," *Grantland*, September 29, 2015, http://grantland.com/hollywood-prospectus/genius-a-conversation-with-hamilton-maestro-lin-manuel-miranda. See also Leah Libresco, "'Hamilton' Is the Very Model of a Modern Fast-Paced Musical," *FiveThirtyEight*, October 5, 2015, https://fivethirtyeight.com/features/hamilton-is-the-very-model-of-a-modern-fast-paced-musical/ (calculating that at just under two-and-a-half hours, the musical has 20,520 words, sung at an average pace of 144 words per minute, about twice as many as its closest competitor).
7. 42 U.S.C. § 2000e-2(a) (2012). Title VII is not the only civil rights law to apply to race discrimination in employment. Employment is also governed by 42 U.S.C. § 1981 (2012), which prohibits race discrimination in contracts and which was originally enacted during Reconstruction to help enforce the Thirteenth, Fourteenth, and Fifteenth Amendments. Courts

treat cases under either statute interchangeably when it comes to defining discrimination, so this chapter primarily focuses on Title VII.

8. 42 U.S.C. § 2000e-3(b) (2012).

9. 42 U.S.C. § 2000e-2(e) (2012).

10. 42 U.S.C. § 2000-3(b) (2012).

11. 42 U.S.C. § 2000e-2(e) (2012); see Senator Cellar, speaking on H.R. 7152, on February 8, 1964, 88th Cong., 2nd Sess., *Congressional Record*, part 2, 2550 (1964) ("We did not include the word 'race' because we felt that race or color would not be a bona fide qualification, as would be 'national origin.' That was left out. It should be left out."); Senator Cellar, speaking on H.R. 7152, on February 8, 1964, 88th Cong., 2nd Sess., *Congressional Record*, part 2, 2556 (1964). (on an amendment to add race as a BFOQ: "The basic purpose of title VII is to prohibit discrimination in employment on the basis of race or color. Now the substitute amendment, I fear, would destroy this principle. It would permit discrimination on the basis of race or color. It would establish a loophole that could well gut this title.")

12. 29 C.F.R. §§ 1606.1, .4 (2017).

13. Senator Clark, speaking on H.R. 7152, on April 8, 1964, 88th Cong., 2nd Sess., *Congressional Record*, part 6, 7217 (1964); emphasis added.

14. Ibid. (using the example of a film "extravaganza on Africa"). One court has also suggested that a different defense, business necessity, which applies to discriminatory effects but not usually intentional consideration of race, might "be appropriate in the selection of actors to play certain roles" if the call is phrased as having to " 'bear a sufficient likeness' " to the particular character they were to play. Miller v. Texas St. Bd. of Barber Examiners, 615 F.2d 650, 654 (5th Cir. 1980) (citing Larson's Employment Discrimination § 72.10 [1979]).

15. Michael J. Frank, "Justifiable Discrimination in the News and Entertainment Industries: Does Title VII Need a Race or Color BFOQ," *University of San Francisco Law Review* 35, no. 3 (2001): 473.

16. See Russell K. Robinson, "Casting and Caste-ing: Reconciling Artistic Freedom and Antidiscrimination Norms," *California Law Review* 95, no. 1 (2007): 2.

17. See, e.g., Jennifer L. Sheppard, *Theatrical Casting—Discrimination or Artistic Freedom, Columbia-VLA Journal of Law & The Arts* 15, no. 2 (1991): 268–71 (describing the controversy over casting a white British actor to play a French-Vietnamese character); Morgan Greene, "A White Actor Is Cast in 'In the Heights,' Setting off a Complicated Debate," *Chicago Tribune*, August 14, 2016, http://www.chicagotribune.com/entertainment/theater/ct-latino-casting-porchlight-in-the-heights-ent-0815-20160814-story.html (describing accusations of whitewashing a play by casting an Italian-American actor to play the part of Usnavi, a Latinx character in Lin-Manuel Miranda's first musical, *In the Heights*, and also describing steps playwright Katori Hall took in response to a white actor being cast to play Martin Luther King in her play, *The Mountaintop* to prevent that from happening in the future).

18. Heekyung Esther Kim, "If Laurence Olivier Was Rejected for the Role of Othello in Othello, Would He Have a Valid Title VII Claim?," *Hastings Communications and Entertainment Law Journal* 20, no. 2 (1998): 413–15.

19. See Steven DiPaola, "2016–2017 Theatrical Season Report," *Actors' Equity Association*, https://www.actorsequity.org/aboutequity/annualstudy/2016-2017-annual-study. pdf (reporting that of the 51,636 union members, 18,422 worked an average of 16.7 weeks and had median earnings of $7,730). Only 11 percent of equity members earned more than $50,000 in 2016–17. Ibid. at 15. The Bureau of Labor Statistics estimated that about 43,470 people in acting jobs in 2017 with a mean hourly wage of $32.89—annual wages were not reported because actors generally do not work year-round, full-time. Bureau of Labor Statistics, "Occupational Employment and Wages, May 2017," https://www.bls.gov/oes/current/oes272011.htm#nat.

20. 29 C.F.R. § 1604.2(a)(2) (2017).

21. Lyra D. Monteiro, "Race-Conscious Casting and the Erasure of the Black Past in Lin-Manuel Miranda's Hamilton," *Public Historian* 28, no. 1 (2016): 89.

22. Miranda, "Yorktown (The World Turned Upside Down)," *Hamilton*.

23. Caitlin Huston, "Lin-Manuel Miranda on Creating Diversity on Broadway, in 'Hamilton,'" *Broadway News*, April 23, 2018, https://broadway.news/2018/04/23/lin-manuel-miranda-creating-diversity-broadway-hamilton/.

24. Mead, "All about the Hamiltons."

25. Lilly Workneh, "Meet April Reign, the Activist Who Created #OscarsSoWhite," *HuffPost*, February 27, 2016, https://www.huffingtonpost.com/entry/april-reign-oscarsso white_us_56d21088e4b03260bf771018.

26. Michael Paulson, "After #OscarsSoWhite, Broadway Seeks a #TonysSoDiverse," *New York Times*, April 27, 2016, https://www.nytimes.com/2016/04/28/theater/after-oscarsso white-broadway-seeks-a-tonyssodiverse.html.

27. Huston, "Lin-Manuel Miranda on Creating Diversity."

28. *United Steelworkers of Am. v. Weber*, 443 U.S. 193 (1979).

29. The Internet Broadway Database lists more than fifty members of the production staff in the Broadway production alone. "Hamilton: An American Musical," IBDB, https://www.ibdb.com/broadway-production/hamilton-499521.

30. Miranda, "The Schuyler Sisters," *Hamilton*; Miranda, "That Would Be Enough," *Hamilton*.

31. Ibid.

13. *Hamilton* and the Power of Racial Fables in Examining the U.S. Constitution

1. Michael Dale, "HAMILTON's Lin-Manuel Miranda Speaks on Race and Casting," *Broadway World*, December 3, 2015, https://www.broadwayworld.com/article/HAMILTONs-Lin-Manuel-Miranda-Speaks-On-Race-and-Casting-20151203.

2. Ibid.

3. Lin-Manuel Miranda, "Non-Stop," *Hamilton: An American Musical* (Atlantic Records 2015).

4. Derrick Bell, *And We Are Not Saved: The Elusive Quest For Racial Justice* (New York: Basic Books, 1987), 7.

5. Miranda, "My Shot," *Hamilton*.

6. Ibid.

7. Miranda, "Washington On Your Side," *Hamilton*.

8. Spencer Kornhaber, "Hamilton: Casting After Colorblindness," *Atlantic*, March 31, 2016, https://www.theatlantic.com/entertainment/archive/2016/03/hamilton-casting/476247/.

9. Ibid.

10. Rebecca Onion, "A Hamilton Skeptic on Why the Show Is Not as Revolutionary as It Seems," *Slate*, August 5, 2016, https://slate.com/culture/2016/04/a-hamilton-critic-on-why-the-musical-isnt-so-revolutionary.html.

11. Ibid.

12. Ibid.

13. Ibid.

14. Ankeet Ball, "Ambition and Bondage: An Inquiry on Alexander Hamilton and Slavery," Seminar Paper, Columbia and Slavery, 2015.

15. Katey Rich, "George Washington Never Mentions Slavery in Hamilton, but the Actor Who Plays Him Does," *Vanity Fair*, April 29, 2016, https://www.vanityfair.com/culture/2016/04/christopher-jackson-hamilton-interview.

14. On Women's Rights, Legal Change, and Incomplete Sequels

Epigraph: Lin-Manuel Miranda, "The Schuyler Sisters," *Hamilton: An American Musical* (Atlantic Records 2015).

1. Miranda, "Take a Break," *Hamilton.*
2. Miranda, "Cabinet Battle #1," *Hamilton.*
3. Miranda, "Cabinet Battle #2," *Hamilton.*
4. Ibid.
5. Office of Management and Budget, "Uniform Administrative Requirements, Cost Principles, and Audit Requirements for Federal Awards," *Federal Register* 78, no. 248 (December 2013), https://www.govinfo.gov/content/pkg/FR-2013-12-26/pdf/2013-30465.pdf.
6. Miranda, "Non-Stop," *Hamilton.*
7. Ibid.
8. Ibid.
9. Miranda, "The Story of Tonight," *Hamilton.*
10. Miranda, "My Shot," *Hamilton.*
11. Miranda, "Cabinet Battle #1," *Hamilton.*
12. Miranda, "Who Lives, Who Dies, Who Tells Your Story?," *Hamilton.*
13. Miranda, "Alexander Hamilton," *Hamilton.*
14. Miranda, "What'd I Miss?," *Hamilton.*
15. Miranda, "The Schuyler Sisters," *Hamilton.*

15. When Your Job Is to Marry Rich

Epigraph: Stephanie Coontz, "World Historical Transformation of Marriage," *Journal of Marriage and Family* 66, no. 4 (2004): 977

1. Lin-Manuel Miranda, "Satisfied," *Hamilton: An American Musical* (Atlantic Records 2015).
2. Ibid.
3. Ibid.
4. Ibid.
5. Ibid.
6. Ibid.
7. Coontz, "World Historical Transformation of Marriage," 977.
8. Ibid.
9. Stephanie Coontz, *Marriage, a History: How Love Conquered Marriage* (New York: Penguin Books, 2005), 7.
10. Rosemarie Zagarri, *Revolutionary Backlash: Women and Politics in the Early American Republic* (Philadelphia: University of Pennsylvania Press, 2008), 51; Mary Beth Norton, "The Evolution of White Women's Experience in Early America," *American Historical Review* 89, no. 3 (1984): 617.
11. Coontz, "World Historical Transformation," 977.
12. *Bradwell v. State*, 83 U.S. 130, 131 (1872).
13. Allison Anna Tait, "The Beginning of the End of Coverture: A Reappraisal of the Married Woman's Separate Estate," *Yale Journal of Law & Feminism* 26, no. 2 (2014): 167.
14. Ibid.
15. Hon. Richard A. Dollinger, "Judicial Intervention: The Judges Who Paved the Road to Seneca Falls in 1848," *Judicial Notice* 12 (2017): 11.
16. Ruth Colker, "The Freedom to Choose to Marry," *Columbia Journal of Gender and Law* 30, no. 2 (2016): 409.

17. Joan R. Gundersen, "Independence, Citizenship, and the American Revolution," *Signs* 13, no. 1 (1987): 72.

18. Harriet Ann Jacobs, *Incidents in the Life of a Slave Girl* (Boston, MA: Thayer & Eldridge, 1861), 44–47. Thomas E Will, "Weddings on Contested Grounds: Slave Marriage in the Antebellum South," *Historian* 62, no. 1 (1999): 100–101.

19. Gary B. Nash, *Forging Freedom: The Formation of Philadelphia's Black Community, 1720–1840* (Cambridge, MA: Harvard University Press, 1988), 75–76.

20. Kenneth Stampp, *The Peculiar Institution: Slavery in the Ante-Bellum South* (New York: Knopf, 1956), 7, 350–51.

21. Annette Gordon-Reed, "Did Sally Hemings and Thomas Jefferson Love Each Other?," *American Heritage* 58, no. 5 (2008), https://www.americanheritage.com/content/did-sally-hemings-and-thomas-jefferson-love-each-other.

22. United States Department of Labor—Office of Planning and Research, *The Negro Family: The Case For National Action*, 1965, https://www.dol.gov/general/aboutdol/history/webid-moynihan.

23. Ibid., 29.

24. Linda C. McClain, "Federal Family Policy and Family Values from Clinton to Obama, 1992–2012 and Beyond," *Michigan State Law Review* 2013 (May 2014): 1644.

25. Laura Doyle, "The Long Arm of Eugenics," *American Literary History* 16, no. 3 (2004): 533–34.

26. See Tim Henderson, "For Many Millennials, Marriage Can Wait," *Pew Charitable Trusts,* December 20, 2016, https://www.pewtrusts.org/en/research-and-analysis/blogs/stateline/2016/12/20/for-many-millennials-marriage-can-wait; Victor Tan Chen, "America, Home of the Transactional Marriage," *Atlantic,* August 20, 2017, https://www.theatlantic.com/business/archive/2017/08/marriage-rates-education/536913/.

27. Naomi Cahn and June Carbone, *Marriage Markets: How Inequality Is Remaking the American Family* (Oxford: Oxford University Press, 2014); Richard Banks, *Is Marriage for White People?: How the African American Marriage Decline Effects Everyone* (New York: Dutton, 2011).

28. New Netherland Institute, "Angelica Schuyler Church [1756–1814]—Notable Dutch-American," https://www.newnetherlandinstitute.org/history-and-heritage/dutch_americans/angelica-schuyler-church1/.

29. Tom Cutterham, "The Revolutionary Transformation of American Merchant Networks: Carter and Wadsworth and Their World, 1775–1800," *Enterprise & Society* 18, no. 1 (2017): 9.

30. Mia Weber, "Telling Her Story," *New York Family,* September 2, 2016, http://www.newyorkfamily.com/renee-elise-goldsberry-telling-her-story/.

31. Ibid.

32. Coontz, *Marriage, A History,* 9.

33. Miranda, "The Schuyler Sisters," *Hamilton.*

16. "Love" Triangles

1. Lin-Manuel Miranda, "Say No To This," *Hamilton: An American Musical* (Atlantic Records 2015).

2. "Say Yes To This," YouTube video, 3:50, April 8, 2017, https://www.youtube.com/watch?v=Jj8FMujbRQU.

3. *Hamilton* paints Alexander as a victim of James Reynolds's plot to blackmail him of money, minimizing the notion that Maria was complicit in the blackmail. According to Hamilton's biographer, Ron Chernow, both Maria and her husband were likely working together

on the extortion plot. "There seems little question that [Maria] approached Hamilton as part of an extortion racket, delivering an adept performance as a despairing woman." Ron Chernow, *Alexander Hamilton* (New York: Penguin Group, 2004), 366–67.

4. Sally F. Goldfarb, "Violence against Women and the Persistence of Privacy," *Ohio State Law Journal* 61, no. 1 (2000): 6; Rachel Bangser, "Criminalizing Nonconsensual Pornography through Amending and Applying the Federal Cyberstalking Statute 18 U.S.C. S2261a," *Syracuse Journal of Science & Technology Law* 32 (2015–16): 9; Danielle Elyce Hirsch, "A Foundation upon which Justice Is Built: The Chicago Bar Foundation's Innovations to Improve Access to Justice during Tough Economic Times," *Maine Law Review* 62, no. 2 (2010): 522.

5. U.S. Library of Congress, Congressional Research Service, *The Violence Against Women Act (VAWA): Historical Overview, Funding, and Reauthorization*, by Lisa N. Sacco, R45410 (2019), 12–14.

6. Robert C. Alberts, "The Notorious Affair of Mrs. Reynolds," *American Heritage* 24, no. 2 (1973), https://www.americanheritage.com/notorious-affair-mrs-reynolds.

7. Jacob K. Cogan, "The Reynolds Affair and the Politics of Character," *Journal of the Early Republic* 16, no. 3 (1996): 417.

17. Hamilton's Dissent to the Travel Ban

Epigraph: K'naan, Snow Tha Product, Riz MC, and Residente, "Immigrants (We Get the Job Done)," track 11, *The Hamilton Mixtape*, Atlantic Records, 2016 (video: https://youtu.be/6_35a7sn6ds). 1. "Immigrants (We Get the Job Done)," YouTube video

2. Priscilla Frank, "Immigrants, They Get the Job Done in Amazing New 'Hamilton Mixtape' Video," *Huffington Post*, June 28, 2017, https://www.huffpost.com/entry/hamilton-mixtape-immigrants-video_n_5953ce88e4b0da2c73205a48.

3. Jenna Johnson, "Trump Calls for 'Total and Complete Shutdown of Muslims Entering the United States,'" *Washington Post*, December 7, 2015, https://www.washingtonpost.com/news/post-politics/wp/2015/12/07/donald-trump-calls-for-total-and-complete-shutdown-of-muslims-entering-the-united-states/?utm_term=.cbf408125ae3.

4. Leonard Pitts, Jr., "Bigotry against Muslims? Supreme Court Says, 'Tough,'" *Miami Herald*, June 30, 2018, https://www.miamiherald.com/opinion/opn-columns-blogs/leonard-pitts-jr/article214104179.html.

5. "Executive Order No. 13769 of February 1, 2017, Protecting the Nation from Foreign Terrorist Entry into the United States," *Code of Federal Regulations*, title 3 (2018): 272–77, https://www.govinfo.gov/content/pkg/CFR-2018-title3-vol1/pdf/CFR-2018-title3-vol1-eo13769.pdf.

6. Lin-Manuel Miranda, "Alexander Hamilton," *Hamilton: An American Musical* (Atlantic Records 2015).

7. Miranda, "Non-Stop," *Hamilton*.

8. Miranda, "Alexander Hamilton," *Hamilton*.

9. Miranda, "Non-Stop"; Alexander Hamilton," *Hamilton*.

10. Miranda, "Alexander Hamilton," *Hamilton*.

11. Alexander Hamilton, "My Shot," *Hamilton*.

12. Aaron Burr, "Non-Stop," *Hamilton*.

13. Miranda, "Washington on Your Side," *Hamilton*.

14. Miranda, "We Know," *Hamilton*.

15. Miranda, "Alexander Hamilton," *Hamilton*.

16. Miranda, "Who Lives, Who Dies, Who Tells Your Story," Hamilton.

17. Miranda, "The Schuyler Sisters," *Hamilton*.

18. "Thomas Paine publishes Common Sense," *History,* January 9, 2009, https://www.history.com/this-day-in-history/thomas-paine-publishes-common-sense.

19. Ibid.

20. David Bier, "America's Founders Supported Immigration," *Huffington Post,* November 20, 2012, https://www.huffingtonpost.com/david-bier/founding-fathers-on-immigration_b_1898163.html.

21. Ibid.

22. Frank, "Immigrants: They Get the Job Done."

23. "Immigrants (We Get the Job Done)," YouTube video.

24. Ibid.

25. Ibid.

26. Ibid.

27. Ibid.

28. Ibid.

29. Ibid.

30. Ibid.

31. Roisin O'Connor, "Immigrants (We Get The Job Done): Lin-Manuel Miranda Unveils Powerful Video ft. K'naan, Riz MC and K'naan," *Independent,* June 29, 2017, https://www.independent.co.uk/arts-entertainment/music/news/immigrants-we-get-the-job-done-video-lyrics-lin-manuel-miranda-riz-mc-residenta-knaan-watch-a7813786.html.

32. Frank, "Immigrants: They Get the Job Done."

33. "Immigrants (We Get the Job Done)," YouTube video.

34. Veronica Villafañe, "The Power of Lin-Manuel Miranda Makes 'Immigrants (We Get The Job Done)' Video Go Viral," *Forbes,* June 29, 2017, https://www.forbes.com/sites/veronicavillafane/2017/06/29/the-power-of-lin-manuel-miranda-makes-immigrants-we-get-the-job-done-video-go-viral/.

35. Leigh Blickley, "Lin-Manuel Miranda Believes the Muslim Ban Is 'Deeply Un-American,'" *Huffington Post,* February 3, 2017, https://www.huffingtonpost.com/entry/lin-manuel-miranda-muslim-ban-protests_us_58938f5ae4b09bd304ba4016.

36. Miranda, "History Has Its Eyes on You," "The Schuyler Sisters," and "Yorktown (The World Turned Upside Down)," *Hamilton.*

37. Ibid.

38. Michael D. Shear and Julie Hirschfeld Davis, "Trump Moves to End DACA and Calls on Congress to Act," *New York Times,* September 5, 2017, https://www.nytimes.com/2017/09/05/us/politics/trump-daca-dreamers-immigration.html.

39. Salvador Rizzo, "The Facts about Trump's Policy of Separating Families at the Border," *Washington Post,* June 19, 2018, https://www.washingtonpost.com/news/fact-checker/wp/2018/06/19/the-facts-about-trumps-policy-of-separating-families-at-the-border/.

40. Joel Rose, "Attorney General Denies Asylum to Victims of Domestic Abuse, Gang Violence," National Public Radio, June 11, 2018, https://www.npr.org/2018/06/11/618988483/attorney-general-denies-asylum-to-victims-of-domestic-abuse-gang-violence.

41. Editor's Note: After he completed this chapter, Mr. Katyal argued the case in the Court of Appeals and successfully obtained an injunction against Trump's sanctuary city policy. See https://www.courthousenews.com/wp-content/uploads/2019/02/philly-sanctuary.pdf.

42. Ben Railton, "DACA, The 1924 Immigration Act and American Exclusion," *Huffington Post,* September 7, 2017, https://www.huffingtonpost.com/entry/daca-the-1924-immigration-act-and-american-exclusion_us_59b1650ee4b0bef3378cde32.

43. Ibid.

44. *Trump v. Hawaii,* 138 S. Ct. (2018), 2447 (Sotomayor, J., joined by Ginsburg, J., dissenting).

45. Neal Kumar Katyal, "Men Who Own Women: A Thirteenth Amendment Critique of Forced Prostitution," *Yale Law Journal* 103, no. 3 (1993): 801.

46. Linda Hyman, "The Greek Slave by Hiram Powers: High Art as Popular Culture," *Art Journal* 35, no. 3 (1976): 222.

47. Katyal, "Men Who Own Women," 801.

48. Richard Hildreth, *The Slave: Or, Memoirs of Archy Moore* (Boston: Whipple & Damrell 1840), 7.

49. Victoria Moll-Ramirez, "Lin-Manuel Miranda, Celebrities Campaign to Raise Money for Immigrant Groups," NBC News, July 7, 2017, https://www.nbcnews.com/news/latino/lin-manuel-miranda-celebrities-campaign-raise-money-immigrant-groups-n78052.

50. Ibid.

51. Miranda, "History Has Its Eyes on You," *Hamilton*.

18. *Hamilton* and the Limits of Contemporary Immigration Narratives

Epigraph: K'naan, Snow Tha Product, Riz MC, and Residente, "Immigrants (We Get the Job Done)," track 11, *The Hamilton Mixtape*, Atlantic Records, 2016 (video: https://youtu.be/6_35a7sn6ds).

1. Lin-Manuel Miranda and Jeremy McCarter, *Hamilton: The Revolution* (New York: Grand Central Publishing, 2016), 33.

2. Julian Lim and Maddalena Marinari, "Laws for a Nation of Nativists and Immigrants," *Modern American History* 2, no. 1 (March 2019): 49.

3. Lin-Manuel Miranda, "Yorktown (The World Turned Upside Down)," *Hamilton: An American Musical*, Atlantic Records, 2015.

4. Lin-Manuel Miranda, verified annotation to lyrics for K'naan, Snow Tha Product, Riz MC, and Residente, "Immigrants (We Get the Job Done)," *Genius*, https://genius.com/10818685.

5. A Tribe Called Quest, "We the People . . .," *We Got It from Here . . . Thank You 4 Your Service*, track 2, Epic Records, 2016 (video: https://youtu.be/vO2Su3erRIA).

6. John Sides, Michael Tesler, and Lynn Vavreck, *Identity Crisis: The 2016 Presidential Campaign and the Battle for the Meaning of America* (Princeton: Princeton University Press, 2018), 69–96.

7. Anil Kalhan, "Deferred Action, Supervised Enforcement Discretion, and the Rule of Law Basis for Executive Action on Immigration," *UCLA Law Review Discourse* 63 (July 2015): 58–97; Rebecca Sharpless, "Immigrants Are Not Criminals: Respectability, Immigration Reform," *Houston Law Review* 53, no. 3 (February 2016): 691–765.

8. Sarah Pierce, Jessica Bolter, and Andrew Selee, Migration Policy Institute, *U.S. Immigration Policy under Trump: Deep Changes and Lasting Impacts*, July 2018; Tom Jawetz, Center for American Progress, *Restoring the Rule of Law Through a Fair, Humane, and Workable Immigration System*, July 2019. Many of the Trump-Pence presidency's initiatives have faced legal challenges, a number of which are pending and remain unresolved.

9. Asian Dub Foundation, "Journey," *Facts and Fictions*, track 5, Nation Records, 1995 (audio: https://open.spotify.com/track/7L3MTdvyf1UpwR5eSFVbu9).

10. Miranda, "Alexander Hamilton," *Hamilton*; Ron Chernow, *Alexander Hamilton* (New York: Penguin Books, 2005), 4.

11. Miranda and McCarter, *Hamilton: The Revolution*, 15, 38.

12. Miranda, "Alexander Hamilton," *Hamilton*; Miranda, "My Shot," *Hamilton*; Miranda, "The World Was Wide Enough," *Hamilton*.

13. Miranda, "We Know," *Hamilton*. Notably, even as it unsympathetically portrays Hamilton's antagonists as xenophobes, the musical, unlike Chernow's biography, overlooks

the real-life Hamilton's own xenophobia, including his support for the Alien and Sedition Acts. Chernow, *Alexander Hamilton*, 476, 570–72, 599–600, 658.

14. Renee C. Romano, "Hamilton: A New American Civic Myth," in *Historians on Hamilton: How a Blockbuster Musical Is Restaging America's Past*, ed. Renee C. Romano and Claire Bond Potter (New Brunswick, NJ: Rutgers University Press, 2018), 311; Dara Lind, "America's Immigration Agency Removes 'Nation of Immigrants' From Its Mission Statement," *Vox*, February 22, 2018, https://www.vox.com/2018/2/22/17041862/uscis-removes-nation-of-immigrants-from-mission-statement.

15. Aaron S. Fogleman, "From Slaves, Convicts, and Servants to Free Passengers: The Transformation of Immigration in the Era of the American Revolution," *Journal of American History* 85, no. 1 (June 1998): 43–76; Bernard Bailyn, *Voyagers to the West: A Passage in the Peopling of America on the Eve of the Revolution* (New York: Alfred A. Knopf, 1986), 24–28.

16. Aziz Rana, *The Two Faces of American Freedom* (Cambridge, MA: Harvard University Press, 2014); Aristide Zolberg, *A Nation by Design: Immigration Policy in the Fashioning of America* (New York: Harvard University Press, 2006); Emberson Proper, *Colonial Immigration Laws* (New York: Columbia University Press, 1900).

17. Kunal M. Parker, *Making Foreigners: Immigration and Citizenship Law in America, 1600–2000* (New York: Cambridge University Press, 2015), 24–25.

18. Ibid.

19. Zolberg, *A Nation by Design*; Rana, *The Two Faces of American Freedom*.

20. Lim and Marinari, "Laws for a Nation of Nativists and Immigrants."

21. Ibid.

22. Los Rakas, "Sueño Americano," *Free Musik 2012*, track 3, Bandcamp, 2012 (video: https://youtu.be/q3M-wri0HZg).

23. Hidetaka Hirota, *Expelling the Poor: Atlantic Seaboard States and the Nineteenth-Century Origins of American Immigration Policy* (New York: Oxford University Press, 2017).

24. Miranda, "Alexander Hamilton," *Hamilton*.

25. Walter J. Nicholls, *The DREAMers: How the Undocumented Youth Movement Transformed the Immigrant Rights Debate* (Stanford: Stanford University Press, 2013); Elizabeth Keyes, "Defining American: The DREAM Act, Immigration Reform and Citizenship," *Nevada Law Journal* 14, no. 1 (Fall 2013): 101–44.

26. Nicholls, *The DREAMers*; Sharpless, "Immigrants Are Not Criminals"

27. Nicholls, *The DREAMers*; Joel Sati, "How DACA Pits 'Good Immigrants' against Millions of Others," *Washington Post*, September 7, 2017, https://www.washingtonpost.com/news/posteverything/wp/2017/09/07/how-daca-pits-good-immigrants-against-millions-of-others/.

28. Calle 13, "Pa'l Norte," featuring Orishas, *Residente o Visitante*, track 10, Sony BMG, 2007 (video: https://youtu.be/SBYO1ZfxxSM).

29. Jillian Capewell, "Protesters Are Using 'Hamilton' Lyrics to Defend Rights across the Country," *HuffPost*, February 1, 2017, https://www.huffpost.com/entry/hamilton-lyrics-make-pretty-good-muslim-ban-protest-signs_n_58920abce4b02772c4ea8582; Romano, "Hamilton: A New American Civic Myth," 297.

30. Miranda, "The World Was Wide Enough," *Hamilton*.

31. Ibid.

19. Hamilton's Immigrant Story Today

1. For her safety, I have changed Sandra's name. I use Juan's name with his permission.

2. Lin-Manuel Miranda, "My Shot," *Hamilton: An American Musical* (Atlantic Records 2015).

3. Miranda, "Alexander Hamilton," *Hamilton*.

4. Miranda, "The World Was Wide Enough," *Hamilton*.

5. Miranda, "Alexander Hamilton," *Hamilton*.

6. Miranda, "Helpless," *Hamilton*.

7. Puerto Rico is part of the United States, but Miranda characterizes his parents' transition to New York as an immigrant experience. Two of Philippa Soo's grandparents were born in China. Oke Onaoduwan's parents are from Nigeria. And so on.

8. In contrast to immigration laws (controlling entry and exit), Congress explicitly racialized naturalization and citizenship starting in 1790, with a naturalization law limited only to "free white men." *An Act to Establish an Uniform Rule of Naturalization*, chapter III, U.S. Statutes at Large 1 (1845): 103–4.The racialization of citizenship continued through to the infamous *Dred Scott* decision, excluding enslaved and formerly enslaved people and their descendants from citizenship (Dred Scott v. Sandford, 60 U.S. 393 [1856]), a wrong rectified only by the ratification of the Fourteenth Amendment in 1868.

9. Ron Chernow, *Alexander Hamilton* (New York: Penguin Group, 2004), 59.

10. Ibid., 92.

11. This phrasing riffs off a familiar structure from Hamilton. First, General Washington tells the eager-to-fight Hamilton that "dying is easy, young man. Living is harder." And later, in "Cabinet Battle #1," the president echoes this, telling Hamilton that "winning was easy, young man. Governing's harder." Miranda, "Cabinet Battle #1," *Hamilton*.

12. "Margaret Stock, Class of 2013," MacArthur Foundation, https://www.macfound.org/fellows/904/.

13. Lin-Manuel Miranda's Hamilton "prob'ly shouldn't brag, but dag" he amazed and astonished. Miranda, "My Shot," *Hamilton*.

14. U.S. Department of State—Bureau of Consular Affairs, "Diversity Visa Program—Entry," https://travel.state.gov/content/travel/en/us-visas/immigrate/diversity-visa-program-entry.html.

15. Asylum applicants can get employment authorization once their claims have been pending 180 days, and the Trump Administration is taking steps as of this writing to undo even this. It needs to be renewed (at a $495 cost) every two years, and the renewal takes so many months that people inevitably fall between the cracks, and (illegally) lose jobs and lose their driver's licenses, too. Trust me when I say you do not want to argue with someone at the Motor Vehicle Administration about the ongoing validity of a person's status under the law when the actual work permit card is expired.

16. The average wait time in Maryland is 1,013 days, just shy of three years, and it is longer in other locations. Relief Granted by Immigration Judges in FY 2019, TRAC|Immigration, https://trac.syr.edu/phptools/immigration/court_backlog/apprep_relief.php.

17. Syracuse University's Transactional Records Access Clearinghouse has great tools for sifting through the massively disparate grant rates across immigration courts. The grant rate in Charlotte in FY2018 was 6.1 percent, and in Atlanta it was 4.5 percent, compared to Baltimore's 57.3 percent. See "Asylum Decisions," TRAC|Immigration, https://trac.syr.edu/phptools/immigration/asylum/.

18. Miranda, "Yorktown (The World Turned Upside Down)," *Hamilton*.

19. Miranda, "My Shot," *Hamilton*.

20. Miranda, "Non-Stop," *Hamilton*.

21. Miranda, "Alexander Hamilton," *Hamilton*.

22. All the grounds of inadmissibility that prevent someone from obtaining lawful immigration status in the United States are found in 8 U.S.C.A. 1182.

23. Miranda, "Blow Us All Away," *Hamilton*.

24. Immigration lawyers often hear people talk about the *ley de diez años* (the ten-year law), which would be like this kind of magic wand. But it doesn't exist. A narrow group of people can leave immigration court with a green card if they have lived here for more than ten years, but only if they can show "exceptional and extremely unusual hardship" to a U.S. citizen spouse or child. 8 U.S.C. 1229b(b)(1). That hardship needs to be substantially beyond the hardships that normally exist in deportations, like separation from family, loss of income, and more: A hard standard to meet.

25. Thomas K. McCraw, *The Founders and Finance: How Hamilton, Gallatin, and Other Immigrants Forged a New Economy* (Cambridge, MA: Belknap Press of Harvard University Press, 2012), 39.

26. Miranda, "The World Was Wide Enough," *Hamilton*.

27. Miranda, "That Would Be Enough," *Hamilton*.

28. Miranda, "Who Lives, Who Dies, Who Tells Your Story?," *Hamilton*.

20. *Hamilton*, Hip-Hop, and the Culture of Dueling in America

1. For more on the Hamilton–Burr fuel and the events leading up to it, see Ron Chernow, *Alexander Hamilton* (New York: Penguin Group, 2004), 680–722; Thomas Fleming, *Duel: Alexander Hamilton, Aaron Burr, and the Future of America* (New York: Basic Books, 1999).

2. See, e.g., Tennessee Constitution, Art 9, Sec. 3: "Any person who shall, after the adoption of this Constitution, fight a duel, or knowingly be the bearer of a challenge to fight a duel, or send or accept a challenge for that purpose, or be an aider or abettor in fighting a duel, shall be deprived of the right to hold any office of honor or profit in this state, and shall be punished otherwise, in such manner as the Legislature may prescribe." This provision was added during the constitutional convention of 1834.

3. Clayton E. Cramer, *Concealed Weapon Laws of the Early Republic: Dueling, Southern Violence, and Moral Reform* (Westport, CT: Praeger, 1999), 5–7.

4. Annie Sweeney, "Gangs Increasingly Challenge Rivals Online with Postings, Videos," *Chicago Tribune*, August 17, 2015, https://www.chicagotribune.com/news/breaking/ct-gangs-violence-internet-banging-met-20150814-story.html.

5. William Oliver Stevens, *Pistols at Ten Paces: The Story of the Code of Honor in America* (Boston: Houghton Mifflin, 1940).

6. Fleming, *Duel*, 287.

7. Joanne B. Freeman, "History as Told by the Devil Incarnate: Gore Vidal's *Burr*," in *Novel History: Historians and Novelists Confront America's Past (and Each Other)*, ed. Mark C. Carnes (New York: Simon & Schuster, 2001), 29.

8. Lin-Manuel Miranda, "Ten Duel Commandments," *Hamilton: An American Musical* (Atlantic Records 2015).

9. Stevens, *Pistols at Ten Paces*, 148.

10. Joanne B. Freeman, "Dueling as Politics: Reinterpreting the Burr-Hamilton Duel," *William and Mary Quarterly* 53, no. 2 (1996): 289.

11. Ibid., 294.

12. Ibid., 295.

13. Ibid., 296.

14. Ibid., 310–11.

15. Miranda, "The Reynolds Pamphlet," *Hamilton*.

16. Lin-Manuel Miranda and Jeremy McCarter, *Hamilton: The Revolution* (New York: Grand Central Publishing, 2016), 270.

17. Fleming, *Duel*, 303.

18. Ibid.

19. Miranda, "It's Quiet Uptown," *Hamilton.*

20. Miranda, "The World Was Wide Enough," *Hamilton.*

21. Fleming, *Duel*, 331.

22. Miranda, "The World Was Wide Enough," *Hamilton.*

23. Fleming, *Duel*, 340.

24. Miranda, "The World Was Wide Enough," *Hamilton.*

25. Fleming, *Duel*, 340.

26. Ibid., 341.

27. Stevens, *Pistols at Ten Paces*, 159.

28. Ibid., 163–64.

29. Ibid., 160–61.

30. Harwell Wells, "The End of the Affair? Anti-Dueling Laws and Social Norms in Antebellum America," *Vanderbilt Law Review* 54, no. 4 (2001): 1823. Wells also notes the advice given to duelist/President Andrew Jackson by his mother: "Never tell a lie, nor take what
is not your own, nor sue anybody for slander, assault and battery. *Always settle them cases
yourself.*" (Quoted in Charles Synor, "The Southerner and the Laws," *Journal of Southern
History* 6, no. 1 [1940]: 12.)

31. "Pistol Dueling in the Olympics," *Lock, Stock and History*, August 12, 2016, http://pea
shooter85.tumblr.com/post/148613868822/pistol-dueling-in-the-olympics-one-of-the-lesser.

32. Philip Wegmann, "That Time Zell Miller Challenged Chris Matthews to a Duel,"
Washington Examiner, March 23, 2018, https://www.washingtonexaminer.com/opinion/
that-time-zell-miller-challenged-chris-matthews-to-a-duel-on-air.

33. See Glenn Harlan Reynolds, *The Social Media Upheaval* (New York: Encounter
Books, 2019), 27–29, for a discussion of the role of social media in making today's political
class more combative and sensitive to personal insults.

21. Alexander Hamilton, Citizen-Protector?

1. Jennifer Carlson, *Citizen-Protectors: The Everyday Politics of Guns in an Age of Decline* (Oxford: Oxford University Press, 2015).

2. Lin-Manuel Miranda, "My Shot," *Hamilton: An American Musical* (Atlantic Records
2015).

3. The first American law mandating carry of firearms was a 1619 Virginia statute stating, "all suche as beare armes shall bring their pieces, swords, pouder, and shotte." The law
was revised in 1632 to state, "All men that are fittinge to beare arms, shall bring their pieces
to church." Nicholas Johnson et al., *Firearms Law and the Second Amendment: Regulation,
Rights, and Policy*, 2nd ed. (New York: Wolters Kluwer, 2018), 183–85.

4. Ibid., 185–86.

5. Ibid., 285.

6. Miranda, "My Shot," *Hamilton.*

7. Ibid.

8. Ibid.

9. Johnson et al., *Firearms Law*, 285.

10. Ibid., 283–85.

11. Ibid., 185–86.

12. Ibid., 175–86.

13. Ibid., 292.

14. Ibid., 283.

15. Miranda, "The Room Where It Happens," *Hamilton*. Dueling in revolutionary times was regarded as misuse of firearms, and banned in a number of states, including New York and Rhode Island. Later, in the antebellum South, many states banned concealed carry, most likely to prevent dueling. Open carry was appropriate for honest citizens; "concealed carry was a dubious practice characteristic only of thugs, robbers, duelers, and other deplorables." Johnson et al., *Firearms Law*, 297, 372, 381. Recent precedents still reference these antidueling regulations as the type of "presumptively lawful" laws that passed muster under *District of Columbia v. Heller*.

16. Miranda, "My Shot," *Hamilton*.

17. Ibid.

18. Miranda, "You'll Be Back," *Hamilton*.

19. Miranda, "Right Hand Man," *Hamilton*.

20. Johnson et al., *Firearms Law*, 332.

21. Miranda, "Right Hand Man," *Hamilton*.

22. Miranda, "A Winter's Ball," *Hamilton*.

23. Miranda, "Ten Duel Commandments," *Hamilton*.

24. Lin-Manuel Miranda and Jeremy McCarter, *Hamilton: The Revolution* (New York: Grand Central Publishing, 2016), 95.

25. Miranda, "Ten Duel Commandments," *Hamilton*.

26. Ibid.

27. Miranda, "Meet Me Inside," *Hamilton*.

28. Miranda, "Yorktown (The World Turned Upside Down)," *Hamilton*.

29. Ibid.

30. Miranda, "Dear Theodosia," *Hamilton*.

31. Miranda, "Non-Stop," *Hamilton*.

32. Ibid.

33. Miranda, "The Room Where It Happens," *Hamilton*

34. Miranda, "Washington On Your Side," *Hamilton*.

35. Miranda, "The Adams Administration," *Hamilton*.

36. Miranda, "Hurricane," *Hamilton*.

37. Miranda, "Blow Us All Away," *Hamilton*.

38. Ibid.

39. Ibid.

40. Ibid.

41. Miranda, "Your Obedient Servant," *Hamilton*.

42. Ibid.

43. Fla Stat. § 790.338. The Eleventh Circuit struck down key provisions of this act in *Wollschlaeger v. Governor of Florida*, 843 F.3d 1293 (11th Cir. 2017) (en banc).

44. Ind. Code § 34-38-8-6.

45. Corinne Segal, "'Hamilton' Cuts Guns from Tony Performance," PBS NewsHour, June 12, 2016, https://www.pbs.org/newshour/arts/hamilton-cuts-guns-from-tony-performance.

46. Daniel Kreps, "See Lin-Manuel Miranda, Ben Platt Perform at March for Our Lives Rally," *Rolling Stone*, March 24, 2018, https://www.rollingstone.com/music/music-news/see-lin-manuel-miranda-ben-platt-perform-at-march-for-our-lives-rally-201906/.

22. We Will Never Be Satisfied

Epigraph: Lin-Manuel Miranda, "Cabinet Battle #1," and "Take a Break," *Hamilton: An American Musical* (Atlantic Records 2015).

1. Miranda, "What'd I Miss," *Hamilton.*

2. Miranda, "Cabinet Battle #1," *Hamilton.*

3. Ibid.

4. Miranda, "What'd I Miss," *Hamilton.*

5. Ibid.

6. Ibid.

7. Alexander Hamilton, "Hamilton's Opinion as to the Constitutionality of the Bank of the United States: 1791," Yale Law School Lillian Goldman Law Library, https://avalon.law.yale.edu/18th_century/bank-ah.asp.

8. Ibid.

9. Thomas Jefferson, "Jefferson's Opinion on the Constitutionality of a National Bank: 1791," Yale Law School Lillian Goldman Law Library, http://avalon.law.yale.edu/18th_century/bank-tj.asp.

10. *McCulloch v. Maryland*, 17 U.S. (4 Wheat.) 421 (1819).

11. 22 U.S. (9 Wheat.) 1 (1824), 197.

12. Jefferson, "Jefferson's Opinion on the Constitutionality of the Bank."

13. *Nat'l Fed'n of Indep. Bus. v. Sebelius*, 132 S. Ct. 2588 (2012) (opinion of Roberts, C.J.).

14. Ibid., 2589.

15. See Ian Millhiser, "Worse Than Lochner," *Yale Law & Policy Review Inter Alia*, November 15, 2011, https://ylpr.yale.edu/inter_alia/worse-lochner. ("The genius of the legal arguments against the ACA . . . is that they construct a rule that fingers just one provision of the United States Code—the ACA's minimum coverage provision—as unconstitutional, while leaving constitutionally similar laws—such as the ban on whites-only lunch counters or Congress's power to condemn land—intact.")

16. *United States v. Butler*, 297 US 65 (1936).

17. U.S. Constitution, Art. 1, Sec. 8.

18. See Andrew Jackson, "President Jackson's Veto Message Regarding the Bank of the United States; July 10, 1832," Yale Law School Lillian Goldman Law Library, http://avalon.law.yale.edu/19th_century/ajveto01.asp ("many of the powers and privileges conferred on it can not be supposed necessary for the purpose for which it is proposed to be created, and are not, therefore, means necessary to attain the end in view, and consequently not justified by the Constitution").

19. See James Buchanan, "February 24, 1859: Veto Message Regarding Land-Grant Colleges," University of Virginia Miller Center, https://millercenter.org/the-presidency/presidential-speeches/february-24-1859-veto-message-regarding-land-grant-colleges (claiming that the tax and spending power is "confined to the execution of the enumerated powers delegated to Congress").

20. Confederate States Constitution, Art. 1, Sec. 8.

21. Melville Fuller, "Jefferson and Hamilton," *Dial* 4 (May–April 1883–1884): 4, https://babel.hathitrust.org/cgi/pt?id=mdp.39015030979515&view=1up&seq=18.

22. Ibid.

23. Miranda, "Washington on Your Side," *Hamilton.*

24. Ian Millhiser, *Injustices: The Supreme Court's History of Comforting the Comfortable and Afflicting the Afflicted* (New York: Nation Books, 2015), 53.

25. Ibid., 20.

26. Ibid., 45.

27. U.S. Constitution, Art. 1, Sec. 8.

28. See, e.g., *United States v. Lopez*, 514 U.S. 586 (1995) (Thomas, J., concurring). ("Alexander Hamilton, for example, repeatedly treated commerce, agriculture, and manufacturing as three separate endeavors.")

29. Jefferson, "Jefferson's Opinion on the Constitutionality of the Bank."

30. *Nat'l Fedn. of Indep. Business v. Sebelius*, 132 S. Ct. 2643 (2012) (joint dissent of Scalia, Kennedy, Thomas, and Alito, JJ.).

31. Ibid., 114 (quoting Gibbons v. Ogden, 22 U.S. (9 Wheat.) 1, 196 (1824)).

32. Ibid., 119. Indeed, *Darby* is one of the most important decisions of the New Deal era because it lays out the textual basis for modern commerce and necessary and proper clause jurisprudence.

33. Miranda, "Cabinet Battle #1," *Hamilton*.

34. Millhiser, *Injustices*, 203.

35. Ibid., 209.

36. Ian Millhiser, "How Conservatives Abandoned Judicial Restraint, Took Over the Courts and Radically Transformed America," *ThinkProgress*, November 19, 2013, https://thinkprogress.org/how-conservatives-abandoned-judicial-restraint-took-over-the-courts-and-radically-transformed-3da3115c81c0/.

37. Miranda, "Cabinet Battle #1," *Hamilton*.

23. Hamilton, Burr, and Defamation

1. Lin-Manuel Miranda, "Your Obedient Servant," *Hamilton: An American Musical* (Atlantic Records 2015).

2. Miranda, "The Election of 1800," *Hamilton*.

3. Ron Chernow, *Alexander Hamilton* (New York: Penguin Group, 2004), 681.

4. Miranda, "Your Obedient Servant," *Hamilton*.

5. Chernow, *Alexander Hamilton*, 681–82.

6. Joseph J. Ellis, *Founding Brothers: The Revolutionary Generation* (New York: Vintage Books, 2000), 34.

7. Ibid., 42–43.

8. Ibid., 42.

9. You can read the first of Cicero's Orations against Catiline here: Cicero, "The First Oration Against Catiline," in *The World's Famous Orations*, vol. 2, ed. William Jennings Bryan (New York: Funk and Wagnalls, 1906), https://www.bartleby.com/268/2/11.html.

10. Miranda, "Non-Stop," *Hamilton*.

11. Chernow, *Alexander Hamilton*, 681.

12. Miranda, "Non-Stop," *Hamilton*.

13. Shannon M. Heim, "The Role of Extra-Judicial Bodies in Vindicating Reputational Harm," *CommLaw Conspectus* 15 (2007): 402.

14. Robert T. Langdon, "The Communications Decency Act § 230: Make Sense or Nonsense?," *St. John's Law Review* 73, no. 54 (1999): 839.

15. J. Skelly Wright, "The Federal Courts and the Nature and Quality of State Law," *Wayne Law Review* 13 (1967): 333.

16. William L. Prosser, "Interstate Publication," *Michigan Law Review* 51 (1955): 971–78.

17. *New York Times v. Sullivan*, 376 U.S. 254 (1964).

18. See Stephen Holden, "Putting the Hip-Hop in History as Founding Fathers Rap," *New York Times*, January 12, 2012, https://www.nytimes.com/2012/01/13/arts/music/hamilton-mixtape-by-lin-manuel-miranda-at-allen-room.html. ("[Hamilton's] fatal duel with Burr echoes the kind of verbal and territorial skirmishes that preceded the deaths of Biggie Smalls and Tupac Shakur.")

19. Miranda, "Your Obedient Servant," *Hamilton*.

20. Miranda, "The World Was Wide Enough," *Hamilton*.

21. John C. Miller, *Alexander Hamilton and the Growth of the New Nation* (New Brunswick, NJ: Transaction Publishers, 2017), 570.

22. Miranda, "Your Obedient Servant," *Hamilton*.

23. Ibid.

24. Chernow, *Alexander Hamilton*, 684.

25. Miranda, "The World Was Wide Enough," *Hamilton*.

24. Elections as Duels

Thanks to my student Maddie Loeffler for providing valuable research assistance as I wrote this chapter and to Kati Alford, Will Carroll, Ned Foley, and Paul Salamanca for comments on an early draft (they had "some questions, a couple of suggestions"). Lin-Manuel Miranda, "Right Hand Man," *Hamilton: An American Musical* (Atlantic Records 2015).

1. Miranda, "The Election of 1800," *Hamilton*.

2. Ibid.

3. Ibid.

4. Ibid.

5. Miranda, "The Room Where It Happens."

6. See Nathan L. Colvin and Edward B. Foley, "The Twelfth Amendment: A Constitutional Ticking Time Bomb," *University of Miami Law Review* 64, no. 2 (2010): 485.

7. John Ferling, *Adams vs. Jefferson: The Tumultuous Election of 1800* (Oxford: Oxford University Press, 2004), 180.

8. Miranda, "The Election of 1800," *Hamilton*.

9. Ibid.

10. Jeremy D. Bailey, *Thomas Jefferson and Executive Power* (Cambridge: Cambridge University Press, 2007), 143–45.

11. Ibid., 140.

12. Joshua D. Hawley, "The Transformative Twelfth Amendment," *William & Mary Law Review* 55, no. 4 (2014): 1538–39.

13. Ibid., 1539.

14. Ibid., 1538.

15. Miranda, "Hurricane," *Hamilton*.

16. *The Federalist* No. 68 (Hamilton).

17. Ibid.

18. Ibid.

19. Ibid.

20. "From Alexander Hamilton to John Jay, 7 May 1800," Founders Online, https://founders.archives.gov/documents/Hamilton/01-24-02-0378. [Originally published in *The Papers of Alexander Hamilton*, vol. 24, *November 1799–June 1800*, ed. Harold C. Syrett (New York: Columbia University Press, 1976), 464–67.]

21. Hamilton, *The Federalist* No. 68 (Hamilton).

22. Hawley, "The Transformative Twelfth Amendment," 540.

23. "From Thomas Jefferson to Albert Gallatin, 18 September 1801," Founders Online, https://founders.archives.gov/documents/Jefferson/01-35-02-0245. [Originally published in *The Papers of Thomas Jefferson*, vol. 35, ed. Barbara B. Oberg (Princeton: Princeton University Press, 2008), 314–15.]

24. Tadahisa Kuroda, *The Origins of the Twelfth Amendment: The Electoral College in the Early Republic, 1787–1804* (Westport, CT: Greenwood Press, 1994), 129.

25. Ibid., 172.

26. Miranda, "The Election of 1800," *Hamilton*.

27. For additional thoughts on how to fix our current elections, see Joshua A. Douglas, *Vote for US: How to Take Back Our Elections and Change the Future of Voting* (Amherst, NY: Prometheus Books, 2019).

28. Miranda, "The Election of 1800," *Hamilton*.

25. Modern-Day Protests

Thank you to my husband, Ronald Alan Norwood, Esquire, to my former research assistants Martin Martinez and David Reck, and to my former colleague Katherine Goldwasser. All provided valuable insights and edits.

Epigraph: Patrick Henry, Virginia House of Burgesses, Speech delivered on March 23, 1775, http://www.ushistory.org/declaration/related/henry.html.

1. "A Biography of Alexander Hamilton (1755–1804): 'I wish there was a war,'" American History from Revolution to Reconstruction and Beyond, http://www.let.rug.nl/usa/bio graphies/alexander-hamilton/i-wish-there-was-a-war.php.

2. Lin-Manuel Miranda, "Right Hand Man," *Hamilton: An American Musical* (Atlantic Records 2015).

3. "Rare Books, Special Collections and Preservation," Frederick Douglass Project Writings: West India Emancipation, University of Rochester, https://rbscp.lib.rochester.edu/4398.

4. Chris Hayes, "Policing the Colony: From the American Revolution to Ferguson," *Nation*, March 29, 2017, https://www.thenation.com/article/policing-the-colony-from-the-american-revolution-to-ferguson/.

5. "Roughly 1,264,000 American soldiers have died in the nation's wars—620,000 in the Civil War and 644,000 in all other conflicts. It was only as recently as the Vietnam War that the number of American deaths in foreign wars eclipsed the number who died in the Civil War." "Civil War Facts," American Battlefield Trust, https://www.battlefields.org/learn/articles/civil-war-facts.

6. Terence McArdle, "'Night of Terror': The Suffragists Who Were Beaten and Tortured for Seeking the Vote," *Washington Post*, November 10, 2017, https://www.washingtonpost.com/news/retropolis/wp/2017/11/10/night-of-terror-the-suffragists-who-were-beaten-and-tor tured-for-seeking-the-vote/?utm_term=.e95e60aeae5e. Black women would not gain the right to vote until the Voting Rights Act of 1965. See Raquel Solla, "The 19th Amendment Did Not Affect All Women: The Fight for Voting Rights Is still a Struggle," Odyssey, August 16, 2016, https://www.theodysseyonline.com/the-19th-amendment-did-not-allow-women-to-vote.

7. Katie Nodjimbadem, "The Long, Painful History of Police Brutality in the U.S.," Smithsonian.com, July 17, 2017, https://www.smithsonianmag.com/smithsonian-institution/long-painful-history-police-brutality-in-the-us-180964098/. See also "Selma to Montgomery March," History.com, January 28, 2010, https://www.history.com/topics/black-history/selma-montgomery-march.

8. Nick Carbone, "Civil Rights," *Time*, October 12, 2011, http://content.time.com/time/specials/packages/article/0,28804,2096654_2096653_2096693,00.html.

9. Sophie Gilbert, "Hamilton's Peaceful Protest," *Atlantic*, June 29, 2017, https://www.theatlantic.com/entertainment/archive/2017/06/hamiltons-peaceful-protest/532212.

10. Eric Bradner, "Pence: 'I wasn't offended' by Message of 'Hamilton' Cast," CNN, November 20, 2016, https://www.cnn.com/2016/11/20/politics/mike-pence-hamilton-message-trump/index.html.

11. Marlene Lenthang, "Hamilton actor reveals he's received HUNDREDS of death threats after telling Mike Pence at his show 'diverse America does not believe the administration will protect them,'" *Daily Mail*, June 21, 2018, https://www.dailymail.co.uk/news/article-5872091/Hamilton-actor-reveals-received-HUNDREDS-death-threats-following-Mike-Pence-address.html.

12. Jane Coaston, "2 Years of NFL Protests, Explained," *Vox*, September 4, 2018, https://www.vox.com/2018/8/15/17619122/kaepernick-trump-nfl-protests-2018, ¶ 3.

13. Will Brinson, "Here's How Nate Boyer Got Colin Kaepernick to Go from Sitting to Kneeling, HBO's 'Real Sports' Spoke to the Former Green Beret," CBS Sports,

September 27, 2016, https://www.cbssports.com/nfl/news/heres-how-nate-boyer-got-colin-kaepernick-to-go-from-sitting-to-kneeling/. Kaepernick's teammate, Eric Reid joined Kaepernick in his protest that day. As Reid recalled: "After hours of careful consideration, and even a visit from Nate Boyer, a retired Green Beret and former N.F.L. player, we came to the conclusion that we should kneel, rather than sit. . . . We chose to kneel because it's a respectful gesture." Eric Reid, "Eric Reid: Why Colin Kaepernick and I Decided to Take a Knee," *New York Times*, September 25, 2017, https://www.nytimes.com/2017/09/25/opinion/colin-kaepernick-football-protests.html.

14. Coaston, "2 Years of NFL Protests."

15. Bryan Graham, "Donald Trump Blasts NFL Anthem Protesters: 'Get that son of a bitch off the field,'" *Guardian*, September 23, 2017, https://www.theguardian.com/sport/2017/sep/22/donald-trump-nfl-national-anthem-protests.

16. Ibid.

17. Anne Branigin, "4 of out 5 Kennesaw State University Cheerleaders Who Protested during National Anthem Cut from 2018 Squad," Root, August 29, 2018, https://www.theroot.com/4-out-of-5-kennesaw-state-university-cheerleaders-cut-f-1828690214; Ashley Johnson, "College Cheerleaders Who Knelt during National Anthem Cut from Squad," WCNC, August 23, 2018, https://www.wcnc.com/article/news/politics/college-cheerleaders-who-knelt-during-national-anthem-cut-from-squad/275-586849535.

18. See, e.g., Johnson, "College Cheerleaders." A lawsuit filed by Kaepernick against the NFL for conspiring to keep him from being rehired settled. Edvard Pettersson, "Colin Kaepernick Settles Blacklisting Lawsuit Against NFL," Bloomberg, February 15, 2019, https://www.bloomberg.com/news/articles/2019-02-15/colin-kaepernick-settles-blacklisting-lawsuit-against-nfl.

19. Paul Szoldra and Christopher Woody, "Soldiers Speak Out on Kaepernick: His Protest 'makes him more American than anyone,'" *Business Insider*, September 25, 2017, https://www.businessinsider.com/veterans-colin-kaepernick-2016-9.

20. Emily Sullivan, "Laura Ingraham Told LeBron James to Shut Up and Dribble; He Went to the Hoop," NPR, February 19, 2018, https://www.npr.org/sections/thetwo-way/2018/02/19/587097707/laura-ingraham-told-lebron-james-to-shutup-and-dribble-he-went-to-the-hoop.

21. Ibid.

22. Harry Edwards, *The Revolt of the Black Athlete* (Urbana: University of Illinois Press, 2017).

23. Joseph M. Sheehan, "2 Black Power Advocates Ousted From Olympics," *New York Times*, October 18, 1968, http://movies2.nytimes.com/learning/general/onthisday/big/1018.html#article.

24. "Muhammad Ali," History.com, December 16, 2009, https://www.history.com/topics/black-history/muhammad-ali.

25. Jeff Zillgitt, "'Shut Up and Dribble': LeBron James-Produced Documentary Looks at Alternative History of NBA," *USA Today*, November 2, 2018, https://www.usatoday.com/story/sports/nba/2018/11/02/lebron-james-shut-up-and-dribble-documentary/1857312002/.

26. "From Youth to College Football, Lynching Threats Reported over Anthem Kneeling," CBS News, September 28, 2016, https://www.cbsnews.com/news/youth-college-football-beaumont-nebraska-national-anthem-kneel-death-lynching-threats/.

27. Jasmine Washington, "Roc Nation Gets Case Dismissed for Sixth-Grade Pledge Protester," *Ebony*, March 6, 2019, https://www.ebony.com/news/roc-nation-gets-case-dismissed-for-sixth-grade-pledge-protester/.

28. *West Virginia State Board of Education v. Barnette*, 319 U.S. 624 (1943).

29. Bloomberg, "The Trump Administration's Latest Idea to Hit Back at Its Opponents: Charge Them for Protesting," *Fortune*, October 12, 2018, http://fortune.com/2018/10/12/trump-protests-white-house-national-mall/.

30. Arthur Spitzer, "Trump Administration Seeks to Stifle Protests Near White House and on National Mall," ACLU, October 9, 2018, https://www.aclu.org/blog/free-speech/rights-protesters/trump-administration-seeks-stifle-protests-near-white-house-and.

31. Christopher Ingraham, "Republican Lawmakers Introduce Bills to Curb Protesting in at Least 18 States," *Washington Post*, February 24, 2017, https://www.washingtonpost.com/news/wonk/wp/2017/02/24/republican-lawmakers-introduce-bills-to-curb-protesting-in-at-least-17-states/?utm_term=.46c38320160b.

32. Elizabeth Day, "#BlackLivesMatter: the Birth of a New Civil Rights Movement," *Guardian*, July 19, 2015, https://www.theguardian.com/world/2015/jul/19/blacklivesmatter-birth-civil-rights-movement.

33. Ibid.

34. A.L., "Black Lives Matter Is Not a Terrorist Organization," *Economist*, August 9, 2018, https://www.economist.com/open-future/2018/08/09/black-lives-matter-is-not-a-terrorist-organisation.

35. Aileen B. Flores, Construction of Trump Border Wall to Begin Saturday in El Paso, Border Patrol Announces," *El Paso Times*, September 21, 2018, https://www.elpasotimes.com/story/news/2018/09/21/construction-trump-border-wall-begin-el-paso-chihuahuita-september/1379571002.

36. Joe Heim, Marissa Lang, and Susan Svrluga, "Thousands of Students Walk Out of School in Nationwide Gun Violence Protest," *Washington Post*, March 14, 2018, https://www.washingtonpost.com/news/education/wp/2018/03/14/students-have-just-had-enough-walkouts-planned-across-the-nation-one-month-after-florida-shooting/?utm_term=.a55a542a4fc6.

37. Auditi Guha, "Republicans Rush to Outlaw Protests Against Oil Pipeline in South Dakota (Updated)," *Rewire*, March 19, 2019, https://rewire.news/article/2019/03/19/republicans-rush-to-outlaw-protests-against-oil-pipeline-in-south-dakota.

38. Brian Freeman, "LGBTQ Groups to Hold Protests Over Reported Trump Plan on Gender Policy," Newsmax, October 21, 2018, https://www.newsmax.com/politics/lgbtq-demonstrations-donald-trump-gender/2018/10/21/id/887294.

39. Amanda C. Coyne, "Large Crowd Marches at Capitol against Georgia's 'Heartbeat' Abortion Law," *Atlanta Journal-Constitution*, May 25, 2019, https://www.ajc.com/news/happening-now-protesters-begin-march-capitol-against-georgia-heartbeat-abortion-law/hcYPzgvWWquoQsf3BkSyQN/.

40. Sasha Ingber, "Protesters across the Country Rally against Trump's Immigration Policies," NPR, June 30, 2018, https://www.npr.org/2018/06/30/624950726/protesters-across-the-country-rally-against-trumps-immigration-policies.

41. Lauren Gambino, Steven Thrasher, and Kayla Epstein, "Thousands March to Protest against Police Brutality in Major US Cities," *Guardian*, December 14, 2014, https://www.theguardian.com/us-news/2014/dec/13/marchers-protest-police-brutality-new-york-washington-boston.

42. Rex Huppke, "Muslims Are Not Welcome in America, and That Is Exactly Who We Are," *Chicago Tribune*, June 28, 2018, http://www.chicagotribune.com/news/opinion/huppke/ct-met-travel-ban-trump-huppke-20180627-story.html; Emma Whitford, "Racist Rant on Q Train: 'Get The F**k Out Of My Country," *Gothamist*, August 11, 2017, http://gothamist.com/2017/08/11/subway_q_train_racist_rant.php; Peter Wade, "Watch This Trump Supporter Yell, 'Go Back to Africa!' at African American Protestors," *Esquire*, March 12, 2016, https://www.esquire.com/news-politics/news/a42966/trump-protester-go-back-to-africa.

43. AP, "Man Who Drove through Protest and Killed Activist Heather Heyer Convicted of First-Degree Murder," *London Free Press*, December 7, 2018, https://lfpress.com/news/world/closing-arguments-expected-in-white-nationalist-trial/wcm/dd645d4c-a164-4402-831d-9b8efdf4c0eb.

44. Huppke, "Muslims Are Not Welcome."

45. Brett Samuels, "Trump Ramps up Rhetoric on Media, Calls Press 'the Enemy of the People,'" The Hill, April 5, 2019, https://thehill.com/homenews/administration/437610-trump-calls-press-the-enemy-of-the-people.

46. *Martin v. Gross*, 340 F. Supp. 3d 87 (D. Mass. 2018); *Glik v. Cunniffe*, 655 F.3d 78 (1st Cir. 2011); *ACLU v. Alvarez*, 679 F.3d 583 (7th Cir. 2012); *Gericke v. Begin*, 753 F.3d 1 (2014).

47. "Dick Gregory: I Chose to Be an Agitator," 60 Minutes, August 21, 2017, https://www.cbsnews.com/news/dick-gregory-i-chose-to-be-an-agitator/.

48. Ishmael Reed, "CounterPunch on Stage: The Haunting of Lin-Manuel Miranda," Counterpunch, April 12, 2019, https://www.counterpunch.org/2019/04/12/counterpunch-on-stage-the-haunting-of-lin-manuel-miranda/:

> Like The Star Spangled Banner, "Hamilton, The Revolution" is some noisy, brassy state art, which pushes the creation myth that Alexander Hamilton and others were abolitionists. When, like the writer of The Star Spangled Banner, they were hypocrites. Next time you sing the lines, . . . "and the land of the free," remember that those lines were penned by Francis Scott Keyes, a wealthy slave owner. Historians who make a living lionizing those who, if they were around today, would be charged with war crimes, offer Hamilton and his father-in-law, Philip Schuyler, membership in The New York Manumission Society as proof of Hamilton's devotion to emancipation. The members of the Manumission Society were abolitionists who refused to give up their slaves.

26. "Every Action's an Act of Creation"

1. In the United States, the fair use doctrine considers several factors: (1) What's the purpose of the new use, including whether it's transformative and whether it's commercial? (2) How creative was the original work, and how much was factual? (3) How much of the original did the new work use? (4) Finally, what's the effect of the new use on the market for the original work? 17 U.S.C. § 107.

2. Alexis Petridis, "Break It Down: How Hamilton Mashed Up Musical Theatre and Hiphop," *Guardian*, December 1, 2017, https://www.theguardian.com/stage/2017/dec/01/hamilton-mashed-up-musical-theatre-and-hiphop-lin-manuel-miranda (noting reliance on Broadway conventions as well as on hip-hop antecedents).

3. Ron Chernow, *Alexander Hamilton* (New York: Penguin Group, 2004).

4. Aja Romano, "Hamilton is Fanfic, and Its Historical Critics Are Totally Missing the Point," *Vox*, July 4, 2016, https://www.vox.com/2016/4/14/11418672/hamilton-is-fanfic-not-historically-inaccurate.

5. Ibid.

6. Audre Lorde, "The Master's Tools Will Never Dismantle the Master's House," in *Sister Outsider: Essays and Speeches* (Berkeley, CA: Crossing Press, 2007), 110–14.

7. Romano, "Hamilton Is Fanfic."

8. Essay originally appeared as Richard Primus, "Will Lin-Manuel Miranda Transform the Supreme Court?," *Atlantic*, June 4, 2016, https://www.theatlantic.com/politics/archive/2016/06/lin-manuel-miranda-and-the-future-of-originalism/485651/.

9. Ibid.

10. Ibid.

11. Ibid.

12. Forrest Wickman, "All the Hip-Hop References in Hamilton: A Track-by-Track Guide," *Slate*, September 24, 2015, http://www.slate.com/blogs/browbeat/2015/09/24/hamilton_s_hip_hop_references_all_the_rap_and_r_b_allusions_in_lin_manuel.html; Alex Beggs, "Read Lin-Manuel Miranda's Genius Annotations for Hamilton," *Vanity Fair*,

November 2, 2015, https://www.vanityfair.com/culture/2015/11/hamilton-lyrics-genius-lin-manuel-miranda (noting that LL Cool J, the author of one licensed work, tried to get a removed line reinstated, but it wasn't because Miranda decided that it generated a laugh at the wrong point in the scene, which introduces Maria Reynolds and "Say No to This").

13. "The model of a modern major general" is an echo of Gilbert & Sullivan's song with nearly the same phrase, but with a better (in Miranda's view) rhyme.

14. "Here Are All the Classical Music References in Hamilton," Classic FM, December 6, 2017, https://www.classicfm.com/discover-music/classical-music-hamilton-lin-manuel-miranda/.

15. Larry Iser, "'Hamilton' Part II—Why Lin-Manuel Miranda Didn't Really Need to Clear the Music," *Forbes*, June 27, 2016, https://www.forbes.com/sites/legalentertainment/2016/06/27/hamilton-part-ii-why-lin-manuel-miranda-didnt-really-need-to-clear-the-music/#7fec5faf45d5.

16. A court reasoned similarly when a criminal named Rick Ross sued a rapper who'd adopted the same name and a corresponding criminal persona: the rapper had added a huge amount of creativity and meaning to the original.

17. Kajikawa, Loren. "'Young, Scrappy, and Hungry': Hamilton, Hip Hop, and Race," *American Music* 36, no. 4 (2018): 474.

18. Beggs, "Read Lin-Manuel Miranda's Genius Annotations" (quoting Miranda).

19. Lin-Manuel Miranda, "My Shot," *Hamilton: An American Musical* (Atlantic Records 2015).

20. Richard Rodgers and Oscar Hammerstein II, "You've Got to Be Carefully Taught," *South Pacific* (1949).

21. Jason Robert Brown, "Nobody Needs to Know," *The Last Five Years* (2002).

22. Copyright Office regulations provide that "words and short phrases such as names, titles, and slogans" are "not subject to copyright." Material Not Subject to Copyright, 37 C.F.R. § 202.1 (2018). Recent lawsuits that have allowed liability findings based on small similarities between songs make this conclusion a bit more uncertain, See, e.g., *TufAmerica, Inc. v. Diamond*, 968 F.Supp.2d 588 (S.D.N.Y. 2013) (denying motion to dismiss copyright claim against defendant who used the lyrical phrase and recording "say what" sampled from plaintiff's song). But both normatively and descriptively, especially in the absence of repetition or musical similarity, it's still the best rule to say that infringement requires more than copying a short phrase.

23. Jim Gibson, "Risk Aversion and Rights Accretion in Intellectual Property Law," *Yale Law Journal* 116, no. 5 (2007).

24. Iser, "'Hamilton' Part II" (reporting that Deborah Mannis-Gardner, who cleared the music references, agreed that Hamilton was making fair use but understood that "Miranda specifically wanted to license all of his references to prior music out of respect").

25. Richard Morgan, "How Hamilton's Cast Got Broadway's Best Deal," Bloomberg, September 28, 2016, https://www.bloomberg.com/features/2016-hamilton-broadway-profit/.

26. Ibid.

27. Ibid. (quoting understudy Sascha Hutchings).

28. Terry Teachout, "'Hamilton' Review: A Star-Spangled Success," *Wall Street Journal*, February 19, 2015, https://www.wsj.com/articles/hamilton-review-a-star-spangled-success-1424385184.

29. Roland Barthes, *S/Z*, trans. Richard Miller (New York: Hill and Wang, 1974), 4–5.

27. Hollering to Be Heard

1. Lin-Manuel Miranda, "Guns and Ships," *Hamilton: An American Musical* (Atlantic Records 2015).

2. 17 U.S.C.§ 102.

3. Oren Bracha, "Not De minimis: (Improper) Appropriation in Copyright," *American University Law Review* 68, no. 1 (2018): 156–57.

4. Ibid., 157.

5. Miranda, "Take a Break," *Hamilton.*

6. Ibid.

7. Ibid.

8. Ibid.

9. Ibid.

10. Cases that found infringement and rejected the de minimis doctrine include *Bridgeport Music Inc. v. Dimension Films*, 410 F.3d 800–01 (6th Cir. 2005) (unauthorized sampling of a sound recording); *Ringgold v. Black Entm't Television, Inc.*, 126 F. 3d 77 (2d Cir. 1997) (unauthorized display of artwork in television program). Cases that applied the de minimis doctrine and found no infringement include *Newton v. Diamond*, 388 F.3d 1193 (9th Cir. 2004) (authorized use of sound recording with unauthorized use of musical composition); *Sandoval v. New Line Cinema Corp.*, 147 F.3d 218 (2d Cir. 1998) (unauthorized background use of photos in film); *Gottlieb Dev. LLC v. Paramount Pictures Corp.*, 590 F. Supp. 2d 631 (S.D.N.Y. 2008) (unauthorized display of pinball machine's copyrighted logo in the background of film shots); *VMG Salsoul, LLC v. Ciccone*, 824 F.3d 890 9th Cir. 2016.

11. Robert W. Clarida and Robert J. Bernstein, "Judges Gonna Judge: When Are Short Phrases Protectable?" *New York Law Journal*, December 03, 2019, https://www.law.com/newyorklawjournal/2019/12/03/judges-gonna-judge-when-are-short-phrases-protectable/?slreturn=20200027155703.

12. Michael Donaldson, "Refuge from the Storm: A Fair Use Safe Harbor for Non-Fiction Works," *Journal of the Copyright Society of the USA* 59, no. 3 (2012): 546.

13. Bruno Latour, "Why Has Critique Run Out of Steam? From Matters of Fact to Matters of Concern," *Critical Inquiry* 30, no. 2 (2004): 225–48.

14. Lin-Manuel Miranda and Frank DiGiacomo, "'Hamilton's' Lin-Manuel Miranda on Finding Originality, Racial Politics (and Why Trump Should See His Show)," *Hollywood Reporter*, August 12, 2015, https://www.hollywoodreporter.com/features/hamiltons-lin-manuel-miranda-finding-814657.

15. "When you durst do it, then you were a man; / And, to be more than what you were, you would / Be so much more the man." *Macbeth* 7.1.49–51.

16. See Tushnet's chapter in this volume ("interpretive use is clearly a transformative purpose; the original is no longer an end in itself, but rather a waystation that helps us learn and experience new things").

17. "The Mob Song," *Beauty and the Beast* (Alan Menken, Howard Ashman, and Tim Rice 1993).

28. Taking Law School Musicals Seriously

The title of this chapter is a riff on the work of Ronald Dworkin from whom I took a seminar as a second-year law student. Despite my best efforts, I was not able to convince my fellow Law Revue writers and producers that a spoof of the Ronnie Show and the famous Hart/Dworkin Debate on legal philosophy and judicial rule-making would be immediately recognizable as hilarious to the entire law student body.

1. *Hamilton* is not the only musical to take on history and the Founding (*1776* comes to mind). However, the specificity of its subject and unbelievable success of the project came as a great surprise to the many people who, prior to its opening, heard only about *Hamilton* in concept.

2. Lin-Manuel Miranda, "The Story of Tonight," *Hamilton: An American Musical* (Atlantic Records 2015).

3. See, e.g., Alex Petridis, "Break It Down: How Hamilton Mashed Up Musical Theatre and Hiphop," *The Guardian,* December 1, 2017, https://www.theguardian.com/stage/2017/dec/01/hamilton-mashed-up-musical-theatre-and-hiphop-lin-manuel-miranda; Joel Eastwood and Eric Hinton, "How Does 'Hamilton,' the Non stop, Hip-Hop Broadway Sensation Tap Rap's Master Rhymes to Blur Musical Lines?," *Wall Street Journal,* http://graphics.wsj.com/hamilton/.

4. Lin-Manuel Miranda, "The Room Where It Happens," *Hamilton.*

5. *Shady Grove Orthopedic Associates, P.A. v. Allstate Ins. Co.*, 559 U.S. 393 (2010) is the latest pronouncement from the Supreme Court on the dimensions of the *Erie* doctrine in which the courts have attempted to discern whether federal or state procedural law applies when state law cases are litigated in federal court. Naturally, as a folk music maven, I always hear the traditional "Shady Grove" bluegrass tune in my head whenever I teach the case. Shady Grove is also the last stop on the Red Line on the Washington, D.C., metro subway system. So when this banjo-playing, civil-procedure-teaching, D.C.-area-native searches for Shady Grove, I am proud to report that I thoroughly confuse the Google search algorithm.

29. "The World Turned Upside Down"

1. J. M. Balkin, "Deconstructive Practice and Legal Theory," *Yale Law Journal* 96, no. 4 (1987): 744.

2. Ibid., 745, 755.

3. Ibid., 764, 786.

4. Ibid., 746–47.

5. Lin-Manuel Miranda, "Alexander Hamilton," *Hamilton: An American Musical* (Atlantic 2015).

6. Ibid.

7. Ibid.

8. Miranda, "Take a Break," *Hamilton.*

9. Miranda, "I Know Him," *Hamilton.*

10. Miranda, "That Would Be Enough," *Hamilton.*

11. Miranda, "Who Lives, Who Dies, Who Tells Your Story," *Hamilton.*

12. Ibid.

13. Michael Schuman, "The Women of 'Hamilton,'" *New Yorker*, August 6, 2015, https://www.newyorker.com/culture/cultural-comment/the-women-of-hamilton.

14. *Eight Mile*, directed by Curtis Hanson (Imagine Entertainment, 2002).

15. Notorious B.I.G., "Ten Crack Commandments," *Life After Death*, Bad Boy Records, disc 2, track 5, 1997.

16. Notorious B.I.G., "Going Back to Cali," *Life After Death,* Bad Boy Records, disc 2, track 4, 1997.

17. Beastie Boys, "Hey Ladies," *Paul's Boutique*, Capitol, track 8, 1989.

18. Miranda, "Satisfied," *Hamilton.*

19. Miranda, "Helpless," *Hamilton.*

20. Miranda, "Satisfied," *Hamilton.*

21. Ibid.

22. Balkin, "Deconstructive Practice and Legal Theory," 777.

23. Jonathan Culler, *On Deconstruction: Theory and Criticism after Structuralism* (Ithaca, NY: Cornell University Press, 1982) (cited in ibid, 774).

24. Mobb Deep, "Shook Ones, Part II," *The Infamous*, Loud Records, track 15, 1995.

25. Ibid.

26. Miranda, "My Shot," *Hamilton.*

27. Miranda, "Blow Us All Away," *Hamilton*.

28. Miranda, "My Shot," *Hamilton*.

29. Miranda, "Blow Us All Away," *Hamilton*.

30. Miranda, "The Schuyler Sisters," *Hamilton*.

31. Ibid.

32. Balkin, "Deconstructive Practice and Legal Theory," 778.

33. Miranda, "One Last Time," *Hamilton*.

34. Balkin, "Deconstructive Practice and Legal Theory," 779.

35. Miranda, "Alexander Hamilton," *Hamilton*.

30. "Cabinet Battle #1"

1. Lin-Manuel Miranda, "Cabinet Battle #1," *Hamilton: An American Musical* (Atlantic Records 2015).

2. Ibid.

3. Ibid.

4. Ibid.

5. Ibid.

6. Miranda, "Washington on Your Side," *Hamilton*.

7. A thorough discussion of the history of the Bank of the United States can be found in Charles Warren, *The Supreme Court in United States History* (Boston: Little, Brown, 1922), 499–540.

8. Miranda, "Who Lives, Who Dies, Who Tells Your Story," *Hamilton*.

9. 17 U.S. (4 Wheat.) 316 (1819).

10. The case reached conclusions on the tax question but the discussion here covers only the congressional power issue.

11. Miranda, "Cabinet Battle #1," *Hamilton*.

12. *McCulloch, 17 U.S. at* 404.

13. Ibid. at 401.

14. Ibid. at 402.

15. Ibid.

16. As Chief Justice Marshall described it: "The powers of the general government, it has been said, are delegated by the states, who alone are truly sovereign; and must be exercised in subordination to the states, who alone possess supreme dominion." *McCulloch*, 17 U.S. at 402.

17. "The government proceeds directly from the people; is 'ordained and established' in the name of the people. . . . The assent of the States, in their sovereign capacity, is implied, in calling a convention, and thus submitting that instrument to the people. But the people were at perfect liberty to accept or reject it; and their act was final. It required not the affirmance, and could not be negatived, by the state governments." *McCulloch*, 17 U.S. at 403–4.

18. *McCulloch*, 17 U.S. at 407.

19. Ibid. (emphasis added). Felix Frankfurter described this sentence as "the single most important utterance in the literature of constitutional law—most important because [it was] most comprehensive and most comprehending." Felix Frankfurter, "John Marshall and the Judicial Function," *Harvard Law Review* 69 (1955): 219.

20. Quoted in Warren, *The Supreme Court*, 501.

21. U.S. Constitution, Art. 1, Sec. 8. concludes by granting Congress the power "to make all Laws which shall be necessary and proper for carrying into Execution the foregoing Powers, and all other Powers vested by this Constitution in the Government of the United States, or in any Department or Officer thereof."

22. *McCulloch*, 17 U.S. at 421.

23. Ibid. at 420.

24. Ibid. at 415.

25. Ibid. at 423.

26. According to Hamilton, the clause has "been held up to the people in all the exaggerated colors of misrepresentation as the pernicious engines by which their local governments were to be destroyed and their liberties exterminated; as the hideous monster whose devouring jaws would spare neither sex nor age, nor high nor low, nor sacred nor profane." *The Federalist* No. 33.

27. Ibid.

28. Miranda, "The World Was Wide Enough," *Hamilton*.

31. Hamilton's Bank and Jefferson's Nightmare

Parts of this chapter are drawn from the Introduction to my book *How the Other Half Banks: Exclusion, Exploitation, and the Threat to Democracy* (Cambridge, MA: Harvard University Press, 2015).

1. Lin-Manuel Miranda, "Stay Alive," *Hamilton: An American Musical* (Atlantic Records 2015).

2. Bray Hammond, *Banks and Politics in America from the Revolution to the Civil War* (Princeton: Princeton University Press, 1991), 40.

3. "Final Version of the Second Report on the Further Provision Necessary for Establishing Public Credit (Report on a National Bank), December 13, 1790," Founders Online, National Archives, https://founders.archives.gov/documents/Hamilton/01-07-02-0229-0003. [Originally published in *The Papers of Alexander Hamilton*, vol. 7, *September 1790—January 1791*, ed. Harold C. Syrett (New York: Columbia University Press, 1963), 305–42.]

4. Ibid.

5. Alexander Hamilton, "Report on a National Bank," Communicated to the House of Representatives, December 14, 1790 (quoted in Joseph Gales, ed., *The Debates and Proceedings in the Congress of the United States* [Washington, DC: Gales and Seaton, 1834], 2101).

6. Ibid.

7. Miranda, "Cabinet Battle #1," *Hamilton*.

8. Miranda, "Washington on Your Side," *Hamilton*.

9. Ibid.

10. Richard R. John, *Spreading the News* (Cambridge, MA: Harvard University Press, 1998), 25.

11. Edwin W. Kemmerer, "The United States Postal Savings Bank," *Political Science Quarterly* 26, no. 3 (1911): 493.

12. U.S. Congress, House, Committee on Post-Office and Postal Roads, Postal Savings Depositories (to Accompany H.R., 4198),47th Cong., 1st sess., 1882, H. Rep. 47-473, 1.

13. Mehrsa Baradaran, *How the Other Half Banks: Exclusion, Exploitation, and the Threat to Democracy* (Cambridge, MA: Harvard University Press, 2015), 189.

14. Senator Butler, speaking on amendments to S. 2369, on December 13, 1897, 55th Cong., 2nd sess., Congressional Record 112, pt. 1:112.

15. Gerald C. Fischer, *American Banking Structure* (New York: Columbia University Press, 1968), 27.

16. Paul Kahan, "The Bank War: Andrew Jackson, Nicholas Biddle and the Fight for American Finance," *Financial History* 116 (Winter, 2016): 28–30.

17. Miranda, "Who Lives, Who Dies, Who Tells Your Story," *Hamilton*.

18. Ibid.

19. Ibid.

32. Alexander Hamilton's Legacy

Some of the ideas in this piece derive from my work on boards found in Stephen M. Bainbridge and M. Todd Henderson, *Outsourcing the Board: How Board Service Providers Can Improve Corporate Governance* (Cambridge, UK: Cambridge University Press, 2018).

Epigraph: Lin-Manuel Miranda, "What'd I Miss," *Hamilton: An American Musical* (Atlantic Records 2015).

1. "What'd I Miss," *Hamilton.*

2. Tench Coxe assisted Hamilton in the drafting of the report, providing much of the statistical data. Coxe was a strong proponent of industrialization, and was called by some the "father of the American cotton industry." John B. McMaster, "Coxe, Trench," in *Appletons' Cyclopædia of American Biography,* ed. James G. Wilson and John Fiske (New York: D. Appleton, 1900), 14. See also Jacob Cooke, *Tench Coxe and the Early Republic* (Chapel Hill: University of North Carolina Press, 1978).

3. Miranda, "Cabinet Battle #1," *Hamilton.*

4. Ibid.

5. Ibid.

6. Alexander Hamilton, "Prospectus of the Society for Establishing Useful Manufactures, [August 1791]," Founders Online, National Archives, https://founders.archives.gov/documents/Hamilton/01-09-02-0114.

7. Miranda, "Cabinet Battle #1," *Hamilton.*

8. Ibid.

9. Ibid.

10. Ibid.

11. Ibid.

12. Franklin A. Gevurtz, "The Historical and Political Origins of the Corporate Board of Directors," *Hofstra Law Review* 33, no. 1 (2004): 109.

13. Stephen M. Bainbridge and M. Todd Henderson, *Limited Liability: A Legal and Economic Analysis* (Cheltenham, UK: Edward Elgar, 2016), 33.

14. David J. Cowan, "William Duer and America's First Financial Scandal," *Financial History* 97 (2009): 20–35.

15. Russell Roberts, "The Society for Establishing Useful Manufacturers," *Financial History* 64 (1998): 20.

16. "An Act Relative to Incorporations for Manufacturing Purposes," Laws of New York, chap. LXVII, March 22, 1811.

17. The Bank was the agent of the government in collecting taxes, making payments, and issuing loans.

18. Bank Act, ch. 10, § 4 (1791).

19. Franklin Gevurtz, "Historical and Political Origins," 110 (citing Cyril O'Donnell, "Origins of the Corporate Executive," *Bulletin of the Business Historical Society* 26 [1952]: 61).

20. The Bank of England was nationalized in 1946, and is now the central bank of the United Kingdom.

21. Gevurtz, "Historical and Political Origins," 128.

22. Gevurtz, "Historical and Political Origins," 129.

23. Ibid., 125.

24. Miranda, "The World Was Wide Enough," *Hamilton.*

33. "I Never Thought I'd Live Past Twenty"

1. Lin-Manuel Miranda, "Right Hand Man," *Hamilton: An American Musical* (Atlantic Records 2015).

2. Miranda, "Stay Alive," *Hamilton.*

3. Miranda, "My Shot," *Hamilton*.

4. Miranda, "Wait for It," *Hamilton*.

5. Ibid.

6. See Marie Skubak Tillyer, "Victimization, Offending, and Perceived Risk for Early Violent Death," *Criminal Justice and Behavior* 42, no. 5 (2015): 539 (prior victimization and witnessing violence can increase the risk of developing an anticipated early death); Tara D. Warner and Raymond R. Swisher, "The Effect of Direct and Indirect Exposure to Violence on Youth Survival Expectations," *Journal of Adolescent Health* 55, no. 6 (2014): 821 (those who experienced physical abuse are more likely to develop an anticipated early death); Arna L. Carlock, "Live Fast, Die Young: Anticipated Early Death and Adolescent Violence and Gang Involvement" (PhD diss., University at Albany, SUNY, 2016), 123 (dangerous and unpredictable environments are associated with the development of an anticipated early death).

7. Miranda, "Alexander Hamilton," *Hamilton*.

8. Miranda, "That Would Be Enough," *Hamilton*.

9. This phenomenon has been explained using self-control theory. See Michael R. Gottfredson and Travis Hirschi, *A General Theory of Crime* (Stanford: Stanford University Press, 1990) (explanation of self-control theory); see also Alex R. Piquero, " 'Take My License n' All That Jive, I Can't See . . . 35': Little Hope for the Future Encourages Offending Over time," *Justice Quarterly* 33, no. 1 (2016) (applying self-control theory to anticipated early death).

10. See Daniel S. Nagin and Raymond Paternoster, "Enduring Individual Differences and Rational Choice Theories of Crime," *Law & Society Review* 27, no. 3 (1993): 468–69 (provides an explanation of rational choice theory); Dana L. Haynie, Brian Soller, and Kristi Williams, "Anticipating Early Fatality: Friends', Schoolmates' and Individual Perceptions of Fatality on Adolescent Risk Behaviors," *Journal of Youth and Adolescence* 43, no. 2 (2009): 189 (applying rational choice theory to anticipated early death).

11. See Lauren D. Brumley, Sara R. Jaffee, and Benjamin P. Brumley, "Pathways from Childhood Adversity to Problem Behaviors in Young Adulthood: The Mediating Role of Adolescents' Future Expectations," *Journal of Youth and Adolescence* 45, no. 1 (2017): 9; Carlock, "Live Fast Die Young," 139–41.

12. Miranda, "Alexander Hamilton," *Hamilton*.

13. Miranda, "Right Hand Man," *Hamilton*.

14. Timothy Brezina, Erdal Tekin, and Volkan Topalli, " 'Might Not Be a Tomorrow': A Multimethods Approach to Anticipated Early Death and Youth Crime," *Criminology* 47, no. 4 (2009): 1113.

15. Elijah Anderson, *Code of the Streets: Decency, Violence, and the Moral Life of the Inner City* (New York: W. W. Norton), 2000, 92.

16. See Brezina, Tekin, and Topalli, "Might Not Be a Tomorrow."

17. In 2016, only 1.3 percent of juvenile cases where the youth were sixteen years old or older and 0.1 percent of cases where they were younger than 16 years old, were adjudicated through the adult system. See Sarah Hockenberry and Charles Puzzanchera, *Juvenile Court Statistics 2016* (Pittsburgh: National Center for Juvenile Justice, 2018), 40, https://www.ojjdp.gov/ojstatbb/njcda/pdf/jcs2016.pdf.

18. "Youth" are generally legally defined as individuals younger than eighteen years old. However, it has long been recognized that decision-making capabilities continue to mature into the mid-twenties. See Alexandra O. Cohen et al., "When Does a Juvenile Become an Adult: Implications for Law and Policy," *Temple Law Review* 88, no. 4 (2016): 779, 783.

19. See Michael E. Newton, *Alexander Hamilton: The Formative Years* (Eleftheria, 2015), 130. Hamilton would still have been considered immature when he was twenty-one years old at the Battle of Monmouth (1778) and twenty-four at the Battle of Yorktown (1781). Ibid., 283 and 500.

20. See Bryan Hogeveen and Joanne Minaker, "Juvenile Justice System," *Encyclopedia of Prisons and Correctional Facilities*, ed. Mary Bosworth (Thousand Oaks, CA: Sage, 2005).

21. See *Roper v. Simmons*, 543 U.S. (2005), 570.

22. See *Graham v. Florida*, 560 U.S. (2010), 68.

23. See *Miller v. Alabama*, 567 U.S. (2012), 489.

24. See Miranda, "My Shot," *Hamilton*. ("I never thought I'd live past twenty. / Where I come from some get half as many.")

25. See Raymond R. Swisher and Tara D. Warner, "If They Grow Up: Exploring the Neighborhood Context of Adolescent and Young Adult Survival Expectations," *Journal of Research on Adolescence* 23, no. 4 (2013): 691.

26. Miranda, "Yorktown (The World Turned Upside Down)," *Hamilton*.

27. Ibid.

28. Ibid.

29. Samantha S. Clinkinbeard, "What Lies Ahead: An Exploration of Future Orientation, Self-Control, and Delinquency," *Criminal Justice Review* 39, no. 1 (2014): 30–31.

30. See Sarah Fishel, "Anticipated Death and Offending Patterns: A Retrospective Self-Report Study" (MS thesis, Drexel University, 2019), 6.

31. Ibid.

32. Miranda, "Right Hand Man," *Hamilton*.

33. See Clinkinbeard, "What Lies Ahead."

34. Ibid., 31.

35. Miranda, "Non-Stop," *Hamilton*.

36. Miranda, "My Shot," *Hamilton*.

Contributors

Bret D. Asbury is professor of law and associate dean of academic affairs at the Drexel University Thomas R. Kline School of Law, Philadelphia. His research interests include jurisprudence, bioethics, and the intersection of law and literature.

Mehrsa Baradaran is professor of law at the University of California—Irvine School of Law. Her research interests include banking law, financial inclusion, inequality, and the racial wealth gap. She is the author of *How the Other Half Banks* (2015) and *The Color of Money: Black Banks and the Racial Wealth Gap* (2017).

John Q. Barrett is professor of law at St. John's University School of Law, New York, and Elizabeth S. Lenna Fellow and board member at the Robert H. Jackson Center, Jamestown, New York. His specialties include constitutional law, criminal procedure, and legal history.

Benjamin Barton is the Helen and Charles Lockett Distinguished Professor of Law at University of Tennessee, Knoxville School of Law. He is the author of the books *Fixing Law Schools* (2019), *Rebooting Justice* (2017), *Glass Half Full: The Decline and Rebirth of the Legal Profession* (2015), and *The Lawyer-Judge Bias* (2011).

Erwin Chemerinsky is the dean and Jesse H. Choper Distinguished Professor of Law at the University of California, Berkeley School of Law. He is the author of eleven books, including leading casebooks and treatises about constitutional law, criminal procedure, and federal jurisdiction. His most recent books are *Closing the Courthouse Doors: How Your Constitutional Rights Became Unenforceable* (2017); *Free Speech on Campus* (2017, with Howard Gillman); and *We the People: A Progressive Reading of the Constitution for the Twenty-First Century* (2018).

Joshua A. Douglas is the Thomas P. Lewis Professor of Law at the University of Kentucky J. David Rosenberg College of Law. He teaches and researches election law and voting rights, civil procedure, constitutional law, and judicial decision making. Douglas is the author of *Vote for US: How to Take Back Our Elections and Change the Future of Voting* (2019), a popular press book that provides hope and inspiration for a positive path forward on voting rights.

Robin J. Effron is professor of law at Brooklyn Law School. She writes and teaches courses on civil procedure, litigation, and international business law.

Anthony Paul Farley is the Matthews Distinguished Professor of Jurisprudence at Albany Law School, New York, and the Peter Rodino Distinguished Visiting Professor at Rutgers Law School—Newark (2020). His areas of expertise include constitutional law, criminal procedure, human rights, civil rights, and legal theory. He is a member of the American Law Institute and the board of governors of the Society of American Law Teachers.

Sarah Fishel is a JD/PhD student in law and psychology at Drexel University and Drexel University Thomas R. Kline School of Law, Philadelphia.

Her areas of interest include the reentry process for individuals involved in the legal system, prison reform, and changes in offending patterns over the lifespan.

Rosa Frazier served as supervising attorney for the University of Wisconsin Law School Domestic Violence Immigration Clinic in Madison between 2009 and 2013. She now writes romance novels under a pseudonym.

Gregory G. Garre served as the forty-fourth solicitor general of the United States and has argued forty-four cases before the U.S. Supreme Court. He is now a partner in the Washington, D.C., office of Latham & Watkins and global chair of the firm's Supreme Court & Appellate Practice.

Michael Gerhardt is the Burton Craige Distinguished University Professor of Jurisprudence, University of North Carolina at Chapel Hill. His specialties include civil rights, the legislative process, and constitutional conflicts. He has served as special counsel, public commentator, and expert witness before Congress on all the major constitutional conflicts between presidents and Congress over the past twenty-five years.

Jill Goldenziel is associate professor of international law and international relations at Marine Corps University Command and Staff College in Quantico, and an affiliated senior scholar at Fox Leadership International, University of Pennsylvania. Her award-winning scholarship focuses on international and comparative law, constitutional law, refugees and migration, information warfare, lawfare, and human rights. She cochairs the American Society of International Law's Human Rights Interest Group and blogs at *Balkinization*.

M. Todd Henderson is the Michael J. Marks Professor of Law at the University of Chicago Law School. His research interests include corporations, securities regulation, and law and economics. He has taught classes ranging from Banking Regulation to Torts to American Indian Law.

Danielle Holley-Walker is dean and professor of law at Howard University School of Law, Washington, D.C. Her research interests include the governance of public schools and diversity in the legal profession. She has published articles on issues of civil rights and education, including recent articles on No Child Left Behind Act, charter school policy, desegregation plans, and affirmative action in higher education.

Anil Kalhan is professor of law at the Drexel University Thomas R. Kline School of Law, Philadelphia. His scholarly interests lie in the areas of immigration law, U.S. and comparative constitutional law, international human rights law, privacy and surveillance, criminal law, and law and South Asian studies. From 2015 to 2018, he served as chair of the New York City Bar Association's International Human Rights Committee.

Neal Katyal is a partner at Hogan Lovells and the former acting solicitor general of the United States, focusing on appellate and complex litigation. In December 2017, *American Lawyer* magazine named him Litigator of the Year.

Elizabeth B. Keyes is associate professor of law and director at the Immigrant Rights Clinic, University of Baltimore School of Law. Her teaching, scholarship, and practice have all focused on improving access to justice for immigrants. She is currently turning her work to the challenges posed by climate change for migrants within and across borders.

Jody Madeira is professor of law, Louis F. Niezer Faculty Fellow, and co-director of the Center for Law, Society & Culture at Indiana University Maurer School of Law, Bloomington. Her scholarly interests involve empirical research; the role of emotion in law; the sociology of law; law, medicine, and bioethics; and the Second Amendment. Her most recent book, *Taking Baby Steps: How Patients and Fertility Clinics Collaborate in Conception* (2018), focuses on the infertility experience.

Marcia L. McCormick is professor of law and women's and gender studies at Saint Louis University and is currently the associate dean for Academic Affairs. Her scholarship explores the areas of employment and labor law, federal courts, and gender and the law.

Ian Millhiser is a senior correspondent at Vox.com and the author of *Injustices: The Supreme Court's History of Comforting the Comfortable and Afflicting the Afflicted* (2015).

Christina Mulligan is vice dean and professor of law at Brooklyn Law School, New York. She teaches Internet law, intellectual property law, and trusts and estates. Recently, she has written about the Internet of Things, robot punishment, and early translations of the Constitution.

Kimberly Mutcherson is co-dean and professor of law at Rutgers Law School in Camden, New Jersey. Her scholarly work is at the intersection of family law, health law, and bioethics. She writes on issues related to reproductive justice, with a focus on assisted reproduction, abortion, and maternal-fetal decision making.

Kimberly Jade Norwood is the Henry H. Oberschelp Professor of Law at Washington University, St. Louis, Missouri. Her research focuses on blackthink, colorism, implicit bias, and the intersection of race, class, and public education in America. She lectures around the world on colorism, various social justice/civil rights issues, implicit (and explicit) bias issues and was part of the national team of experts consulted to advise Starbucks on its national implicit bias training agenda.

Eloise Pasachoff is professor of law, Agnes N. Williams Research Professor, and associate dean for careers at the Georgetown University Law Center. She teaches and writes about administrative law, public administration, and education law.

Richard Primus is the Theodore J. St. Antoine Collegiate Professor of Law at the University of Michigan Law School, Ann Arbor. He teaches the law, theory, and history of the U.S. Constitution.

Glenn Harlan Reynolds is the Beauchamp Brogan Distinguished Professor of Law at The University of Tennessee, Knoxville School of Law. His interests are law and technology and constitutional law issues. A songwriter and producer for such bands as Mobius Dick, The Nebraska Guitar Militia, and The Defenders of The Faith, Reynolds is a member of the American Society of Composers and Performers and the National Academy of Recording Arts and Sciences.

Kermit Roosevelt III is professor of law at the University of Pennsylvania, Philadelphia. His work focuses on constitutional law and conflict of laws.

He is the author of *The Myth of Judicial Activism: Making Sense of Supreme Court Decisions* (2006) and *Conflict of Laws* (2010).

Zahr K. Said is associate dean for research and faculty development at the University of Washington School of Law. Her research applies humanistic methods, theories, and texts to problems in legal doctrine and policy. Her current work examines the role of the jury in copyright law and jury instructions in copyright litigation.

Paul M. Secunda is professor of law and director of the Labor and Employment Law Program at Marquette University Law School, Milwaukee. He teaches employee benefits law, labor law, employment discrimination law, employment law, education law, civil procedure, and trusts and estates.

Lisa A. Tucker is an associate professor of law at Drexel University Thomas R. Kline School of Law, Philadelphia. Her scholarly work focuses on the federal courts, legal education, family law, and law and literature. She is the author of the law school novel *Called On* (2015), as well as eleven books for children.

Rebecca Tushnet is the Frank Stanton Professor of the First Amendment at Harvard Law School, Cambridge. Her current work focuses on copyright, trademark, and false advertising law. She helped found the Organization for Transformative Works, a nonprofit dedicated to supporting and promoting fanworks, and currently volunteers on its legal committee. Contact herrtushnet@law.harvard.edu

Elizabeth B. Wydra is president of the Constitutional Accountability Center. She served as its counsel from 2008 to 2016, representing the center as well as clients including preeminent constitutional scholars and historians, state and local government organizations, and groups such as the League of Women Voters and the AARP. She frequently participates in Supreme Court litigation and her legal brief writing has been recognized as "exemplary" by the Green Bag Almanac & Reader. Email: elizabeth@theuscon stitution.org.

INDEX

Page numbers followed by f or n indicate figures or notes.

CPSIA information can be obtained
at www.ICGtesting.com
Printed in the USA
LVHW090900021220
673142LV00006B/52

31192022082190

9 781501 753381